GODS, GHOSTS & GOBLINS: FOLKLORE & BEYOND

By Eric L Fitch

Published by

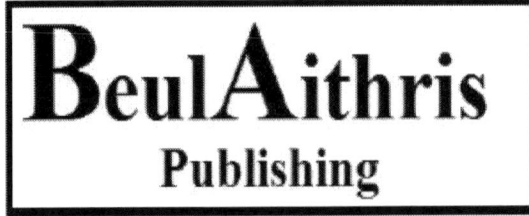

Scotland

www.beul-aithris-publishing.com

This book is dedicated to the late Maidenhead historian Michael Bayley for his pertinent researches, to Mary Orange for her encouragement, and last but not least, to my wife Valerie for her tireless overseeing of my scripts.

CONTENTS

PREFACE

Over the past 30 years or so I have contributed articles to various magazines and journals on topics such as King Arthur, traditional customs, folklore, witchcraft, ghosts, ancient sites, local history and H G Wells. This book gathers together a number of these uncollected articles, with some previously unpublished, including a follow-up chapter to my book *In Search of Herne the Hunter*.

As a number of the original articles were written some time ago, I have edited some to take into account new research, deleted out of date material and in a few cases expanded them. To help the reader I have placed them under sections where similar topics are gathered together. There is a little bias here and there to the locality of the Windsor/Slough/Maidenhead area where I was born and bred, but apart from that I feel that the reader will appreciate that the nature of each chapter is of interest in its own right, and fitting to the overall flavour of the book.

Eric L. Fitch

2018

Note:

For dates I use the modern terms CE (Common Era) and BCE (Before the Common Era), corresponding to AD and BC respectively

MYTHS, LEGENDS AND MYSTERIES

1 - Nodens, Lydney & Tolkien: Celtic God, A Temple, Romans, And Author Link

Introduction

The three names heading this chapter title are all linked, with threads connecting the Celts, Romans, a temple, 1920s excavations, a legendary archaeologist, etymology, and the writer of perhaps the most read fantasy book of all time. The unravelling of the threads begins here.

Nodens

The Celtic god Nodens was worshipped in Britain, in particular at Lydney in Gloucestershire, as well as elsewhere in Europe, and was primarily a god of healing. He also was associated with the sun, water, hunting and fertility, and his totem animal appears to have been the dog. In Germany an inscription found at Mainz refers to a deity named Noadatus, which may be the same god, and the place name of Maynooth in Ireland derives from the Gaelic "*Magh Nuad*", meaning the "plain of Nuadu". The latter name ("*Nuadha Argat-lam*" in full, meaning "Silver Arm") was the first king of the legendary Tuatha De Danann, the "people of the goddess Danu" of Celtic Ireland. Nuadha lost an arm in battle, which was replaced by one of silver, which gave him the nickname of "Silver Hand". Nodens is also equated with the Welsh Gwynn ap Nudd/Llud, the master of the wild hunt, although this is tentative. It has been suggested that the name Llud forms the first part of Lydney, but this is not universally accepted. The "official" derivation is that Lydney comes from "Lida's Island", made up from the Anglo-Saxon personal name "Lida" meaning a sailor, and "eg", meaning an island, thus "Sailor's Island".

Nodens is also known from a silver statuette discovered at Cockersand Moss in Lancashire in 1718 which had a base with the following inscription (in Latin): "To the god Mars Nodontis, the College of Lictors and Lucianus Aprilis the traveller, in fulfilment of a vow". And an inscription from Vindolanda on Hadrian's Wall read *"DEO NO/NEPTU"*, which is assumed to have meant "To the god Neptune Nodons". In Romano-Britain times it was often the case that their gods were equated with a local Celtic god/goddess, Mars and Neptune being two examples. But the most well-known site where Nodens was worshipped was at Lydney Park in the Forest of Dean, where a temple once stood on a steep bluff which overlooked the Severn Estuary, the excavations of which will be discussed in the following section.

The name Nodens, or Nodons, has been interpreted as meaning "cloud-maker" or "wealthy one", although these are speculative. There were two inscriptions from Lydney linking Nodens with the Roman god Mars. One reads: "To the god Mars Nodens, Flavius Blandinus the drill-instructor willingly and deservedly fulfils his vow". The other read: "Pectillus dedicates this votive offering which he had promised to the god Nudens Mars". The linking with Mars ties in with Mars's association with protectiveness and healing which was common in Continental Europe.

Although the association of the god Neptune with Nodens, it could be that the latter was worshipped as a sea god as well. Nodens was also associated with Silvanus, a woodland/hunting Roman god, and in this role he would have been seen as a fertility deity, as this would have been appropriate to a healing cult. A figure of a mother-goddess with two cornucopiae was found at Lydney, supporting the fertility aspect. In addition a pavement frieze on which were depicted sea monsters and fish, together with a broken part of a bronze relief of some kind of sea god, point to there being an association with the sea, perhaps linking with the name of Lydney as described above. The mosaic, now lost, was funded by gift offerings from devotees. Because of the late date of the sanctuary, all the evidence seems to point to a pagan revival at Lydney, and despite there being a pre-Roman iron age presence at the site, it does not appear to have been a place of early ritual or cultic activity.

This sums up the aspects of Nodens that can be adduced from the evidence, scanty though that may be. It is now time to pay attention to the god's most important sanctuary, that at Lydney.

Lydney Temple

Although there were some limited excavations in 1779 and more detailed ones in 1805, it was not until 1928/29 that the site of the Lydney Temple was properly excavated by the legendary archaeologist and TV personality Sir Mortimer Wheeler, who also excavated the famous Celtic hill-fort of Maiden Castle in Dorset. Wheeler and his wife Tessa discovered that the temple site, Camp Hill, was occupied first in the 1st century BCE with the building of a hill-fort. The Romans arrived in Britain in 43 CE and they set about mining for iron, and their workings at Lydney are the only ones of their kind discovered in the British Isles

The Romano-Celtic temple complex was built in about 364 CE, refurbished in the late 4th century CE, and activity seems to have persisted there until the 5th century. The Wheelers unearthed a number of buildings, including evidence of a temple, a baths complex, a guesthouse and a "long building", as well as the sanctuary walls. Some of the structures show above ground, up to two or three feet, to this day, and are well worth a visit via a short climb up to the top of Camp Hill.

The sanctuary walls consisted of arched colonnades, but sometime later these collapsed due to a geological fault underlying the structure, however they were subsequently rebuilt more solidly. The baths complex followed the normal Roman layout of such a feature, with the *frigidarium* (cold bath), *tepidarium* (warm bath) and *calderium* (hot bath), and there was also a furnace for heating the water. There would also have been a gymnasium and an exercise area. The building interpreted as the guesthouse, by far the largest building on the site, indicates that the sanctuary attracted many people to the site, and its situation, as now, is an idyllic spot to commune with the spirits.

The structure of the temple itself is unusual in that it appears to be based on a Romano-Celtic style, but with a rectangular ambulatory taken from the Roman design. The far end of the *cella*, or inner chamber, was split into three sections, probably originally spaces for statues. Although Christianity had arrived in Britain by the time of the building of the sanctuary, it is clear that paganism was far from over yet. The temple was basically a Celtic edifice, as defined by the name of the Celtic god Nodens, and the inscriptions indicated that the Romans equated the god with those of their own. Technically the Roman Empire had been officially made Christian by the Edict of Thessalonica in 380, but this had little impact in the outposts of Britain, and by 410 the Romans pulled out of the country and left Britain to its own defences. The date of the latest coin discovered was of the reign of the Emperor Arcadius who died in 408, and the archaeological evidence shows that activity carried on at Lydney for some decades to come.

And finally the "long" building. About 183 feet in length, it was made up of a dozen or so small rooms which all opened on to a structure interpreted as a veranda. A paved corridor had been laid down beneath this in front of the rooms, all of which were decorated with mosaic floors. Wheeler's interpretation of this unusual structure is discussed in the next section. Artefacts that were excavated at the site included a bronze plaque of a woman, a bronze arm, bronze reliefs portraying what appears to be a sea god, tritons and fishermen, and an oculist's stamp. More numerous items included over 8,000 coins, almost 300 bracelets and around 320 pins, all of which must have been votive offerings. The depictions on some of the artefacts clearly revealed associations with the sea, and others showed evidence that the temple had a healing role. Finds include offerings such as a model arm and an explicit bone plaque of a woman, in the hope that the afflicted area would be healed. In particular afflictions pertaining to the eye were dealt with, the stamps of physicians' stamped ointment boxes having been excavated on site.

A significant discovery were nine bronze or stone statuettes of dogs, and taking into account that in the Roman world dogs were regularly connected with sanctuaries where healing was practised, it can be assumed that this was what took place at Lydney. The most important canine representation excavated was a bronze statuette of a half grown wolfhound, which has come to be the emblem of Lydney Park. As we have seen there are two inscriptions linking Nodens with Mars, the latter often being depicted with dogs, which were symbolic of healing both in the Roman and Celtic worlds. Apparently Classical writers felt that it was important to note that dogs from Britain were reputed to be first-rate, with Strabo writing that British hunting dogs were exported to Rome, and a third century writer Marcus Aurelius Olympius Nemesianus describing them in a poem as being speedy and fit for hunting.

Dog statuette from Lydney

A sanctuary at Nettleton Shrub in Wiltshire, a possible healing centre, was dedicated to Apollo Cunomaglus meaning "Hound-Lord", accentuating the reverence for dogs in Romano-Celtic Britain. This seems to denote the presence of a hunting cult, one of the roles of the Roman god Apollo being that of huntsman. In Irish and Welsh mythology the hunt is closely related to the supernatural, with many stories depicting nobles out for the hunt, often encountering Otherworldly beings. Roman scholar Martin Henig felt that such hounds reminded him of the Celtic/Germanic goddess Nehalennia, who was often portrayed with a dog.

Dogs were often seen to lick their injuries in order to heal them, and portrayals of them are at holy springs in Gaul, and sacred canines were held at the Temple of Asclepius (Roman Aesculapius), the god of healing, at Epidaurus in Greece. According to the anthropologist Mary Elizabeth Thurston, at such centres of healing the patient would be taken into a room full of dogs and asked to lie down on the floor. The dogs would then be allowed to sniff the patient and to lick various parts of his body, thereby diagnosing the person's afflictions and effecting a cure for them. It is of note that in 2017 an amazing hoard of 4th century bronze Roman dog statuettes were discovered by a metal detectorist in Gloucestershire, one of which depicts a licking dog, and it is likely that these were linked the Lydney complex. All in all the Lydney Temple was an important British sacred and healing centre in the late Roman-Celtic period, but there is more to come.

Incubation

Wheeler was adamant that the long building was used as an incubation centre, wherein people came to sleep hoping that their (alcohol or drug-induced?) dreams could be interpreted with a view to heal them of their various conditions. This was supported by the discovery of a fish-covered mosaic upon which was an inscription referring to "Victorius the Interpreter". This is paralleled by a similar structure at the Temple of Asclepius in Epidaurus, mentioned by the Greek writer Pausanius. Wheeler concluded that the building was to supplement the "chapels" in the temple itself, for it was through temple sleep which the god and his priests worked.

The shrine, or abaton, follows the standard Asclepian pattern whereby the pilgrim enters one of the cubicles where he would prepare himself, say prayers and make offerings to the temple before settling down in bed to dream. Upon waking up a priest would hear the subject matter of the dream and interpret its meaning in order that the pilgrim could be healed of whatever condition afflicted him/her. The cure could include the use of the temple's gymnasium or baths, but at Lydney some activity involving dogs could well have been recommended, as described above.

At Epidaurus a number of inscriptions dating to about 350 BCE were discovered, which recorded the healing of about 70 patients. This included their names, afflictions and cures, which sometimes resulted in surgical procedures such as the cutting out of malignant abscesses, with the patient partly anaesthetised by opium. Exactly what procedures took place at Lydney we do not know, but the overall spirit of the sanctuary was clearly that of healing, with practice of incubation playing an important part in the process. However, the quality of the buildings points to the clientele being wealthy, not for the ordinary person.

Ultimately, of course, the Middle Eastern mystery cult of Christianity overtook everything, spelling the death of the ancient world altogether. Apparently, the rise of the new religion was foretold during the reign of the Emperor Tiberius (14-37 CE), who ruled at the time of Christ's crucifixion. A sailor was on his way back to Italy and across the water he heard an ethereal voice calling out the words "when you reach home, make sure that you proclaim that the great god Pan is dead", which was received with monumental lamentations. It is of note that according to the Greek writer Plutarch, Pan was one of only two Greek gods who actually died, the other, interestingly, being Asclepius.

Tolkien and the Ring

J.R.R.Tolkien needs no introduction, but his association with Lydney is not so well known. He was involved with Wheeler's excavations in 1929, his role being adviser on the temple on top of the hill which was known locally as Dwarfs' Hill. (It is of interest here to note that the English plural of the word "dwarf" was always "dwarfs", until *Lord of the Rings* came along using Tolkien's own plural "dwarves", which has caught on ever since.) In addition he was asked by Wheeler to investigate the origin of the name Nodens, so that his findings could be published as an appendix to the archaeological report, which was published in 1932, Tolkien's contribution being entitled 'Note on the Name "Nodens"'.

Examining the inscriptions found at the site, Tolkien used his expertise in comparative literature and etymology in order to delve into the derivation of the name. He believed that its origins were in Irish mythology, particularly Nuadha Argat-lam, as mentioned above. Its appearance as Nodens at Lydney is the only instance of the name appearing anywhere outside Ireland, concluding that it must have been brought over thence to Britain.

Tolkien also saw a connection with the medieval Welsh figure of Lludd Llaw Ereint, speculating that the name of Lydney itself may have been derived from Llud. As to the meaning of Nodens, he delved into Celtic and Germanic philology, arguing that it probably meant hunter, catcher or snatcher. Tolkien had a great interest in the history of early Britain, especially the period where there were interactions between the Celtic, Roman and Germanic peoples and their languages on these islands. Thus, this was ideal material for Tolkien to examine, which covered the period from the late Celtic period up to the so-called Dark Ages.

We now turn to the ring. One of the objects discovered in the early 19th century was a lead curse tablet. Inscribed on it in Latin was the following:

> *"To the god Nodens. Silvianus has lost a ring and promised half of its value to Nodens. Grant no good health amongst those who bear the name Senicianus until it is brought back to Nodens' temple."*

Curse tablets were often used in Romano-Celtic Britain, and throughout the Graeco-Roman world, many being discovered at the Roman baths at Bath, or Aquae Sulis. They were often of a kind as described in the example above, i.e. objects being lost or stolen, and they were sometimes used as love spells, and at Bath they were nearly always concerned with clothes stolen whilst the owner was bathing. It also seems that the south western part of Britain was a major centre for the preparing of lead curses. The messages were scratched onto a thin lead sheet, folded and deposited in sacred wells, graves or at temples, as at Lydney.

By an incredible coincidence, what must be Silvianus's ring was discovered in 1785 in a field close to the Roman town of Silchester, or Calleva Atrebatum, in Hampshire some 100 miles from Lydney. It is a Roman ten-sided gold thumb-ring with the Latin inscription "Senicianus, may you live in God", indicating a Christian owner. However, it was once a pagan ring, since the Christian inscription had been crudely added, the bezel of which shows an image of the Roman goddess Venus.

It was Mortimer Wheeler who made the connection between the curse and the ring, and it seems that this Senicianus stole the ring, ran off with it, before losing it at Silchester. As previously mentioned, Tolkien was called in by Wheeler to use his talents in finding the meaning of Nodens, Tolkien being a Professor of Anglo-Saxon and Celtic Literature. Indeed he was later credited with confirming the Celtic word Sulis as the Celtic goddess equated with Minerva at Bath, thus giving the dual name of Sulis Minerva as the tutelary goddess of Aquae Sulis.

So how much of the Lydney "matter" influenced Tolkien's later works of *The Hobbit* (1937) and *Lord of The Rings* (1954-55)? Two lines regarding the Rings of Power from the latter work read thus:

> *One Ring to rule them all, One Ring to find them,*

One Ring to bring them all and in the darkness bind them.

These words were proclaimed by Sauron the Dark Lord at the time he forged the One Ring as part of his plan to dominate Middle Earth. To summarise Lord of the Rings, (very briefly!), it tells of the quest to destroy the Ring so that Sauron is unable to achieve his evil purposes.

First a clarification. Bilbo Baggins' ring in the first book has a different nature from that of Frodo Baggins' in the later trilogy. *In The Hobbit* the only magic the Ring possesses is the invisibility of the wearer, whereas in the trilogy it gives the wearer exceptional sight and longevity, but it also leads to corruption for the unfortunate wearer, as evidenced by Gollum, who had been in possession of the Ring for many centuries. However, he had lost it in a cavern in the Misty Mountains, only to be found by Bilbo Baggins, and later his nephew Frodo inherited the Ring from his uncle.

So the tale of Silvianus's ring, and the idea of a ring lost and rediscovered, may well have been at the back of Tolkien's mind when writing his epic fantasy, and this question is much discussed in Tolkien circles. However, Tolkien could have been influenced by more than just the ring, Lydney providing him with a backdrop for his saga.

As already described, the Lydney Temple was built at the top of Camp Hill, but to the locals the hill was referred to as Dwarfs' Hill, and Tolkien must have been aware of this. The hill was punctuated with the tunnels made by the Roman iron workings, known as scowles, and Tolkien was said to have been quite smitten by the locality. Apparently over the centuries the locals came to believe that the tumbledown ruins were the dwelling places of hobgoblins and dwarves, and they were fearful of going near them.

Tolkien's account of the origins of the name Nodens was full of mythological characters, ancient gods and heroes, together with stories of everlasting battles, themes which all appear in his works. At the time of his involvement with the excavations he was working on The Hobbit, and the magical Lydney landscape, with its ruins, deer park, wooded valley and lakes bear a close likeness to The Shire, the home of the Hobbits.

It must be apparent that Lydney had a profound effect on Tolkien and it would be churlish to deny that the area had no effect on his writings concerning the One Ring. He was already a scholar of ancient languages, especially the Celtic and Germanic families of tongues, of ancient Britain, of the myths and legends of the British Isles as well as its folklore. Tolkien would also have been aware of Wagner's *Ring Cycle*, the plot of which the composer drew from Norse mythology, especially *The Ring of the Nibelung* which involved a magical golden ring forged by the dwarf Alberich which granted the possessor great power. Also he would have known about the ring Draupnir from the Norse legends, which was forged by two dwarven brothers and possessed by the god Odin.

Without all these interests and influences, would *The Hobbit* and *Lord of the Rings* ever have turned out the way they did, or even have been written at all? Only Tolkien himself could have answered that question.

Works Consulted:

Religion in Late Roman Britain, by Dorothy Watts (1998)
Gods with Thunderbolts: Religion in Roman Britain, by Guy de la Bedoyere (2002)
Religion in Roman Britain, by Martin Henig (1984)
Animals in Celtic Life and Myth, by Miranda Green (1992)
http://www.bbc.co.uk/gloucestershire/films/tolkien.shtml
https://en.wikipedia.org/wiki/Ring_of_Silvianus

Visiting:

Lydney Park Estate Gardens and Roman Ruins are normally open on certain days from April to June.
The Silvianus Ring is on show at the National Trust stately home The Vyne at Sherborne St John in Hampshire.

2 - The Whiteleaf and Bledlow Crosses: The Enigma Of The Chiltern Hill Figures

Introduction

Two large crosses highlighted in white from the underlying chalk of the Chiltern Hills near Princes Risborough - the handiwork of pagans, monks or parliamentarians? The Whiteleaf and Bledlow Crosses have long been an enigma, subject to many theories, some fantastic, some mundane, some plausible and others merely wrong. This chapter is an attempt to consider the diverse conjectures about these mysterious figures.

First a note on hill figures in England. There are a number of large, sometimes gigantic, figures cut into the turf of English hillsides, revealing various distinctive shapes in chalk. Horses abound, the most famous being at Uffington, Oxfordshire. Human figures include the Priapic Cerne Abbas Giant in Dorset and the Long Man of Wilmington in Sussex, and it is probable that others once existed; it is known that there were once two giants on Plymouth Hoe.

The 18th century seems to have produced many of these figures, especially horses, but those at Cerne and Wilmington may well have been cut many centuries ago. Indeed the White Horse of Uffington was dated in 1990 with a new dating method by the Oxford Archaeological Unit to the late bronze age about 1000 BCE. Their art is almost exclusively English and is not yet extinct, the 20th century producing a number including regimental badges at Fovant in Wiltshire, the Whipsnade Lion and a huge depiction of a Kiwi at Bulford again in Wiltshire, a county with many hill figures. There was even a suggestion, in 1981, of siting a figure of Marilyn Monroe near the Cerne Giant!

However two hill figures in particular should be mentioned. About six miles south west of Bledlow in Buckinghamshire lies the Watlington White Mark, which resembles an obelisk or church spire. This feature is fairly positively dated to 1764, when it was cut as a folly by a certain Edward Horne. There is also one large cross at Ditchling in Sussex, which measures about 100 feet across, which is traditionally associated with Henry III's defeat by Simon de Montfort in 1264, but this is unverified and any date is possible.

This introduction now paves the way for a consideration of the origins and purpose of the two Chiltern Crosses.

Beginnings

The two crosses are recorded for certain no earlier than the 18th century. The Whiteleaf Cross is first mentioned in 1742 in a work written by the

Rev Francis Wise, who makes no reference to the Bledlow Cross, and whose first definite appearance in print is in an edition of the Gentleman's Magazine of 1827. In addition there are four instances in which the crosses are not referred to when one would expect a reference.

In the 16th century John Leland, Henry VIII's chaplain and librarian, embarked upon a tour of England and published his *Itinerary*, recording many ancient monuments. He made no mention of the crosses, although he may be excused since his recorded journey did not actually pass the immediate vicinity. On the other hand, he failed to mention the Uffington White Horse. The second omission was by the Elizabethan antiquarian William Camden in the first guide to Britain's antiquities published as *Britannia* in 1586 (but again the first edition also ignored the great stone circle at Avebury).

The third instance concerns the magnum opus of the poet Michael Drayton, which appeared in 1612 and entitled *Polyolbion*. Inspired by Camden's work the poem is a topographical description of England in twelve syllabled verse with the incredible subtitle of 'A Chorographical Description of the Tracts, Rivers, Mountains, Forests and Other parts of this Renowned Isle of Great Britain, with Intermixture of the Most Remarkable Stories, Antiquities, Wonders, Rarities, Pleasures and Commodities of the Same'! He knew the area well and portrayed the Vale of Aylesbury as the "Goodly Vale", but he fails to remark upon the crosses.

Finally a letter written in 1757 to the prolific field archaeologist of the 18th century William Stukeley fails to mention the Bledlow Cross, even though referring to a Danish Camp at Bledlow and the Whiteleaf Cross itself. Prima facie, there appears to be a strong case against their antiquity, but this point is discussed below.

The Whiteleaf Cross

This cross is on a steep west facing slope, east of Monks Risborough. The cross itself is mounted on top of a large, triangular base which reaches the foot of the hill at an oblique angle, although viewed from a distance it appears perpendicular. It can be seen for 15 miles, and Wise even claimed he could see it from Uffington 30 miles away. The cross has been measured over the centuries with the following results (all in feet):

	Height	*Base*	*Arms (end to end)*
1742	*200*	*189*	*12*
1848	*230*	*340*	*20*
1936	*246*	*400*	*17*
1985	*216*	*380*	*81*

As can be seen there are some wide discrepancies in the measurements, but this author helped out at the 1985 measuring and can vouch for the figures. It has been argued that the tapering shaft recorded by Wise in 1742 would not have survived much weathering, thereby indicating a comparatively recent origin, although the measurements taken then cannot be now verified.

Whiteleaf Cross

Scouring, of course, would have helped enlarge the figure and a report from 1837 stated that this "is now borne by the neighbourhood and never without merry-making". Scouring festivities are a common feature of hill figures, often carried out at seven-year intervals on specific dates, but that for Whiteleaf is not known. This is unfortunate since a date may indicate a Christian or pagan festival, thus giving a possible clue to its origins and purpose.

The base was locally termed the "globe", which may be derived from "glib" or "glide" referring to the habit of the children sliding down the cross on faggots in the 19th century. If there was in fact a globe at one time, then the figure may have represented a Roman victory cross, the globe deteriorating into a triangle over the years. Alternatively it could have been the washout from the cross's lower limb.

Dating the whole figure presents similar speculations. A Saxon charter of 903 CE refers to Whiteleaf Hill as the "eastern brushwood covered hill". The first indication of anything white comes in 1541, when the hill is referred to as Whitt Light (appearing as Whitcliffe in 1766), thus indicating the presence of something white at that date, even if only a patch caused through natural weathering. However, the Saxon charter also contains an intriguing entry - a reference to a boundary mark at Whiteleaf called "Weland's stoc" (Wayland's stock or pole), whose approach was along a "straet", which normally denotes a Roman or other paved road.

The question is, of course, whether this refers to the cross. It cannot be proved, but there are indications that it may well do so. Wayland the Smith was a character in Saxon mythology, the equivalent of the Greek Hephaestus or Roman Vulcan, who forged magical weapons for the gods. His name is associated with other places throughout Britain, notably Wayland's Smithy, a Neolithic tomb on the Ridgeway near the Uffington White Horse. A local legend says that a traveller may have his horse's shoes shod if he leaves a coin on the tomb's capstone overnight and his horse alongside. The White Horse is said to have been shod by Wayland, who is reputed to have possessed a white horse himself. This fits in very well with his attributes, since everything associated with him is on a gigantic, supernormal scale.

So here we have two pointers - Wayland's connection with another hill figure only 30 miles away, and with anything colossal; and what else Wayland's stock be but his mighty (phallic?) pole, subsequently modified in Christian times? It may, of course, date from earlier times than the Saxon, although the position of the paved way is a mystery, as none is known in the area. The Icknield Way may be intended, but it does not fit the description. Such an identification, whether originating in Saxon times or before, would however add weight to the cross's purpose being connected with fertility rites. Wise, however, placed it firmly in the Saxon period and attributed it to a commemoration of the Saxons' victory over the pagan Danes in the 10th century, pinpointing the battlefield near Bledlow. He appears to have connected the cutting of nearly all hill figures with Saxon battles, in much the same way that Stukeley associated ancient monuments with the Druids.

Nevertheless the Saxons could have put their own name on to older monuments, as was probably the case with the earthworks called Grim's Ditch near Great Hampden, which seem to be Celtic boundaries raised by the Catuvellauni tribe. Grim was a nickname for the god Woden whose awesome nature has left its mark in such place names as Wednesbury in

Staffordshire, and the day Wednesday (Woden's Day). In fact one 19th century idea was that the name Whiteleaf was derived from Whitgils or Wiglife, Woden's grandson and father of those legendary heroes Hengist and Horsa, but this theory cannot now be considered seriously. The cross has also been ascribed to Wiglaf, a Mercian king of the 9th century, the name subsequently corrupting to Whiteleaf, but this is etymologically unsound.

Turning to the prehistoric periods, not a few writers have ascribed the cross to the iron, bronze or neolithic eras, i.e. from about 2,000 to 6,000 years ago. H.J. Massingham, in his *Chiltern Country* for example, considered the Whiteleaf and Bledlow Crosses the Watlington White Mark, the Icknield Way (which passes close to each) and the hill figures at Uffington, Cerne Abbas and Wilmington to be contemporary, in his opinion of the late Bronze Age, about 1000 BCE. This no doubt represents a confusion of dating, but there may be a case for a prehistoric origin.

The main line of argument is that the Whiteleaf Cross was originally a phallic symbol, of Iron or Bronze Age date, and that in Christian times it was modified to a cross by the addition of the arms, to remove pagan associations. This practice was encouraged by Pope Gregory I, who wrote to Abbot Mellitus in Britain in 601, instructing him to urge the pagan Saxons to convert their heathen shrines into Christian ones.

It has already been stated that the White Horse of Uffington and the giants of Wilmington and Cerne Abbas are very old, and the latter has obvious phallic attributes. It was probably cut in the Romano-British period and appears to be representation of Hercules. Another opinion has been that a pagan altar once existed at the foot of Whiteleaf Hill, and that the chalk figure was originally that of a god, which was later obliterated and recut as a cross by Christians. Indeed there is a strong possibility that many human representations once graced our hillsides in antiquity.

There are historical records of at least four, which are no longer extant. Two, known as Gogmagog and Corineus are recorded on Plymouth Hoe, one on the Gogmagog Hills near Cambridge and one on Shotover Hill in Oxfordshire. Furthermore in the 1950s T.C. Lethbridge, an archaeologist turned paranormal investigator, successfully located the giant near Cambridge by probing and excavation. In fact he claimed to have discovered a set of hill figures: a goddess on a horse pulling a chariot, a sun god, a warrior and the moon, all of which he thought depicted a Celtic mythological scene.

In the 1960s, but not quite so thorough a manner, S.G. Wildman claimed to have discovered, whilst searching for the lost Red Horse of Tysoe in Warwickshire, another set of hill figures, viz a man with a whip, a bird and two horses, which he interpreted as deriving from Saxon mythology. Perhaps this shows that there is a great deal of undiscovered material waiting to be unearthed in relation to ancient hill figures, although it must be pointed out that limited probing around the Whiteleaf Cross in the past has been unpromising.

There is no doubt that the cross is adjacent to some ancient sites. It has already been mentioned that the Icknield Way, possibly the oldest road in Britain, passes close by and its origins probably lie back in the Neolithic Age. Southwards it continues as the Ridgeway past Uffington to Avebury, and northwards to the Norfolk coast. Just above the cross are two burial mounds. To one side is a Neolithic mound, which is one of the earliest monuments in Buckinghamshire. Most of the barrow was excavated in the 1930s, but more recent work has added to the data obtained.

The mound contained the remains of one individual aged about 45 who was buried around 3700-3650 BCE. The individual was placed in between two halves of a tree trunk which had been split, forming a wooden chamber. There was also evidence of a possible ritual feast or ritual scattering of artefacts, with further evidence that the barrow was used in later years, for instance a Bronze Age burial urn was found placed in the side of the barrow. In addition Roman pottery and coins were discovered in the turf at the top of the mound and in the surrounding ditch. Perhaps this important monument was contemporary with the cross in the Neolithic period, and the rites enacted at the mound have some connection with the symbol depicted close by. The cross could even have been some form of memorial to the incumbent of the barrow, but we shall never know of course.

On the other side is a Bronze Age bowl barrow, cut into a curious cross shape, perhaps the result of plundering. To the north are the Iron Age hillfort of Pulpit Hill and Cymbeline's Mount, said to be the British King Cunobelin's stronghold, and to the south lies Grim's Ditch. Indeed one other memorial theory is that the cross was cut to commemorate the battle between Cunobelin's sons and the Romans.

At this point it is appropriate to consider the more adventurous prehistoric conjectures made about the cross. First a theory that it represented the astrological symbol of Mars (the male sexual symbol) can be dismissed, as can the suggestion that it was cut by the Picts or Scots.

Next, in an extraordinary contribution in 1872 to the Journal of British Archaeology came this hypothesis. It was suggested that the Cerne Abbas Giant was fabricated by a Roman surveyor to contain certain secret knowledge. The author claimed that the Giant's measurements, in multiples of 60 feet, either concealed or revealed the distance from the Giant to other significant sites in miles. By ruling lines across a map of England, he discovered that they joined up sites he believed to be of Roman origin. One of these lines ran from East Anglia, through the Whiteleaf Cross and the Cerne Giant to the island of Ushant off the coast of Brittany. It was by using the information contained within the Giant that the Romans were supposed to have surveyed and laid out their British province. Understandably, this idea did not catch on.

However, a fascinating experiment was carried out in 1980 to test a theory that the cross was connected with Celtic ritual. On October 31st, the eve of the Celtic new year Samhain, when bonfires were lit to help strengthen the winter sun (and which eventually led to our Hallowe'en); it was thought that the rising sun's rays would fall on the cross. Unfortunately, this was found not to be the case, the area being illuminated was nearby Beacon Hill. In fact the cross faces due west of the equinoctial sun. The Cerne Giant appears also to have solar connections, his nickname being Helios, the ancient Greek Sun-God.

To come down to earth, one suggestion may be that both the Chiltern Crosses are landmarks for travellers, lying as they do on either side of the Risborough Gap. Wayfarers would presumably be passing along the Icknield Way, and one theory postulates the "Whit" in Whiteleaf is derived from "wich", an Anglo-Saxon word meaning "dwelling place", such habitations often being near salt production, and thus the cross would guide salt trains on their way to Princes Risborough. Alternatively they could be directing travellers to the monks' cell at Monks Risborough, but more of monks later. Finally on this point, the cross could have aided those travellers from the direction of Shotover and Cuddesdon to aim straight for the cross and thence to Amersham and Hertfordshire. At any event, intentional or not, the Whiteleaf Cross is undoubtedly a landmark.

And now to a favourite hypothesis, namely that the figure is a representation of another form of cross. Taking the Medieval standing cross first, these were surmounted on bases consisting of two or three steps and were set up at crossroads, in villages, in churchyards and at other sites as boundary stones, guides for travellers or memorials. They were used for public proclamations to preach at, or to act as venues at which to transact business, or sell wares. Perhaps the town of Gerrards Cross, only a few miles from the cross, has such an origin. It is argued that the triangular base of the cross has deteriorated from a stepped form. The wayside cross was common in medieval times, with many still in existence. These were often boundary markers and the cross could be an imitation of these, especially taking into consideration Wayland's Stock.

Finally there is the religious cross. The monks' cell at nearby Monks Risborough was established from that at Christ Church of Canterbury, and lasted presumably until the time that Missenden Abbey was dissolved in 1539. The monks may have cut the figure as a devotional symbol, as a demarcation of church lands, to denote a right of sanctuary, or a combination of any of these. As mentioned previously it may have been a Christianised pagan image and perhaps the monks were responsible.

There is a reference to St. John's College, Oxford, originally a Bernadine College for students of the Cistercian Order, that the monks there kept the cross scoured and that a mound was raised in their garden from which they would see the cross and pray within sight of it. But apparently the mound does not exist. Indeed one suggestion was that if it was monastic handiwork, then it would be more likely that the monks at Notley Abbey near Long Crendon would be responsible, since an excellent view of the cross is obtained from that spot. It may also be significant to note that religious houses are associated with other hill figures, for example Cerne Abbas, Wilmington and Ditchling.

The last set of theories concerns the 17th and 18th centuries. The Civil War brings us the first, with the idea that both Chiltern Crosses were military beacons made by John Hampden, a Parliamentarian, to defend the Chilterns from the King's forces. The idea is that the Whiteleaf Cross was intended to indicate to the troops in the Vale of Aylesbury the road via Hampden and Missenden, to their Amersham headquarters. Alternatively it could be that, in cutting turfs for a fire beacon during the war, an area of chalk was exposed and then enlarged, forming the cross, which would have been illuminated by the fire lit nearby. However, the mound which would have been used for this purpose appears to be in the aforementioned Neolithic burial mound, which was already in existence.

One last related hypothesis is that the figure was cut to commemorate John Hampden himself, who was killed at Chalgrove Field during the war in 1643. This seems highly improbable, considering the Puritanical abhorrence of idols. The Hampden Estate itself, however, was made responsible for the maintenance of the cross by an Inclosure Act of George IV.

Which leaves us with one final theory. The monks' cell was probably dissolved in the mid-16th century. The shape of Wise's Cross indicated a recent origin, but old enough to be forgotten. In the intervening period, about 100 years, and assuming the monks were not responsible, it must have been cut by persons unknown. Could it be the work of an obscure religious sect or other secret order? And, if so, what was its purpose and what rites were enacted in sight of the strange hillside depiction? Who knows?

Note: Conjecture concerning the Whiteleaf Cross is often relevant to the Bledlow Cross also, thus the emphasis on the former.

The Bledlow Cross

This cross is cut in the hillside on Wain Hill, 3.75 miles south-west of its companion at Whiteleaf, and is a plain cross with almost equal length arms, termed Greek in style, and it has no base. If one stands on this cross one gains a good view of that at Whiteleaf. Measurements made over the years are as follows:

1848	30 ft	by	15 ft
1936	80 ft	by	75 ft
1985	73 ft	by	68 ft

As with the Whiteleaf Cross, this author can vouch for the 1985 measurements, but the 1848 figures seem a bit wayward! Although first recorded in 1827, an entry in the Records of Bucks in 1863 stated that it was discovered by accident by the writer's father sometime after 1802, when he took tenancy of the land. There is nevertheless one possible earlier reference. This is in respect of a wrong-doer recorded as being brought before the Prince of Wales bailiffs in 1350, by the name of Henry atte Crouche of Bledlowe. It could be that the Old French "crouche", or cross, is contained in his name, and that this is a reference to that at Bledlow. However, it could equally refer to Whiteleaf. Alternatively it could refer to another cross elsewhere, perhaps indicative of where the gentleman came from originally. Lastly it could merely be a name, since surnames in that form were not uncommon in the 14th century.

The Rev. Wise attributed the Bledlow Cross to a Saxon commemoration of a victory over the Danes and backed it up with a dubious derivation of the name Bledlow, which he postulated came from the Saxon words meaning "bloody hill", thereby indicating a battlefield. Apparently at the foot of Wain Hill, the Warren, a number of skeletons were once excavated. Etymologists, on the other hand, prefer "Bledda's hill or burial mound", Bledda being a Saxon personal name. If it refers to a burial mound, it must be the bronze mound known as the Bledlow Cop, a bowl barrow excavated in the 1930s. It had one central inhumation and two cremations, as well as two further inhumations and five or six cremations dating to the early Saxon period, which had been inserted into the mound. The site is unfortunate, being bounded nearly all round by trees and vegetation.

Another suggestion was that, as a landmark, it merely pointed out to any travellers to look for the Whiteleaf Cross, but this seems rather pointless. As to the tradition of scouring, there appears to be a confused local tradition that Eton College, to which the manor of Bledlow was attached, was responsible for the cross's scouring. However, on being asked about the matter a 19th century bursar of the college could find no record of it. In 1863, the contributor to the Records of Bucks article mentioned above stated that apparently local shepherds used to scour it for amusement. He started up himself a subscription amongst parishioners to scour the cross and suggested that a base be added to match that at Whiteleaf. As to orientation, the cross faces NNW, which is not indicative of anything astronomically except approximating to the midsummer sunset.

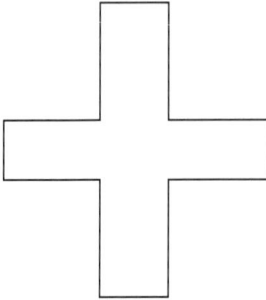

Bledlow Cross (Greek Cross Diagram

Thus this is about all that can be said about the origins of Bledlow Cross, in addition to those mentioned in the Whiteleaf section.

Conclusions

Can we arrive at any conclusions? Starting from hard facts, Bledlow Cross is recorded no earlier than 1827 and Whiteleaf 1742. They both face roughly west, a characteristic they share with many other hill figures. Other crosses exist, such as Ditchling, and two modern war memorials in Kent, and there may well have been others that have now become overgrown and forgotten. It does not take long for this to happen and so it is amazing that the Uffington Horse has been kept scoured for about 3,000 years.

In the case of Whiteleaf, there is a connection with a religious house, a feature common with other hill figures. There is also no reason why they should not date from antiquity, but further than this, much is speculation. Further evidence may come to light in the future, perhaps from manuscripts, local lore or work in the vein of Lethbridge.............

Taking the two Crosses individually, Bledlow does show strong indications of being 18th century, given that Stukeley's correspondent in 1757 mentioned only Whiteleaf. This, coupled with the fact that being fairly small in 1827, would mean that it would have been much smaller when cut and therefore almost invisible if very old, points to a comparatively recent date. The nearby Watlington White Mark is an 18th century folly and Bledlow may well be the result of a country landowner's whim. Whiteleaf is more enigmatic, due to its unusual appearance, its proximity to a monks' cell and the reference to Wayland's Stock.

Therefore, though not by any means ruling out any ancient, ritual or mysterious associations altogether, Whiteleaf can quite likely be medieval and possibly much older, even if not originally a cross. If the two figures are accepted as crosses then it is almost certain that they are Christian, since the symbol was not used in pagan Britain, although it was elsewhere in Europe. The monks must therefore be strong candidates.

It would have been satisfying, nevertheless, to have reached firm conclusions, but the Chiltern Crosses are mysterious puzzles which have kept their secrets.

Works Consulted:

White Horses & Other Hill Figures, by Morris Marples (1970)
The Hill Figures of England, by Sir Flinders Petrie (1926)
The Secret of the White Leaf Cross, by Benjamin Chilton (1921)
Gogmagog, by T.C. Lethbridge (1957)
Records of Bucks (various)

This chapter was my first published article, which appeared in Strange Wycombe, a booklet commemorating the 700th Mayoral Anniversary of High Wycombe in Buckinghamshire. It was published in 1985, edited by Alan Cleaver, and I have revised and updated it for this volume.

3 - Woden And England: The Saxon God's Influence

Introduction and Etymology

The god Woden was a major figure in the Anglo-Saxon pantheon, whose influence in England is still apparent today. To begin with, the name Woden is derived from the hypothetical Indo-European word *awe meaning "to blow", thus indicating that he was primarily a wind god, this then leading to the Proto-Germanic *Wodanaza and ultimately to Woden. It seems that the blowing aspect led to the theme of Woden being associated with "fury". This is supported by a reference by the 11th century German chronicler Adam of Bremen to Wodan being "the furious".

Woden/Odin

The name Woden is the Anglo-Saxon equivalent of the Norse name of Odin, a member of the Germanic pantheon of deities. But there is little written record of Woden himself, so the myths concerning Odin are often considered to apply to Woden as well. He was regarded as the chief of all the gods and with the help of his brothers he was responsible for the formation of the earth and the heavens from the dead body of Ymir the giant. He also created the first man and woman from an alder and an ash tree and set up the laws that governed the universe and directed the fate of humankind.

Woden's attributes included wisdom, learning, magic and poetry and was overseer of the fate of the souls of the dead. The Icelandic saga Havamal describes how Woden was hanged on a tree for nine days and nights and was pierced by a spear. This voluntary sacrifice enabled him to learn the secret of the runes. Some see Christian influence in this, alluding to Christ's hanging on the Cross, but this is disputed. The gaining of the runes and thus great wisdom does, however, suggest an independent Northern tradition. Indeed, it may be that hanging for nine days on a gallows-tree and being pierced by a spear may indicate an ancient initiation rite.

Woden's main role was to oversee those who had died in battle and to welcome them to Valhalla where they would enact battles for eternity. His wife was Frige, goddess of foreknowledge, and sacred to him were the raven and the wolf. He gained his wisdom by drinking water from the well of wisdom named Mimir, but he had to leave one of his eyes behind as a pledge for the drink. As the one-eyed god who wore a hood to disguise his identity, and armed with a spear, he was accompanied by two ravens named Huginn ("Thought") and Muninn ("Memory") and two wolves called Geri and Freki, as he traversed the world on his eight-legged horse Sleipnir. In Norse mythology he is eventually swallowed by the wolf Fenrir who has broken free from his shackles at the destruction of the world known as Ragnarok, probably meaning "the final destiny of the gods".

There is little mention of Woden in English literature, but there are a couple of note. The Nine Herbs Charm from an 11th century English manuscript has the god curing a snake bite by hurling nine "glory-twigs" at the snake, which caused it to fly into nine pieces. "Glory-twigs" were pieces of wood, which had been marked with runic symbols representing the names of the herbs used in the cure. The Exeter Book Maxims of Old English poetry of unknown date also contains a reference to Woden in a poem, which compares Woden unfavourably to the Christian God:

"Woden made idols, the Almighty made glory and the spacious heavens".

Anglo-Saxon Royal Genealogies

It appears that of all the Germanic peoples, the Anglo-Saxons were unique in ascribing their tribes' origins back to Woden. The Venerable Bede, in his *Ecclesiastical History of the English Nation*, tells us that the legendary Anglo-Saxon leaders Hengist and Horsa, whom the Celtic king Vortigern invited to Britain to help defeat marauding tribes, were the sons of one Victgilsus, whose father was Vecta, who himself was Woden's son.

Another example was Ine, King of Wessex, who traced his ancestry from Cerdic, the legendary founder and first king of Wessex who believed he had descended from a line leading back to Woden. In addition the Anglo-Saxon Chronicle tells us that both Mercian kings Penda (died 655 CE) and Offa (died 796 CE) derived their ancestry from Woden. Even King Alfred claimed such descent by the fact that he considered himself to be fourteenth in line from Cerdic and twenty-second from Woden himself. However, being a Christian he also believed he was thirty-ninth from Noah and fiftieth from Adam!

Wednesday

Amazing as it is, the names of pagan Anglo-Saxon gods are still used in the 21st century for our names of days of the week, thus highlighting that tradition can last for millennia. Sunday and Monday are self-explanatory, but still retain the flavour of pre-Christian times when the natural world was revered. Saturday again harks back to pagan days, but this time from the Roman god of time Saturn.

The rest of the days of the week all originate from the following Anglo-Saxon (AS) gods:

Thursday - the thunder god Thor	(AS Thuresdaeg)
Friday - the goddess Frigg, wife of Woden	(AS Frigedaeg)
Tuesday - the war god Tiw	(AS Tiwesdaeg)
Wednesday - the chief god Woden	(ASWodnesdaeg)

Thus the English name Wednesday, as well as the names of the rest the days of the week, has been retained in spite of influence from Christianity and from Norman French and Latin.

Woden Place-Names

Place-name evidence shows that Woden-based names are common in northern Germany, Denmark, southern Sweden and England. There is evidence that, despite the conversion of the English to Christianity begun by St Augustine in 597, the old religion was not swept aside immediately. For instance Harrow in Middlesex derives from the Anglo-Saxon word 'hearg' meaning "pagan temple or shrine". Similarly Weedon Beck in Northamptonshire and Wye in Kent have as their origins the Anglo-Saxon word 'weoh' denoting a "heathen temple" or "idol". So it appears that temples, or memories of temples, lingered on enough in the landscape for their pagan attributes to be fixed in their place-names. Perhaps we can envisage the local village people observing the decay of these structures and over time shunning them or their locality as "heathen" or even "devilish".

Wednesbury in Shropshire (Woden's fort) refers possibly to a now obliterated Iron-Age hill-fort where once a temple dedicated to Woden stood and which subsequently became the site of the parish church. Alternatively, the ancient fortifications could have led the Anglo-Saxons to believe that, due to its once monumental earthworks, it must have been made by a god. Adam's Grave, a long barrow near Alton Priors in Wiltshire, was earlier called Wodnesbeorh meaning Woden's Barrow, and Woden was also associated with the huge earthwork called Wandsyke, which stretches from Hampshire to Somerset. An early record refers to this as Wodnes dic.

Excavations at Woodnesborough in Kent, "Woden's Mound", have revealed remains of feasting and cremation, and it may indicate a cult of Woden in the area, as these activities were associated with the god. Similarly Wiltshire may well have been an area of Woden worship, since four Woden place-names are situated close to each other. They are Wanborough (Wodnes-beorg – Woden's Barrow), Wansdyke (Woden's dyke or embankment), and two early place-names Woddesgeat (Woden's gate or gap) and Wodnesdene (Woden's valley). Indeed it seems that the Vale of Pewsey was a centre of ritual Woden veneration. Such cult places had so much influence that Woden's name was remembered for some until it was eventually transmuted into the names we use today.

Woden's hanging on the tree probably influenced the names of trees and groves in the landscape. In England there are two possible recorded instances, a Woden's Oak in Worcestershire and a Woden's Trunk in Chieveley in Berkshire. Other Woden-derived place-names include Wambrook in Somerset (Woden's brook), Wednesfield in Derbyshire (Woden's field), Wednesham in Cheshire (Woden's enclosure), Woden Hill in Hampshire and Woodbridge in Suffolk (Woden's bridge). Wormshill in Kent is unusual in that it derives not from a prehistoric site but a topographical feature, i.e. Woden's Hill. However the god was also known by a "nickname", which is explored in the following section.

Grim

The name Grim, from the Norse word Grimr meaning "the hooded one", is another name by which Odin/Woden is known because of his practice of changing shape and disguising himself. The name Grim is often to be found applied to prehistoric features in the landscape.

To begin with there are several earthworks called Grim's Ditch, including those in Wiltshire, Oxfordshire, Hertfordshire and Middlesex. In Herefordshire, the iron-age hill fort at Credenhill is recorded to have the earlier name of Grimsworth. In addition Gryme's Dyke in Essex and Grimsburyburh in Oxfordshire are further examples and these refer to prehistoric earthworks. It is not unusual for such structures to be named after otherworldly figures, which existed before the Anglo-Saxons arrived and which required a name. Similar instances attribute their names to the Devil, such as the Devil's Dyke in Sussex.

Sometimes Woden and the Devil have been confused. After the Anglo-Saxons were converted to Christianity it appears that they wished to renounce any references to their previous pagan religion. This led to place-names such as Grimsby (the Devil's abode) and Grimsthorpe (the Devil's village) being so named. The Anglo-Saxons referred to the famous neolithic flint mines in Suffolk known as Grime's Graves, the landscape of which is dotted about with "pock holes", residues of shafts now filled in, by this name, which literally means "the graves, or quarries, of the hooded one". It seems that huge, ancient prehistoric earthworks were believed by the Anglo-Saxons to have been dug out and worked by primeval and powerful beings.

Names of other otherworldly figures are not uncommon in England's place-names, including the Celtic gods Bran and Lugh and umpteen Christian saints, but those are another story. It just goes to show how various peoples have regarded the features in the landscape, whatever their belief system, the Anglo-Saxons being no different. Speaking of beliefs, there was one king, however, who was taking no chances. King Raedwald of East Anglia died around 624 and is assumed to have been the occupant of the ship burial at Sutton Hoo in Suffolk. It is recorded that he kept in his temple one altar dedicated to Christ and another to a pagan god, who is usually identified as Woden. The Venerable Bede later wrote that King

Ealdwulf of East Anglia recalled that when he was a boy he visited Raedwald's temple complete with the two altars.

Folklore

In English folklore Woden mainly appears in the guise of Grim. An example is the Bronze Age enclosure containing hut circles on Dartmoor which according to tradition has been called Grimspound. The archaeologist Leslie Grinsell points out that the name came "from the heathen Grim, which can mean the Devil, Woden, or any goblin or spectre". Grim's Ditch near Streatley in Oxfordshire is an earthwork also known as Grim's Bank and the Devil's Ditch, and tradition has it that it was ploughed by the Devil in the course of one night. It was also said that two nearby round barrows were scrapings from his ploughshare and that he hurled another, smaller, mound at one of his imps for not driving straight.

Over near Naphill in Buckinghamshire is another Grim's Ditch where once upon a time it was thought by the locals that it should be filled in, but apparently, such was the reputation of the earthwork that it was never carried out, because they were too fearful of the consequences. And going back to Grimes Graves, there is a barrow not far from the site that is known as Grim's Hoe, which folklore suggests that it was the meeting-place of the local Hundred in Saxon times. The aforementioned Wansdyke in Wiltshire is said by locals to have been built on a Wednesday, indicating that Woden had performed this tremendous feat in one day.

Traditionally Woden was one-eyed and wore a cloak and a wide-brimmed hat and rode his eight-legged horse Sleipnir. In this garb he was often seen as leader of the Wild Hunt, as were the Devil, King Arthur and Herne the Hunter, that horned demon who led the Hunt in Windsor Forest. On these spectral hunts he gathers the souls of the dead and delivers them to Valhalla, thus making him a psychopomp in the same vein as the Roman god Mercury and the Angel Gabriel.

Belief in the Wild Hunt was particularly prevalent in North West Europe, being known as Wodende Jager in the Germanic parts of the Continent and Odinsjagt in Scandinavia. However, in this guise Woden became a target for the Church and in Medieval times he was actually equated with the Devil himself. In his guise as hunt leader, Woden was also known as Herian, and Walter Map (1140-1210) in his work entitled *De Nugis Curialium* uses the variant Herla, a mythical ancient British king who became leader of the Wild Hunt, whose retinue were referred to as " the troop of Herlethingus".

Returning to Adam's Grave long barrow near Alton Priors in Wiltshire, formerly known as Woden's Barrow, and Old Adam by the 19th century, there was a stone at its base which was known as Little Eve. Up until at least 1950, there was a local superstition that if anyone runs round the barrow seven times a giant will emerge. This does not refer to Woden as such, but it is an interesting folklore survival.

Folk memory of Woden in everyday life, especially up to modern times, is sparse. However there is a healing rhyme recorded in the 19th century from Lincolnshire where an old woman tries to cure her grandchild of a fever. First a kind of ritual was enacted consisting of nailing three horseshoes in the centre of a footboard with a hammer which was fixed crosswise on them. Then, removing the hammer the grandmother tapped each horseshoe whilst chanting the following verse:

Father, Son and Holy Ghost,

Nail the Devil to this post -

With this mell I thrice do knock,

One for God, and one for Wod, and one for Lok.

A mell is an archaic Northern dialect word for a hammer. It is interesting to note that the names of two Germanic gods are quoted here, Woden and Loki, but such linguistic survivals like this are rare.

Conclusion

To close, it must be pointed out that one aspect of Woden was his ability to draw strength from his contradictions. On one hand he was the creator of humanity and lord of the trees, hills, wind and the sky, and the ancestor of kings, but on the other he was lord of the gallows and the god who chose the fate of warriors engaged in battles.

Thus Woden has proved to be a durable feature of England's history, culture and landscape and there has been a revival of interest in the god in neo-pagan circles today. Wodenism, or Anglo-Heathenism, is a small English branch of "heathens who follow the Germanic tradition", which brings us up to the present day.

Finally, an imaginative portrayal by author Brian Branston:

The Anglo-Saxon Woden stalked the rolling downland, one-eyed and wise beyond all knowing in cloak and hood when the weather was fine, stopping at cross-roads to recognize his own dangling from the gallows: but on black and stormy nights he racketed across the sky at the head of his wild hunt of lost and noisy souls.

Works Consulted:

Anglo-Saxon Paganism, by David Wilson (1992)
The Lost Gods of England, by Brian Branston (1957)
The Lore of the Land, by Jennifer Westwood & Jacqueline Simpson (2005)
Herne the Hunter, by Michael John Petry (1972)
Folklore of Prehistoric Sites in Britain, by Leslie V. Grinsell (1976)

This chapter first appeared in Merry Meet Magazine no. 55, Winter 2015

4 - Montem Mound: A Prehistoric Burial Mound In Slough

Montem Mound (Author Photo)

There is a mysterious feature to be found in that oft-maligned town of Slough in Berkshire. Surrounded by 20th century office blocks, a leisure centre and an ice rink, it exudes strange and ancient vibrations in an otherwise concrete jungle. What can this structure be, one asks? Some think it is just a grass-covered hillock of no importance, but others see it as an important archaeological site in a place where there is little in the way of historical structures to be seen. As I conclude in this chapter, the Montem Mound[1] was constructed long before Slough became the built up town we see today.

Mounds of various kinds are to be found throughout the countryside of our land, dating from prehistory up until modern times. They have been constructed for a variety of reasons, and often they have attracted folklore and legends. The vast majority can be fairly well dated, but the Montem Mound at Salt Hill in Slough has always been an enigma and has long kept its secrets. First recorded in 1561, it was used by nearby Eton College

---

1 Note: Montem Mound is a scheduled ancient monument, which means that any unauthorised interference at the site, such as digging, is illegal. However, it is accessible to the public at any time to visit and to ponder its antiquity. Just head for the Montem Leisure Centre and Ice Arena.

pupils for their "Salt" ceremony, hence the local name Salt Hill (see chapter 5).

In Victorian times a wooden summer house was built on top of the Montem and the neighbouring area became a pleasure garden. The mound may now look small to support such a structure, but over the centuries it had been enlarged by the Eton boys, but now it has returned to something like its original size by the tender hand of Slough Borough Council.

Now to turn to when the Montem was constructed and by whom. It has variously been described as:

- A Bronze Age tumulus (barrow or burial mound)
- A Roman tumulus
- A Saxon tumulus
- A Medieval moot hill
- A Norman motte & bailey (the official explanation of local archaeologists)

To start with the motte and bailey, the size of the mound eliminates this explanation straight away, as it is only about 20 feet (6 metres) high. These structures built by the Normans soon after the Conquest were wooden keeps (the motte) set up on the top of a large mound, with an enclosed area (the bailey) at the base of the mound reserved for domestic buildings, chapels and workshops. There are many examples to be found in Britain, all of which are larger than the Montem, the smallest being about 50 feet (15 metres) high. A good example is the castle mound at Oxford.

The wooden keeps were often eventually replaced by stone ones and it is highly likely that Windsor Castle, about 2 1/2 miles from Slough, began as a wooden motte and bailey. In 1986, some chance finds of late Saxon pottery shards led archaeologists to date the Montem to the early Norman period, but this does not necessarily mean that it was in fact constructed at that time. So it is clearly obvious that the Montem is far too small to be a motte and can be eliminated without further ado.

As to it being a moot hill, it is quite possible that it could have been reused for this purpose. These were often reused tumuli, which in medieval times were a focus for the local community where various kinds of village business were carried out. It may well be that the Montem was used for this purpose, but sometimes they were purpose built. However, its position points to a much earlier construction date.

It is certain that the Montem was originally a burial mound, since its site at the summit of a hill (Salt Hill), near a stream (Chalvey Brook) and close to a holy well (Queen Anne's Well) on the west side of the brook, but no longer visible, all point to this explanation. Such juxtapositions were common in pre-Christian times, with trees, hills, streams and springs, and the area they occupied, often being considered as sacred. The spring water at Queen Anne's Well in its heyday was renowned as a cure for eye conditions. In fact the Stuart Queen Anne was so pleased with the well's remarkably clear water that she had the spring lined with stone and a headstone constructed which exhibited the royal cipher. The well was still used up until the reign of George III, and apparently, Queen Charlotte was wont to have water collected by her servants and carried to nearby Windsor Castle. In ancient times the area surrounding the well, stream and mound must have been a very sacred spot, with Montem Mound dominating the site, being visible for some distance.

To add support to the theory that it is a burial mound comes from four sources:

1. *Magna Britannia, Volume 1* by Daniel & Samuel Lysons (1813) refers to it as a "tumulus".
2. 2. *The History & Antiquities of the County of Buckingham* by George Lipscomb (1847) describes it as a "small tumulus".
3. *Records of Bucks., volume 4* (1870) again refers to it as a "tumulus".
4. *The Royal Commission on Historic Monuments, Volume 1* (1912) describes it a "mound at Salt Hill, possibly a tumulus".

So, these references certainly are strong evidence that the Montem had always been considered a tumulus, but the question is - which period does it date from?

There are three burial mounds around the Slough area – the Montem Mound, Taeppa's Mound at Taplow Court and a mound on Stoke Park Golf Course. The latter one has been firmly dated to the Bronze Age, so there is no debate about that. As to Taeppa's Mound, when excavated in 1883, it was found to contain the remains of a Saxon chieftain, together with the most important Saxon grave goods found in England until the Sutton Hoo ship burial came along in 1939. So here we have two local mounds, one firmly dated to the Bronze Age, perhaps around 1500 BCE, and another dared to the 7th century CE.

Burial mounds in folklore often have strange associations. Prime examples are tumuli involving dragons guarding treasure within, fairy folklore and the Devil, the latter being particularly connected with Bronze Age mounds. However appealing such folklore may be, unfortunately there appears to be none associated with Montem Mound. Nevertheless the mound was deliberately positioned in a prominent place and, being a hallowed spot, may well have led later on to it being reused as a moot hill and finally by the pupils of Eton College for their Montem Salt Ceremony (see chapter 5). My view has always been that Montem Mound belonged to the Bronze Age, but now it has been accurately dated.

In the 2016/7 academic year, Reading University carried out an investigation on the Mound via a new method of dating by drilling into sites, which enables information to be accessed, whilst causing minimal damage. Radio carbon dating of charred remains of plants retrieved indicate that the Mound dates from about the late 6th or early 7th century CE. At the time, this area came under the kingdom of Mercia, and was probably ruled by a Kentish sub-king. Dr Jim Leary, who led the investigation, spoke of the Anglo-Saxon period as a "time of heroic myth and legend where archaeology fills the gaps of the historic record. This discovery will add so much more to our understanding of the people who lived in Britain at this time. It will also extend our knowledge of the history of Slough".

Slough Borough Council manages the site and has prepared an enhancement scheme, which includes an information board explaining the new interpretation of the Mound's origins. This is a major achievement for the Borough, which does not possess much in the way of archaeological sites, and Montem Mound will now be celebrated as Slough's most important ancient monument.

On a personal note, these findings vindicate my view all along that it was in fact a burial mound, even if I deduced the date incorrectly.

This is a revised article, which was published first in Merry Meet Magazine no. 53 Summer 2014

5 - Ad Montem: The Eton College Salt Custom

Montem ceremony 1825

The title of this chapter, *Ad Montem*, is Latin for "to the hill", which refers to the Montem Mound at Salt Hill, Chalvey in the borough of Slough, as discussed in the previous chapter. The phrase was used by Eton College schoolboys to describe a strange custom which they used to enact at this enigmatic monument until it ceased after 1844. The custom also gave rise to the name of the locality in which the mound is located, i.e. Salt Hill, for reasons which will become clear as we proceed into this investigation of a once popular tradition.

The earliest reference we have dates from 1561 and is recorded in William Malim's Cosuetudinarium, which is worth quoting in full, as it is a quaint example of 16th century writing:

> *"About the Feast of the Conversion of St. Paul, at nine o'clock on a day chosen by the Master, the boys go to the Hill (ad montem), in the customary manner in which they go to gather nuts in the month of September. The Hill is a sacred spot in the boyish religion of Etonians: on account of the beauty of the country, the charm of the greensward, the coolness of the shade, the harmonious song of the birds, they*

dedicate the retreat to Apollo and the Muses, they celebrate it in verses, they call it Tempe[2], and they extol it above Helicon[3].

Here the novices, or freshmen, who have not yet manfully and stoutly stood up to the lash for a whole year in the Etonian ranks, are first seasoned with salt, and then deftly portrayed in little verses having as much wit (salem) and humour as possible. Then they make epigrams on the freshmen, vying with one another in pleasantry and jest. They may say whatever comes uppermost, provided it be in Latin, courteously expressed, and free from offensive buffoonery.

Finally they bedew their faces and cheeks with salt tears, and then at last are initiated into the rites of veterans. Ovations follow, and little triumphs, and the novices rejoice in good earnest that their toils are ended and that they are admitted into the fellowship of such merry fellow-soldiers. When all is over, the boys return about 5 o'clock, and after supper play until eight."

It seems that the prime reason for the tradition was the collection of money or salt. The sum raised was used to fund the festivities, and any surplus was given to the senior scholar elected to Cambridge to pay for his support. Appreciable sums were often collected, sometimes in excess of £1,000. Over the years the custom varied somewhat, but the key elements were consistent, and the following gives some idea of the festivities.

The first part of the tradition entailed the election of the "Captain of the Montem", which usually fell to the Senior Colleger. However, since he could be called up to Cambridge at any moment to fill a vacancy, he was never certain of his captaincy until 20 days before the Montem ceremony. It was the rule that he had to present himself at Cambridge within 20 days, otherwise he would have to forfeit his claim. So on the night following the twentieth day before Montem, all the Collegers stayed up late in the Long Chamber at the College to see if a messenger from Cambridge would arrive.

Then at the last stroke of midnight from the clock in Lupton's Tower, they all slammed window shutters or dropped their beds on the floor, the

2 Tempe is a valley in Greece near Mount Olympus, the abode of the gods.

3 Mount Helicon is sited in Boeotia in Greece, and it was here that the Muses inspired the ancient Greek poets.

noise from which could be heard from neighbouring Windsor. There then occurred a thundering yell of "Montem sure!", and it was not until the early hours of the morning that the revelry ceased. This night was called Montem-Sure-Night and the custom continued until the penultimate one in 1841.

Salt bearer

The next stage consisted of the selection and attiring of those boys who would be engaged in demanding salt or money from passers-by. Two Salt Bearers were chosen and they were assisted by ten or twelve "Runners" or "Servitors", all of whom were dressed in fancy costumes, often richly ornate, and they followed the procession accompanied by two or three military bands. They were followed by fifth-form "Corporals" or "Polemen" who were themselves followed by boys from the lower school dressed in the Eton costume of blue jacket and white trousers. The latter also carried satin money bags and painted staves, the tops of which were engraved with Latin or Greek texts and which were cut in two by the Corporals' swords at the end of the ceremony in the school yard, preceded by a "Marshall". A Lieutenant brought up the rear of the procession, together with a "Parson" and a "Clerk".

And so this collection of pupils made its way from the school across the fields until it reached the Montem Mound itself, also known as Salt Hill. Earlier in the day, often at dawn, the Runners would make their way to their various appointed places. As well as one at Salt Hill, there was one at Slough, Iver, Gerrards Cross, Maidenhead Bridge, Windsor Bridge, Colnbrook and two at Datchet Bridge. It was their duty to collect money from passers-by in exchange for a blue ticket as a receipt, crying "Salt! Salt!" These tickets bore a motto which on alternate years were "*Mos pro lege*" (custom in return for the law) or "*Pro more et monte*" (for custom and the Mound), together with the year. If such a ticket were displayed on the person, such as on their hat, it would protect them from any further demands that day.

Salt has been important in many societies from early times. The Romans paid their soldiers in salt, as it was valuable for such things as food preparation, in fact the Latin word for salt, *sal*, gave us the word salary, although later this was changed to rations and currency. It was also considered to be powerful magically, and the spilling of salt was seen as a bad omen to be averted by throwing the spilt salt over one's left shoulder into the Devil's eye. It was also used in superstitious customs to keep witches away. Thus it is not surprising, perhaps, that salt was caught up in the Ad Montem event, a substance held in awe since time immemorial.

It was said that William III was accosted once by the boys not long after his accession. It appears that he was travelling in his carriage along the Bath Road at Slough when he was stopped by the salt bearers. However his Dutch guards, unaware of the nature of the custom, drew their swords only to be stopped in the nick of time by the King. Monarchs were especially generous and donated what was known as Royal Salt, and it was the custom for the king and queen to give 50 guineas each. Indeed, royalty often attended the festivities in person, including the aforesaid William III, George IV, William IV and Queen Victoria. The forceful demanding of salt was mocked in a magazine published in 1712 when it was an annual event as follows:

When Boys at Eton once a Year

In Military Pomp appear,

He who just trembled at the Rod

Treads it a Heroe, talks a God,

And in an instant can create

A Dozen Officers of State.

His little legion All assail,

Arrest without Release, or Bail;

Each passing Traveller must halt,

Must pay the Tax, and eat the Salt.

You don't love Salt you say-and storm-

Look o' these Staves, Sir-and conform.

Having arrived at the Montem, a boy designated the Ensign climbed to the top of the mound and waved a flag. This ended the ceremony in the latter years, but in earlier days, the two pupils dressed as the Parson and Clerk then said mock prayers in Latin. Occasionally there was much hilarity when, dressed in the ornate costume of a Church dignity, the Parson would proceed to kick the Clerk to the bottom of the mound. In 1778, however, Queen Charlotte was so shocked at this element of the proceedings that she requested it to be stopped, whereupon it was never repeated after that date.

After this was all over, the royal party returned to Windsor and the pupils, together with visitors, retired to two local inns, the Windmill and the Castle. Having dined, everyone filed out into the inns' gardens, where all the fruit and vegetables growing there were wantonly destroyed with the aid of the swords which had been carried all day. Apparently this reached excessive proportions in the latter years when it was used as a means of obtaining bills against an unpopular Captain.

The day ended at about six in the evening when the boys in similar procession made their way back to the great square at the College and, after marching round it, were dismissed. To conclude there was a promenade on Windsor Terrace with entertainment from musical bands, and it was not uncommon for the Royal Family to attend.

Montem Mound (Salt Hill) 1850

One more feature of the Montem day must be described, and which was always popular. This was termed the Ode. Supposedly written by the "Montem Poet", but was often really the work of youngsters from the College, it consisted of a sheet of rhymes and puns about the main participants of the procession and alluded to their characters and idiosyncrasies. It apparently sold very well. A memorable Montem Poet was an eccentric Windsor man named Herbert Stockhore who attended every Montem from 1784 to 1835. He would drive about in a donkey cart, dressed in flamboyant attire, reciting his ode, copies of which he sold to the public. He lived to over 90, and when he was 81 in 1826, his ode was as follows:

I Herbert Stockhore, once more,

In spite of age and pains rheumatic,

Hop down to Montem with verses Attic[4],

4 Attica was a region in ancient Greece comprising the city of Athens.

To make the Muse as have done before

For why should I lie abed groaning and bickering

When I ought to be up to sing Captain Pickering.

Pickering was the Eton College boy who benefited from the salt raised at that particular Montem. All this demonstrates the sense of fun and mayhem the custom generated.

As we have seen in Malim's report of 1561, it was then traditional for the ceremony to take place annually around the feast of the Conversion of St. Paul, which is 25th January. Later on, it became biennial, and in 1759 it changed to triennial and was moved to the Tuesday in Whitsun week, which would have promised more favourable weather. The event then continued until the last was staged on 28th May 1844. At this final procession Prince Albert himself gave the Royal Salt amounting to £100.

With the arrival of the year of 1847 the incumbent provost Mr. Hodgson decided that enough was enough and recommended that the festivities be abolished. This gave rise to an outcry and led to two meetings of Old Etonians in London, at which a letter from Mr. Hodgson was read out. Although he described the Montem day as "a splendid show", he said that it had "immoral tendencies" and that the recent opening of the railway would "cause an influx of objectionable characters", a statement which was "greeted with shouts of derision". In addition, local youths had become a nuisance, fighting with the College boys and causing general mayhem. Thus 1844 marked the end of the event and with it the end of an ancient tradition, Queen Victoria herself reluctantly consenting to its cessation.

It has been suggested that the Eton boys' ceremony has pagan origins, the sprinkling of salt recalling earlier kinds of initiation traditions. In earlier times salt symbolised permanence, immortality and the incorruptible spirit, and it was considered to have magical powers. In fairy lore, sprinkled salt was considered a charm, which would prevent fairies from abducting a newborn child. In Roman times, salt was placed on the lips of eight-day-old babies to ward off evil spirits. However this type of argument is conjecture, as there is no documentary evidence to back it up, but who knows, traditions can sometimes last for a very long time, even though their original purpose may be forgotten. The *Ad Montem* festivities have been discussed over the years as to their origins and there are four versions.

First is the hypothesis that the event developed from the custom of appointing a "boy bishop". This used to take place at various cathedrals, the best known being that at Salisbury, whereby the incumbent was chosen to act as bishop on St Nicholas' day. The Captain of Montem was equated with the Boy Bishop, and the Salt Bearers with the Deacons. The wearing by the

Boy Bishop of clerical attire and the reading of Latin prayers at some of the early processions adds weight to this suggestion. This sounds plausible, but there is no concrete or documentary evidence to support it.

Secondly, the possibility has been suggested that its origins lie in monks', or friars', practice of selling consecrated salt for medical uses, especially in European Catholic countries. This sounds as though it was a ploy by the friars to gain money, playing on the superstitious laity who would not have realised that in fact the holy salt had no remedial effect except, perhaps, as a placebo. Again there is no real evidence for this derivation.

Thirdly an outlandish theory comes from the pen of E.O. Gordon, in whose 1914 book entitled *Prehistoric London: Its Mounds & Circles* he suggested that ancient mounds in and around the London area were structures constructed by the Druids. From here, his theory went on to surmise that the founder of Eton College, Henry VI, was eager to show that he had links with Celtic kings, and that Montem Mound was a meeting place used by the ancient Druids. This is a late appearance of connecting ancient sites to the Celts or Druids. The 18th century antiquary William Stukeley, who wrote copiously about Stonehenge and Avebury, attributed many prehistoric remains to the work of the Druids, but even by Gordon's time this was an outdated view. I leave the reader to make up his own mind on this idea.

And lastly, the setup which ruled at Winchester College was adopted at Eton College, so it has been suggested that the procession was adopted too. At Winchester there was a daily procession called 'Ad Montem' which made its way to nearby St Catherine's Hill, the event being commonly referred to as "going on hills". Winchester College was founded in 1382 by the Bishop of Winchester, William Wykeham, whilst that at Eton was founded in 1440 by Henry VI, who borrowed Winchester's statutes and took its headmaster and a few of its scholars and set them up at Eton. The former's traditions could well have been transferred to the later college as well. This seems to me to be the most plausible explanation, as there is at least documentary evidence here on Winchester College's influence on Eton College.

So it was inevitable that the *Ad Montem* event would eventually cease, especially as since 1847 the Eton/Slough area has been so built up, previously consisting of broad fields as far as the eye could see. It would be very incongruous nowadays to see a stream of Eton College pupils marching from Eton to Salt Hill in Slough dressed up, as they would be and weaving their way round tarmac roads, houses and other modern constructions, which would be in the way. On the other hand it was a custom that was popular and well received on the whole, but it would not really fit into the world we live in today.

Works Consulted:

The History of Slough, by Maxwell Fraser (1973)
Records of Bucks. (various)

6 - The Norse Gods & Fate: A Selection Of Norse Gods

Urdr or Wyrd

The Oxford English Dictionary defines fate as "Power predetermining events unalterably from eternity". The ancient Greeks believed that this power was in the hands of the Fates, three goddesses named Clotho, Lachesis and Atropos, responsible respectively for the winding, spinning and severing of life's thread. These are the most well-known deities of this kind, but Norse mythology also has its own similar triad.

Known as the Norns, they comprised Verdandi (the present), Skuld (the future) and Urdr, who ruled over the past (and who gave her name to fate itself). Urdr, or Wyrd in Anglo-Saxon terminology, is a feminine noun meaning "that which has come to pass". The Norns resided at the foot of the ash tree Yggdrasil, or world-tree, which the trio would water daily from the Well of Urdr. These three goddesses were wont to weave webs not only of great complexity, but also of great haphazardness. Both Urdr and Verdandi showed no animosity towards mortals, but Skuldr could fly off the handle over any perceived insult, however trivial. Nevertheless, at childbirth the Norns always attended the scene and decided the fate of the new-born.

But the Norns had control over not only mere mortals but the gods themselves, so this chapter will now proceed to see how fate intervened in the lives of half a dozen of the gods of the Norse pantheon, or Aesir. There are two points to make initially though. The Norse myths are complex, with differing versions of the same events and cases where one source of an event may not appear in another. I have therefore had to be selective. In addition, I have had to reluctantly omit goddesses such as Freyjar or Frigg as they did not live the eventful lives as their male counterparts. The ultimate fate of everything of course occurred at the apocalyptic climax of Ragnarok, which is dealt with in the last section.

Odin

Born of the giantess Bestla and the god Borr, Odin gradually displaced the latter as leader of the Aesir, the collective name of the twelve gods who lived in Asgard, this realm being broadly the equivalent of the Greek Olympus.

As a war god, Odin presided over Valhalla, the hall where warriors who have fallen in battle and are chosen by the Valkyries, Odin's handmaidens, as fit to join the god's entourage for eternity. One of Odin's titles was "Allfather" and as well as being a god of the dead, he was also god of cunning, poetry and wisdom. Originally, he had been chief of a raven clan, which is why he is often portrayed as being accompanied by two of these birds, Huginn (thought) and Muninn (memory). These two kept Odin informed of news from every corner of the world. In addition he rode far and wide on the eight-legged horse Sleipnir. Odin was married to Freyjar, the goddess of marriage, children and the hearth and who gave birth to Balder.

The Norns

Odin was a shape-shifter and he often wandered around in disguise, especially as an old man with one eye, a grey beard, wearing a wide-brimmed hat and carrying a staff. He carried a spear named Gungnir, which was forged by two dwarfs Brokkr and Sindri, and which had the property of never stopping a thrust once started. In addition, he held a gold ring named Draupnir, which we shall come to when discussing Balder.

And Odin's fate? This is tied up with the wolf Fenrir, spawned by Loki, who was fettered and chained to a rock, with a sword wedged between his jaws. He was left in this state until Ragnarok when he shattered his fetters and devoured Odin entirely, only to be torn in half himself by Odin's son Vidar in revenge.

Balder

Son of Odin and Frigg, Balder was the god of light, wisdom and beauty, who was the first of the gods to die. He was the best loved of the gods, except by the jealous Loki, and the story of his demise is basically all we know about the god, so his fate is as follows.

Balder's tale begins with recurring nightmares in which he dreams of death. He decides to report his troubling dreams to the Aesir, whereupon they call a council meeting to discuss the matter. The outcome was that his mother, Frigg, manages to extract an oath from every living and non-living thing that they would not harm Balder in any way.

Unfortunately the god of strife and evil, Loki, became very jealous of Balder's divine protection and he decided to find a way of killing him. Fortunately for him he discovered that the mistletoe plant had been overlooked when the oath was taken, so he sharpened a twig of the plant and persuaded the blind god Hodr to throw it. Loki, however, guided his arm and aimed the dart at Balder, who was killed outright when the dart reached its unfortunate target.

However, this was not the end of Balder's story. To set the scene we must bring in here the goddess of the dead, Hela, who was the daughter of Loki. She was raised along with the wolf Fenrir and the serpent Midgardsormr, and was described as having one side of her face human and the other totally blank. She may also have been a sybil, as after Balder's death she was visited by Hermodr, another son of Odin and Frigg, who asked her for Balder's return from the underworld in return for a ransom. Hela's answer was that she would allow Balder to live as long as all things in the world would weep for him. This condition was accepted, but there was one individual who refused to weep for Balder, the giantess Thokk. A funeral pyre was constructed on Balder's ship and it was pushed out to sea, and Odin placed the ring Draupnir on the pyre as a final gift. So Balder remained in Hela's domain of Niflheimr, a region of everlasting cold and dark night.

Loki

We have already come across this figure, who was a fire god and a member of the Aesir. Brother of Odin and father of Hela, Fenrir and Midgardsormr, he was also a demonic spirit of evil, and was at the same time both brilliant and devious, as we saw with his involvement in the death of Balder. His other attributes included his charm, his ability to amuse, his continual chattering, and a perverted trait of finding various ways in which to irritate his family, often successfully. He had many mischievous adventures, too many to be told here, so the aftermath of the Balder escapade will suffice.

After the death of Balder the gods pursued Loki as they believed that he had disguised himself as Thokk which, as we saw above, ensured that Balder would remain in Niflheimr. Having run away as quickly as possible, the gods were eventually catching up with him and as his only chance of escape Loki decided to shape-change into a salmon. In the end, however, he was caught in a net and the other gods sealed his fate in punishment for causing the death of Balder. Their judgement was to tie him over three stones with the intestines of one of his sons, whilst a serpent dripped venom from above onto his face.   Loki's wife Sigyn, however, tried to divert the venom by catching it in a vessel, but every time she left him to empty its contents, the poison resumed its continuous dripping onto the face of Loki. This torture was so great that his squirming led to violent earthquakes, and his fate was to suffer in this manner until the end of time.

Thor

Son of Odin, Thor was the thunder god famous for his belt of power which doubled his strength, his iron gloves and his hammer named Mjolnir which came back to him after it had been thrown. As well as symbolising the destructive power of storms, Mjolnir was also important in protecting Asgard from the giants and in warding off evil and savagery. Although he was renowned for bravery, strength and endurance, he was also known to be brutal and stupid on occasion. In the mythology of north western Europe where trees were revered, the oak tree was sacred especially to Thor, as it was the tree that was most often struck by lightning.

Thor fought many battles, mainly with giants and giantesses, but perhaps his most famous and important encounter was with the serpent Midgardsormr, offspring of Loki and Fenrir's sister. Disguised as a young man Thor invited one of the giants named Hymir to accompany him on a fishing trip. Whilst Hymir was away collecting bait, Thor decapitated Hymir's largest ox and secreted its head on the boat out of Hymir's sight. Upon leaving, Thor began to row so fast that Hymir became afraid that they might arouse Midgardsormr, becoming even more fearful when Thor bypassed their fishing ground and headed out to the open sea. Having eventually stopped, Thor placed the ox head on the end of his line as bait and cast it overboard.

It was not long before Midgardsormr took the bait and Thor used all his strength to haul the watery beast up to the surface. He then grasped Mjolnir and aimed a blow at the serpent, but the fearful Hymir cut the line and

Midgardsormr disappeared into the depths of the ocean. In a furious rage, Thor then struck a blow on the side of Hymir's head, which was so hard that Hymir fell overboard and Thor left him writhing and waded back to dry land. So Thor was defeated on this occasion, but perhaps this was all to the good because if Midgardsormr had been slain that would have led to the end of the world, as the serpent held the world together with his coils.

So what was the ultimate fate of Thor? It was at the apocalyptic end of all things that Thor and Midgardsormr had a final battle when in the struggle between the two they managed to slay each other.

Tyr

Son of Odin and brother of Thor, Tyr was the god of war, identified with the Roman god Mars and giving us the week name Tuesday. An alternative origin story has Tyr formed from the sweat of the father of all the giants Ymir. Before becoming the war god, he began as the Sky Father and was described by the Roman writer Tacitus as "the god who holds sway over everything", and was connected with law and order. However as the centuries passed by he lost this peaceful aspect and became the god who could forecast the outcome of battles.

As well as Odin, Tyr also had a tie-in with the wolf Fenrir, although some accounts give the wolf the name of Garmr, a hellhound that could be Fenrir under another name. The legend goes that Fenrir had grown so enormous and fearsome that Tyr was the only individual who was brave enough to feed him. In the end the gods decided that Fenrir had grown so fierce that he had to be bound, and the dwarfs were given the task of forging a chain which, although it looked like a rope made of silver, it was so strong that nothing could break it and its name was Gleipnir.

However, Fenrir refused to be bound in such a way unless a god placed an arm in its jaws as a hostage. And it was then that Tyr met his fate, when he volunteered to perform this perilous deed, as Fenrir straightaway bit off his right hand, and the god had to make do with only one hand thereafter.

Freyr

Brother of Freyja and husband of the giantess Gerdr, Freyr was a god of fertility, crops, rain and shine who became one of the most popular deities in the Norse pantheon. He was worshipped in grandiose temples and his cult stretched far and wide even though it demanded human sacrifice. He travelled in a chariot drawn by a boar named Gullinbursti, wrought out of gold by the dwarfs, which could run so fast that it could easily outrun the fastest horse. Dwarfs also made for him a magical ship named Skidbladnir, which could fly up in the clouds and be folded up when not required.

It is possible that Freyr was originally the chief of a boar clan, and he became one of the three gods who were worshipped at the great temple at Uppsala in Sweden. As well as being associated with boars, he was also linked to horses, both of which were fertility symbols since prehistoric times. Sacred horses were kept at Freyr's sanctuary at Thrandhelm in Norway, and boar images have been discovered fixed to Viking helmets as protection by the god.

And the fate of Freyr? It turns out that it was not the living god who experienced a "fate", but his dead body. He died an unspecified death, and as he lay on his deathbed, Freyr ordered his priests to construct a burial mound and to bury him inside after his demise. However, his death was not announced for three years, for the priests had built a door in the barrow in which they had bored three holes through which they dropped gold, silver and copper to perpetuate the god's glory. Apparently, during that period the land was prodigiously fruitful. However, another source has it that Freyr's death did not occur until Ragnarok, when the fire giant Surtr engaged in combat with Freyr, resulting in Surtr's victory and the demise of the god.

Ragnarok

Also referred to as The Twilight of the Gods, Ragnarok was the end-time when the old world and all its inhabitants were extinguished, the ultimate fate of everything. Prior to this the land would experience a terrible three-year long winter, earthquakes, the obscuring of the sun by the wolf Fenrir, and conflict and strife amongst humankind. On top of these fearful events, monsters like Fenrir would break free from their fetters, and serpents such as Midgardsormr would leave the oceans leading to the flooding of the entire world. After a final great battle between the armies of the gods and those of the giants the world would come to an end.

But after the destruction a new world would emerge and humans will reappear upon the face of the earth and a new golden age will commence. Thus the end of creation would give rise to a new beginning, like the phoenix from the ashes, to quote another myth. But that is another story.

Works consulted:

European Myth & Legend: An A to Z of People & Places, by Mike Dixon-Kennedy (1997)
Gods & Myths of Northern Europe, by H.R. Ellis Davidson (1964)
Everyman's Dictionary of Non-Classical Mythology, compiled by Egerton Sykes   (1962   edition)
Gods of the North, by Brian Branston (1955)

This chapter first appeared in Merry Meet Magazine no. 56 Winter 2015/2016

7 - Horned Figures: Hathor, Pan, Moses, Alexander, and Irish Witches

This chapter is concerned with five cases of persons who have been portrayed as wearing horns, namely a god, a goddess, a legend, a historical person and some Irish witches. Horns have always symbolised power, especially that of nature. They have embodied this primal force throughout history when they have been employed in symbolic ways such as depicting an individual with horns on his/her head. In ancient times, the bull god was worshipped in Sumeria and the ram god in Egypt, both symbolising the might of the deity. In addition, in the Old Testament, after Abel was murdered by his brother Cain for marrying their sister, Jewish tradition told that Cain was doomed to wander the land bearing a horn which God had caused to sprout from his head. He was later killed himself, being mistaken for a wild animal.

It is also known that ancient shamans and priests used horned headdresses, again symbolising power and authority. Going back to Mesolithic Britain, around 9000 BCE at Star Carr in Yorkshire, sets of deer skulls with antlers intact were discovered with two holes punched in them. These seem to have been used to thread rope through so that they could be tied on to a person's head for ritual activities, and in recent times, the horned god has become an important figure in modern paganism and Wicca. Here are five examples of horned individuals, beginning with one from Egypt.

Hathor

The goddess Hathor, daughter of the sun god Ra, was known as the Cow Goddess in ancient Egypt, and was often depicted either as a cow or as a woman with the addition of a pair of cow's horns sprouting from her head which also contained a representation of the sun disc. She represented motherhood, feminine love, fertility, music and joy, and was one of the most revered personages in the Egyptian pantheon, worshipped by the common people and royalty alike. In fact, she was so popular that more festivals were celebrated in her name than any other of the Egyptian deities. Unusually in Egyptian religion she was attended not only by priests, but also priestesses. Her complex relationships within Egyptian mythology included the dichotomy that her father was also her "son", as she gave birth to Ra every morning when the sun rose in the east.

The cow was considered a sacred animal from early times, her fertility being of upmost importance to Egyptian farmers, which is not surprising as Egypt was an agricultural country. She personified the Milky Way, thought by the Egyptians to be milk flowing from the udders of a heavenly cow, and in this aspect Hathor was seen as a sky goddess. As well as being depicted as a woman with horns, she was also sometimes portrayed as an actual cow, and Pharaohs were sometimes shown as suckling from the goddess in this form. The tomb of Tutankhamun contained three funerary couches, one of which had sides made into the form of two long cows, both carrying a sun's disc between their horns.

Hathor (centre) (CC BY-SA 2.0/rowanwindwhistler/Adapted to black and white from original)

Portrayed as a woman, she was shown either as described above with horns or with cow's ears. Importantly Hathor was often portrayed with her head face-on, breaking the Egyptian convention that human heads should be portrayed in profile. She was also called Mistress of the West, as she received the dead, granting them a safe journey to the afterlife. In this guise, she was depicted as a cow emerging from the western mountain. In the underworld, she refreshed the dead with food and drink taken from a sycamore tree, which was sacred to her. In fact, coffins made for the royal family were constructed from sycamore wood in the belief that they would be returned to the womb.

One of her epithets was the Lady of Drunkenness, her ceremonies involving the drinking of wine and beer. Music was also an important feature of her worship, and the most prominent instrument in her worshippers' rituals was the sistrum, which was a kind of rattle. Women in particular revered the goddess, and this is emphasised by her portrayal on the handle of women's mirrors, and she was associated with pregnancy and childbirth. With royalty, however, she not only oversaw the birth of children, acted as their nurse, but also in her cow form she suckled future Pharaohs.

Hathor's most famous temple was that at Denderah in Upper Egypt, where she was worshipped as the wife of the falcon god Horus. Fourteen days before the new moon of the third month, Hathor's statue was taken from the temple and a procession formed accompanying the figure as it was carried to the River Nile. Here it was transferred to her state barge which, accompanied by a flotilla of secondary boats carrying priests and other dignitaries, was towed up the Nile to Edfu some 30 miles away. It was here that the Sacred Marriage of Hathor and Horus took place and the next fortnight became a time of rejoicing and celebration, with visitors arriving from all over Egypt. Every large town also had a shrine where the goddess was worshipped, and her popularity with the Egyptian people was due to her attributes of sexual love, music and the bringer of joyous happiness, the Golden One of the gods.

Pan

Son of the Greek messenger god Hermes, Pan was a pastoral god who presided over nature, whose name derives from the Greek word *paein* meaning "to pasture". This is not to be confused with the Greek word *pan* denoting "all" or everything". There are fourteen accounts of who his mother was, the most well known being Penelope. At his birth he was so ugly with his horns and goat's features that Penelope deserted him, leaving his father to attend to him and taking him up to Mount Olympus where the gods had their abode.

Pan was a shepherd god, looking after the flocks of sheep and goats as well as shepherds themselves, and he was especially associated with mountainous Arcadia situated in central Peloponnese, the Arcadians considering themselves as the original Greek people. His appearance was that of half man and half goat, with horns, shaggy goat's legs, a beard and a tail, and he also had the epithet Aegocerus, meaning goat-horned. Also, as a god of prophecy a number of oracles were founded in his name.

The Greek God Pan

He enjoyed nothing better than an afternoon nap, and if he was ever disturbed whilst asleep he let out a deafening shout which made people's hair stand on end, leading to our word "panic". There are accounts even in modern times of people out and about in the countryside suddenly becoming overcome with panic for no apparent reason, and having to run back to "civilisation". Often joining in revels with various nymphs, Pan once took a fancy to one in particular named Syrinx and chased her to the banks of a river where she transformed into a reed to avoid his advances. Not being able to distinguish her from the other reeds, he plucked several reeds at random and turned them into a Panpipe, with which Pan came to be associated. He was thereafter also seen as a god of rustic music.

Kids, goats and sheep were sacrificed in his honour by shepherds and herdsmen, and as a hunting god he looked after small creatures such as small birds partridges and hares, leaving the larger animals to be presided over by the hunter goddess Artemis. Theocritus, the Greek writer of the 3rd century BCE, tells us that when hunters were unsuccessful in the hunt or their animals became infertile, they would scourge a statue of Pan to influence the god to revive his vitality. Being a rustic god, he was not worshipped in temples, but rather in natural settings such as caves and groves.

Pan was also renowned for his sexuality, often being depicted with a phallus, and his appearance and lecherousness were mirrored by the mythological satyrs, who also were half-goat half-man, who were also associated with the god Dionysos. Pan's eroticism led him to his greatest conquest, that of the moon goddess Selene. He clothed himself in a sheepskin to hide his goatish appearance, lured her from the heavens and seduced her in the cover of a forest. Taking things further, there is a notorious statue, which was found in the Villa of the Papyri in Herculaneum portraying Pan having sex with a goat. The image of the lascivious Pan with his horns, of course, gave us the word horny.

He inherited his lecherous nature from his father Hermes, a god associated with fertility. From the 6th century BCE herms were erected in his honour, consisting of a pillar made from bronze or marble, with a head on top and a phallus on the front, which became very popular as harbingers of good luck to both individuals and cities. Pan's often phallic appearance eventually became that of the Christian Devil, but modern research has questioned this interpretation as deriving from outdated Victorian thinking.

As mentioned in Chapter 1 (Nodens), the reign of Pan was declared to be over when the rise of Christianity was foretold when a sailor named Thamus was on his way back to Italy via the island of Paxi. Across the water he heard an ethereal voice calling out the words "Thamus! when you reach Palodes, make sure you that you proclaim that the great god Pan is dead", which Thamus did and which was met with groans and lamentations from every animal and plant as well as inanimate rocks. The cries were mixed with dismay and astonishment. Robert Graves considered that Thamus had misheard the phrase Thamus Panmegas Tethneke "the all-great Tammuz is dead!" for Thamus, Pan ho megas tethneke "Thamus, great Pan is dead!" Apparently, the writer Plutarch, who was a priest at the oracle of Delphi towards the end of the 1st century CE, believed the Pan version. But when Pausanias toured Greece about a century later, he discovered that Pan's shrines and sacred caves were still being used by worshippers. Pan was also credited to possess prophetic powers at the Corycian Cave at the oracle at Delphi.

In the late 19th century the horned god Pan had a renaissance in literature, and children's stories such as J M Barrie's *Peter Pan*, whose character Barrie described as "betwixt and between". And in 1894 the author Arthur Machen published his novella entitled *The Great God Pan*, which is considered by some, including Stephen King, as being one of the most powerful horror stories ever written, such is the force of the god's personality. The god also features in two short stories, "The Man Who Went Too Far" by E F Benson, and "The Call of Wings" by Agatha Christie.

Aleister Crowley, the notorious occultist, would invoke Pan in his magical rituals, which eventually drove him insane. He wrote a poem entitled Hymn to Pan which he allegedly used in his ceremonies, and which was recited at his funeral in 1947:

Io Pan! Io Pan Pan! Pan.

I am a man:

Do as thou wilt as a great god can,

O Pan! Io Pan!

Io Pan! Io Pan! I am awake

In the grip of the snake.

The eagle slashes with beak and claw:

The gods withdraw:

The great beasts come, Io Pan! I am borne

To death on the horn

Of the Unicorn.

Which brings us to a seemly conclusion to this section on the carnal horned god Pan.

Moses

This legendary figure belonged to the Tribe of Levi, and his discovery as a baby in a basket in a river by Pharaoh's daughter is too well known to repeat here. His name derives from a Hebrew word meaning to "draw or pull out", specifically from water. He later became the leader of his people, often having to bring them back to their true God. He is described in Exodus 34.29-30 as returning from the summit of Mount Sinai with the Ten Commandments, bearing two horns on his head, although some claim that this is a mistranslation which should have read that his "face shone", which is the traditional translation which has come down the centuries. However the former still has support from some researchers, regarding the horns as "horns of light".

Horned Moses

This interpretation, for example, is depicted in two illustrations, one found in the Bury St Edmunds Bible of 1135 and another in a painting by Jusepe de Rivera of 1638. Others regard the word "horns" to be symbolic and not literal, representing authority and wisdom, not evil as they came to be within Christianity. The trouble with these differences of opinion is that there are so many translations of the Bible made over the centuries, from Hebrew to Latin, from Latin to Greek, from Greek to English to name just three, that there is no consensus over the meaning.

Many ancient cultures worshipped a bull-god, and the early Hebrews were no exception. Moses could well have been a manifestation of the bull-god, as the bull was revered as being a powerful beast, a facet required of a religious leader. Moses' descent from the mountain thus adorned, would have been regarded by his people as a mighty individual commanding their respect, who naturally would be depicted with the horns of a bull.

In Exodus 29.1-14 God instructs the Israelites to perform a religious rite involving a young bull, which was to be sacrificed and its blood smeared over the horns of the altar as a sin offering. Similar rituals were also to be enacted with two rams, another animal bearing horns. Thus it is apparent that the bull was an important animal in the Israelites' religious practices. This is evidenced from the incident of the image of a golden calf, probably a full-grown bull, which the people were worshipping at which Moses was horrified and angry. He immediately burnt the image, ground it into powder which he then tipped into a container of water and forced his people to drink it. The fact that Moses carried out these actions, showed how at that time the people had their doubts about him and they had responded by turning their devotion to the bull-god in order to gain guidance.

It seems, though, that Moses' actions did not have any deep effect on the Israelites' beliefs, as when they reached the Promised Land of Canaan, their leader was Joshua of the Ephraim tribe, which means "double fruitfulness", probably called as such from the two horns of the wild bull they used to worship when wandering in the desert. Over the years the Israelites assimilated other religious aspects from various other tribes, including a god of storm and battle, Yahweh, which eventually became their one and only god. His voice sounded like thunder, and this resonated well with the roar of a bull. Upon arriving at Canaan, the Israelites found bull shrines at a number of places, and pilgrimages were made to these cult centres, but eventually the worship of the bull changed its nature from that of power and strength to that of fertility. And finally the bull-element of the Israelite religion vanished from Yahweh altogether.

The idea that Moses wore horns on his head when he brought down the Ten Commandments was immortalised by Michelangelo's statue of the patriarch, finished in 1516, to which the sculptor had appended two horns emerging from his head. This sculpture, housed in the Church of San Pietro-in-Vincoli in Rome, apparently has been accepted as a truthful depiction of Moses, with all Popes from that period until now being quite happy with it.

Alexander the Great

Alexander the Great with the horns of Amun

So now to the historical figure, Alexander the Great (356-323 BCE) was one of the greatest generals in history. His name derives from the Greek name Alexandros meaning "defender of the people". Legend has it that on the day of his birth one of the Seven Wonders of the Ancient World, the Temple of Artemis at Ephesus was destroyed, the reason being that the goddess was away attending Alexander's birth.

At his death he was ruler of land stretching from Macedonia to Kashmir via Egypt, founding or renaming cities as Alexandria on his journeys. But we are concerned not with his victories or his unexplained death, but the portrayal of his head with horns, which largely comes from coins. The most well-known coin discovered is the "Two-Horned Alexander" depicted on a silver coin from around 300 BCE which shows Alexander's head wearing a diadem and the ram's horns of the Egyptian god Ammon. I shall explain why these particular horns were relevant.

In 332 BCE Alexander and his army entered Egypt, camping at Memphis, where he visited the Serapeum which held the shrine and mummified bodies of the sacred bulls of Apis. His aim was to become a Pharaoh, and the priests of Memphis probably advised him to consult the oracle of Zeus-Ammon at the oasis of Siwa in Libya to be officially recognised as such. The Greeks, as was their custom, equated Ammon with their chief god Zeus, thus the temple complex at Siwa was dedicated to Zeus-Ammon. It was founded some time before the 7th century BCE and was considered to be of equal importance to that of Apollo at Delphi and of Zeus at Dodona in its heyday, and it remained a stronghold of paganism until about the 6th century CE.

The Egyptian god Ammon, or Amun, was the chief god whose sacred animal was the ram. The sheep found in the area of Upper Egypt produced rams whose horns were quite larger than other sheep, and they were also curved and down-turned. They were noted for their virility and belligerence, which was why the ram was adopted by the priests of the god. Ammon was never portrayed either as a ram nor as a man with a ram's head, but as a man with a cap with two tall feathers and the sun's disc. Alexander, however, was depicted wearing Ammon's ram's horns, as mentioned above, indicating that his power was as strong as that of the ram itself.

Arriving at the oracle, after marching his army there for six weeks, he was greeted by the high priest and an assembly of women dressed in white who put on a show of singing and dancing. Alexander was then guided to a procession, which took him to the temple and oracle. He then asked his questions, after which he waited for the replies in an anteroom. After a short wait, an old priest came in and greeted him as Alexander, Son of Zeus-Ammon and King, answering Alexander's question about whether he would be ruler of the whole world. The satirical writer Lucian in his Dialogue of the Dead portrayed Alexander in the Underworld where he met his father, former Philip II of Macedonia, who derides him for denying that he was his real father and declaring that he was really the son of Ammon himself.

A horned Alexander also appears in Azerbaijani folklore. He set his sights on conquering the province of Shirvan, which was ruled by a woman queen who refused to capitulate. Alexander then commenced battle, his army finally managing to surround the province, but the queen had her own weapons, sending forth a host of poisonous snakes towards the great leader. He could do nothing to prevent a calamity, so he offered to engage in a face to face fight with anyone from Shirvan. Surprised, Alexander found himself fighting against the queen herself.

A while into the fight Alexander's helmet fell off, revealing a horn sprouting from his head, which the queen immediately grabbed hold of as he fell down, broke it off and it plunged into the ground. All of Alexander's power was encapsulated within his horn and he weakened and collapsed. Eventually recovering, he and his army left Shirvan, having buried the treasure he carried with him within the province. Of course, the Shirvanians tried to find where Alexander had hidden the treasure, in vain as it turned out, as his broken horn stuck in the ground guarded over the treasure and prevented anyone from discovering it. If any person tried to find the treasure the horn would start to shake and an earthquake would be caused, which from then on in popular superstition explained the frequency of earthquakes in that area.

Alexander was keen to publicise his descent from Greek heroes as Heracles and Achilles, and therefore being almost divine to begin with. This was just what Alexander hoped to achieve, and later just before his death, he requested that he be buried at Siwa. However it turned out that he would be buried at the great city he founded, Alexandria, although his tomb has never been discovered, despite much searching. Technically he was a Pharaoh, founding the Greek dynasty which lasted until the suicide of Cleopatra, after which Egypt came under the rule of Rome. Alexander was afterwards known as the Son of God, a title used again some 400 years later.

Twelve Irish Witches

The Irish have a wealth of folklore, myths, legends and fairy stories, and it is the latter we turn to now. A tale entitled "The Horned Women" is of relevance here, as it relates the appearance to a wealthy woman of twelve witches who wear horns on their heads. I paraphrase the story below.

One night the woman stayed awake whilst the rest of the household was asleep, spending her time cleaning and combing wool. All of a sudden, there was a knock on the door and a voice shouting out for her to open up. Asking who was outside, the reply came back stating that it was The Witch of One Horn. Hesitantly the woman let in the witch, who had a horn sprouting from her forehead, and who promptly sat near the fire and began to frantically card the wool herself. There was then another knock at the door and the woman again opened up, this time to another witch who called herself The Witch of Two Horns, wearing as she did two horns upon her forehead. She immediately sat down and began feverishly to spin the wool.

These arrivals continued until twelve horned witches, bearing from one to twelve horns, were seated with their spinning wheels and who were singing together. Although the woman was trembling with fear, she could not call out or move as the witches had placed her under a spell. Eventually one of the witches shouted out to her to get up and make a cake for them, so she looked for a bucket to fetch some water from the well in order to mix it with the necessary ingredients, but could not find one. In response the witches told her to get a sieve for the water, but of course this was useless and she sat down near the well in floods of tears.

The next thing she heard was a disembodied voice, the Spirit of the Well, advising her to gather some moss and yellow clay, to bind them into a paste, and to spread it over the sieve which will stop the water from seeping through. Having carried out this process, the voice told her to go back to her house and to cry out three times "the Fenian[5] women's mountain

---

[5] The word Fenian relates to a legendary Irish band of warriors form the 1st and 2nd centuries CE.

and its sky overhead is afire". As soon as the witches heard her call, they let out a terrible shout and fled shrieking to their abode at Slievanamon[6]. However, the Spirit of the Well told the woman to enter her house and prepare to protect it against any similar occurrences. This involved carrying out folkloric magic of various kinds within the building.

Twelve horned Irish Witches

It was not long before the witches returned, in a vengeful rage. For each piece of magic she had treated inside her home, they tried to undo, calling out each time to be let inside, in vain. Thwarted, the witches cursed the Spirit of the Well and flew into the air back to Slievenamon, leaving the woman in peace thereafter. One of the witches, however, had dropped her shawl, which the woman picked up and hung up in memory of that awful night, the shawl remaining in the same family for five hundred years.

The relevance of the witches' horns in this tale is not apparent, but such stories probably date back into the misty past long before writing, when the horns had a meaning now lost to us. This has now been confirmed by a paper by an anthropologist from Durham University, Dr Jamie Tehrani, and folklorist Sarah Graca Silva, whose innovative research using phylogenetic methods in conjunction with cultural phenomena, has shown that some traditional folktales such as "Beauty & the Beast" and "Rumpelstiltskin" date back over 4,000 years, to the Bronze Age.

Conclusion and Notes

---

6 Slievanamon derives from the Gaelic and means "women's mountain".

So we come to the end of the narratives of horned beings. It is fascinating how in each of the cases the story of how they came to bear horns has been quite different. I just leave you now with three further points of interest:

1. It is a curious fact that ammonites, those fossils of prehistoric sea creatures, obtained their name from the Egyptian god Ammon, or Amun. In ancient times the curved shape of ammonites were seen to be similar to the curves of rams' horns. The Roman writer Pliny the Elder named them *ammonis cornua*, being the Latin for "horns of Ammon", because the ram was sacred to the Egyptian god. A strange derivation for a scientific subject to be sure. To add a mythical British element to this, a mid 1960s excavation was carried out on mystical Glastonbury Tor where a large number of ammonites were discovered. They may have been merely eroded from the top of the Tor where they occur naturally, or were they votive offerings to ancient gods. Who knows?

2. Incidentally Pliny the Elder was watching the eruption of Vesuvius in 79 CE which devastated Pompeii and, because he was so absorbed in the sight that he died suffocating from the matter thrown out by the volcano. His nephew Pliny the Younger recorded this unfortunate   event, pointing out the curiosity and learned investigative nature of his uncle, who was obviously unaware of the danger he was in.

3. As a horn-related issue, it is a fallacy that Vikings wore horned helmets - they did not! - if only because they would have been quite impractical.

Works Consulted:

The Gods of Ancient Egypt, by Barbara Watterson (1984)
Greek Myths, by Robert Graves (1960)
The Oxford Dictionary of Classical Myth & Religion, edited by Simon Price and Emily Kearns (2003)
The Nature of Alexander, by Mary Renault (1975)
Alexander the Great in Azerbaijan's Literature and Folklore, by Seyfaddin Rzasoy
 in Folklore Volume 127 No. 2 August 2016
The Holy Bible
The New Bible Dictionary, edited by J D Douglas (1967)

"Panic! Panic!", by Paul Newman in 3rd Stone magazine issue 30 April-June 1998
Fairy Tale Origins http://www.bbc.co.uk/news/uk-35358487

8 - St. Ursula, A Legend & A Skull: A Saint, Her Legend & A Holy Relic

The place-name of Maidenhead in Berkshire derives from the Celtic Mai Dun, meaning "Great Fortress", which refers to the ancient earthworks atop Berry Hill over the River Thames at the village of Taplow, overlooking the town. However, the spelling of the town's name, which we recognise today, is a result of the "official" derivation meaning "Maidens' Wharf" and ties in with a local legend concerning some other maidens, although this derivation I think is unlikely. Actually, the connection is based round Moor Bridge, which crosses the White Brook just outside the town.

First a little background. The bridge was a toll bridge, the income of which was supplemented by donations made to the resident hermit. During the Middle Ages it was the custom for a hermitage to be constructed adjacent to a bridge, the hermit being licensed by the bishop to accept gifts or money from travellers. He would keep sufficient for his personal needs and use the excess for bridge maintenance. A chapel was built at the end of Moor Bridge in 1269, and one Richard Ludlow installed as hermit, accompanied by church and civic dignitaries as well as the locals. At the induction ceremony Ludlow took an oath to renounce worldly ways, to live a life of devotional prayer and to ensure the upkeep of the bridge.

We now turn to legend. The chapel was once reported to have housed the skull of one of the eleven thousand virgins who were martyred at Cologne along with St. Ursula, the patron saint of that city. She was the daughter of Nothus, a 4th (or 3rd or 5th) century Romano-British king, otherwise known as King Dionotus, a legendary king of Cornwall. The Christian Ursula was betrothed to a prince of the pagan Huns whom she had no intention of marrying, but she agreed to the marriage provided that ten other virgins were chosen to intermarry as well, and that they should all be given one thousand handmaidens each. In order to delay the nuptials, she managed to obtain three years' grace, during which she planned to sail the seas. Ursula inwardly hoped that these conditions would be impossible to achieve, but the chief of the Huns managed to carry them out and they set off from Britain on eleven triremes.

A variant of this story is that Nothus was requested by Conan Meriadoc, King of Brittany, to send over thousands of young women for marriage to his menfolk. Ursula herself was chosen to wed Conan. As to the figure of 11,000 virgins, there are several theories as to how this large number came about. Perhaps the most likely is that one of the handmaidens' names was Undecimilla, which was mistaken for the Latin *undecim millia*, translated as 11,000. However, the earliest reference refers to only ten handmaids.

St Ursula and her Handmaidens

Unfortunately, a storm forced the ships up the Rhine, reaching Cologne and then Basel, from where they began a pilgrimage on foot across the Alps to the Eternal City of Rome, where they visited the tombs of the Apostles. On their return to the Rhine they were accompanied by Pope Cyriacus who had experienced a premonition about the imminent martyrdom. The Roman Emperor of the time was concerned that because many people had been converted to Christianity through Ursula's stay at Rome, the pagan religions of the Roman Empire would be supplanted by the new faith. Furious about this possibility, he sent a messenger to Cologne to persuade the prince of the Huns to kill Ursula and her entourage.

The whole company was attacked and beheaded by the bloodthirsty Huns, not only for being Christians but also for their refusal to lie with them. With Ursula, she was reputed to have been killed by an arrow fired from the Huns' leader. After the slaughter it was said that angels appeared, one for each of the virgins, and they forced the Huns to flee. The virgins' bodies were then buried within the city of Cologne, and in remembrance of the massacre, a small basilica was built near their resting place. It appears that the basis of the legend was the discovery of a 4th or 5th century inscription at the Church of St Ursula in Cologne.

In 1155 a large collection of human bones was discovered at the site of an old Roman town outside Cologne, Colonia Agrippina, and they were declared by a young nun named Elizabeth of Schonau to be the remains of St Ursula and her maidens, despite the fact that some were those of men and children and even dogs! However, an aged English monk named Richard who lived near Cologne at Arnsberg Abbey had a vision that told him that in fact the virgins' married relations had sailed with them and thence on to Rome with their children, and that they also had become martyrs. This satisfied the Church and the martyrs' honour was assured. From then on the Church of St. Ursula in Cologne became an attraction for pilgrims seeking the saint's intercession. An order of nuns, the Ursulines, was founded in 1535 in Brescia by St. Angela Merici making her their patron saint, their chief concern being the education of girls. The order spread throughout Italy and France, and an Ursuline house was later founded in Quebec.

Many of the bones were subsequently despatched as relics to various churches far and wide, and one of the skulls reached Maidenhead, where it was housed in the small chapel on the bridge. In addition another relic of Ursula's handmaidens, in the form of a rib, was recorded to have found its way to St George's Chapel at Windsor Castle. This was venerated in Medieval times, along with such other relics as two fingers of St. George, part of the skull of St. Thomas the Apostle and a section of the table used at the Last Supper. The basilica at Cologne Cathedral to this day also houses a number of the virgins' bones. Also from Germany, the 12th century mystic Hildegard of Bingen composed a number of chants in her honour.

The martyred virgins lend their names to the Virgin Islands, named by Columbus, and Cape Virgenes off the south coast of Argentina, was named by Magellan. London itself has Ursula connections in that there is a street name, St Mary Axe (near the Gherkin), where a church used to be dedicated to St. Mary the Virgin as well as to St. Ursula and her 11,000 virgins. In the early 1500's a rumour went around that an axe wielded by one of the Huns was actually held in the church itself. There is also a church dedicated to St Ursula in the village of Llangwyryfon in Wales, the village name translating as "Church of the Virgins".

St. Ursula was deleted from the Catholic Calendar of Saints in 1969, but her feast day of 21st October is still remembered by Catholics worldwide.

At any rate the Moor Bridge chapel was rebuilt in 1726, but it was eventually demolished in the early 19th century as it had become an impediment to the flow of traffic across the bridge. What became of the skull is not known, but even if it did exist, was it really authentic? Holy relics were the focus of pilgrimages, especially in the Catholic Church, so perhaps it was considered too "Popish" and was destroyed, and its story may just been a legend, like many others dating from the Middle Ages.

Works Consulted:

Curious Myths of the Middle Ages, by Rev. Sabine Baring-Gould (edited E Hardy 1977)
Unknown Taplow & Environs, by Eric Fitch (Windsor Publications, 1988)
Websites: Historic UK, Berkshire History, Wikipedia

This chapter is a revised and much expanded account, which appeared in my book mentioned above.

Note:

There is a fine stained glass portrayal of St Ursula in a Windsor church not far from Maidenhead, All Saints in Dedworth. Crafted by the Pre-Raphaelite Edward Burne-Jones, the window was made by William Morris's Arts & Crafts Company. Installed in 1887, along with others from the Morris works, it depicts St Ursula in blue over red with a green halo.

9 - The Chalvey Stabmonk: A Murdered Monkey And Its Annual "Wake"

The conurbation of Slough may harbour an ancient secret, but what is it? Before we delve, first we must tell the strange story of the Chalvey Stabmonk.

Organ Grinder's Monkey

The term "Stab Monk" refers to the reputed 19th century stabbing of an organ grinder's monkey in revenge for biting a child, and there are various versions of the tale which revolve around this event.

The traditional date for the incident appears to be the mid 19th century. It has been suggested that the organ grinder came from a colony of Italians who lived in Windsor between 1850 and 1880. At all events, he was providing entertainment in Chalvey village, now a district of Slough, whilst his monkey collected the money. Unfortunately, it appears that the monkey suddenly bit one of the children who were standing around, perhaps they were teasing it. Some versions say the victim was a little girl and others a little boy, but whichever the case the father arrived on the scene and stabbed the monkey to death.

Chalvey Stabmonk by Michael Bayley (Berkshire Local History Association

It is here, however, that the divergence between the versions are at the greatest. There are at least five variations:

a) The father, named Lovejoy, stabbed the monkey with a table knife on the spot.

b) Lovejoy chased the monkey to the nearby Montem Mound where it was brought down from a tree and killed with a garden rake.

c) The child ran home and summoned his father who had just sat down to supper having left the Cape of Good Hope public house. Being a bit worse for drink, he immediately dashed out and stabbed the monkey.

d) A local butcher killed the monkey.

e) A labourer in a nearby field stabbed the monkey to death with a pitchfork.

Despite this gruesome act of revenge, it seems that the villagers took pity on the organ grinder and they decided to provide the monkey with a funeral and wake. To finance this they carried the monkey's body round the village, collecting money as they went; in fact they acquired enough to purchase a new monkey and provide free beer for the mourners as well. The monkey was buried in Chalvey Grove and after the funeral, there was general merry-making and games.

The Chalvey Stab Monk was the plaster figure of the monkey which had been painted, and which was held within the village, only to be brought out on certain occasions when it was paraded through the streets of Chalvey. The earliest record of the tradition appeared in the Windsor and Eton Express of 10th June 1865. The report was printed as follows:

The Garibaldi Tea Gardens - These were opened for the second summer season on Monday [2nd June]. An excellent military band performed in the orchestra during the afternoon and dancing was carried on with great hilarity. The drunken ceremony of 'burying the monkey' on Sunday morning was very judiciously omitted, such omission being under the influence of the police. The 'Mayor of Chalvey' was duly elected and installed on the Monday; quarrelling and fighting did not prevail as in former times, and a very pleasant day was spent by a very respectable company. The gardens are tastefully laid out, and open for promenade every evening.

This report is evidence that the tradition had been going on for some time, but for how long is debateable.

The Annual Wake and the Mayor of Chalvey Custom

At the end of twelve months, the festivities were recalled by the villagers and it was decided to re-enact them. A plaster cast of the monkey was made and a mock funeral, wake and burial took place, accompanied by merrymaking. Apparently this was so successful that it became an annual event, usually on Whit Monday. However, this was not all, since there were other customs attached to those mentioned, which may help provide an alternative explanation of the ceremony's origins.

It appeared that a "Mayor of Chalvey" was chosen each year, and his method of election to office was by being the first Chalvey man to get drunk and to fall into Chalvey Brook or, as it was also known, the Black Ditch. Known as Long John, he held office for one year, became chief mourner and had to lie down in the monkey's grave to measure it for size. In order to aid intoxication, two free barrels of beer were made available on the green outside The Garibaldi public house. When part of the green was let off as allotments, the rent therefrom provided the money to supply the beer, brewed at the old Queen Anne public house and the water drawn from nearby Queen Anne's Well (see also chapter 4).

The ritual evolved over the years and two boys with blackened faces who danced like monkeys joined the procession. In 1919, the Stab Monk ceremony was part of the Great War victory celebrations, and the Stab Monk became cited in a court case involving the publican of the Cape of Good Hope public house. Apparently, he was tried for serving drink after hours. However as the drinking had been because of the Stab Monk ceremony and he had invited the "funeral procession" into the pub to celebrate the war's end, he won his case.

When the ceremony was partially revived in 1937, the Stab Monk was paraded on a black draped bier and the "Mayor" wore a scarlet cloak, black cocked hat and a chain of office. Four Stab Monks, as Chalvey-born locals are known, held a canopy over the bier and the monkey was accompanied by an Undertaker, Organ Grinder, the child's father and a mounted Dick Turpin, or Ledger, a local highwayman who was hanged in nearby Ledgers Road.

The procession was headed by the Carnival Master, Mr. Pusey, whose banner depicted a crest with Chalvey's four industries: treacle mines, taking in washing, babies and beer drinking, as well as the Chalvey Motto. The latter is "Courage Sans Peur", or courage without fear, and in the revival year of 1937, the coronation of George VI afforded a celebration at which children were given a medallion brooch with the motto inscribed. However, the graveside ceremony, drinking and mayor making were not carried out, and all later revivals were not complete.

The revival procession of 1961 consisted of the Mayor, Town Clerk, Mace Bearer, Pall Bearer and locals dressed as the monkey, organ grinder, merry widow and washerwoman. On this occasion a monologue was related telling the story of the monkey's death, which was followed by the singing of what is known as the "Chalvey National Anthem". In 1963, the Stab Monk was paraded through the streets and introduced to the Mayor of Slough, and it has often been a feature of local events since, often helping to raise sums for charities.

The full tradition, however, had died out by the time of the Great War, after which the Stab Monk itself disappeared. The story goes that a Londoner was passing through the village in his car, when he stopped for a drink at the Cross Keys public house in the High Street, where the Stab Monk was kept. He happened to notice it in the bar, enquired about it and then asked the landlord if he could buy it. The publican refused on the grounds that it belonged to Chalvey village, but a bargain was eventually reached whereby he could take it away if he bought as much beer as the village could drink. However, when the traveller returned to his car at the end of the drinking, the monkey, which had been placed in the back, had "mysteriously!" disappeared.

Nothing more was heard of it until it was rediscovered in 1937 in an old house in Chalvey Grove, which was being demolished. It was then that the Stab Monk was given a reinforced base and was painted. The custom was re-enacted in 1938, but the Second World War saw an end to its continuance until a brief revival in the early 1960s, as described above. There have also been brief appearances at other times such as visits to the Agars Plough Carnival in Eton and to the Mayor of Slough's Parlour at the Town Hall in 1955 in celebration of the fact that Chalvey-born Alderman Pusey had become elected Mayor of Slough.

Another revival occurred in 1985 when the vicar of St. Peter's Church felt that it would be a good idea to perform the Stab Monk ceremony again at the church fete, as he was in favour of tradition since it helped communities maintain a sense of identity. He therefore organised the event to coincide with the church's fete in June of that year. This opened with the procession the Stab Monk being accompanied by three "pall bearers", which were not the traditional two monkey boys, but in this case three girls and one boy.

Origins

This completes the traditional history of the Stab Monk, but there is a stranger one yet to tell, as there are alternative versions of the origin of this unusual custom.

There are three other ideas as to how the Stab Monk custom arose, and two of them can be dealt with briefly. The first was suggested by an old lady of 84 who was interviewed at the 1937 revival. It was her opinion that the whole thing was set up by the landlord of the Queen Anne public house in order to increase beer sales.

The second theory came from a one-time Mayor of Chalvey, who put forward the idea that the ceremony could be an imitation by the locals of the Eton schoolboys' traditional festivities at the nearby Montem Mound (see chapter 5).

But the most interesting, and contentious, came from the pen of the late local historian and independent thinker, Michael Bayley of Maidenhead, which will now be discussed.

Sacrificial Calf God

Michael Bayley A.R.I.B.A. was a well respected and talented architect, historian, folklorist and illustrator, whose maps of the Slough and Maidenhead area, which included old field names and folklore and legends of the district, were original and full of little-known facts. He was also the author of three books on Celtic origins. His thoughts on the Stab Monk tradition may appear to be far-fetched, but here they are.

Mr. Bayley felt that there was more to the story than met the eye and the yearly ritual death aspect led him to the conclusion that it represented the vestiges of a fertility rite dating back into the mists of time when life was more primitive and closer to nature. In a long article in a local newspaper, he pointed out the affinities between the Stab Monk ceremony and the rites that were enacted in connection with the ancient Greek Dionysus Sabazius, god of wine and beer.

The clues, which led to this conclusion, were firstly that the plaster cast of the monkey's features resembled no known monkey, indeed he thought they looked more like those of a calf. Secondly, the monkey rested in a container not unlike a winnowing basket, and finally the monkey's tail had obvious phallic attributes, which in later years was hidden by a fig leaf.

Dionysus was originally a sacred king of a type common in the Mediterranean lands in prehistoric times. In those days the tribal leader or king had to be sacrificed each year in order to ensure the fertility of the crops. His blood was sprinkled over trees, crops and animals, and his flesh torn and devoured by priestesses. In later times, when the king's reign was extended, a boy-king was killed in his stead, but eventually animals replaced human sacrifice altogether. Echoes of this are to be found in Abraham's intended sacrifice of his son Isaac.

Dionysus' worship seems to have originated in Thrace and consisted of drunken revels with wild music and dancing. He is associated with trees and agriculture, and is said to have been the first to plough the land with the aid of oxen, a fact that explains his representation sometimes with an ox. An ancient hymn refers to him as "noble bull". One of his emblems was the winnowing-fan, a basket used to separate corn from chaff by throwing the grain in the air, which was used in the Chalvey area up to the nineteenth century.

Tradition has it that the god was placed in a winnowing-fan at birth and he is represented in this manner in art. As a vegetation god his death was believed to have been violent and his death and resurrection were a feature of the rites enacted in his honour, which involved tearing into pieces and devouring of live bulls and calves in an orgiastic frenzy. Mr. Bayley pointed out that Sabazius meant "breaker in pieces", and it may be that Stab is a contraction of this name.

The Dionysian rites which appear to have a direct relevance to the Stab Monk are as follows:

a) Worshippers at the ancient Greek sacred site of Delphi adores Dionysus as a new-born child, i.e. the god reborn for another year. They carried his image in a winnowing-basket, referring to him as Liknites, meaning "the child in the harvest basket".

b) The celebrations called the Rural Dionysia involved the carrying in procession sacrificial implements, fruit and a wooden phallus in a winnowing basket to commemorate Dionysus' dismemberment and devouring by the mythical giants the Titans. That the Stab Monk appears to have phallic attributes, with his thick erect tail, it could be that the monkey boys with their blackened faces are the Chalvey equivalent of the Titans.

c) In May the religious king of Athens, the Archaeon, would lead the population to the Dionysus Sabazius sanctuary for a drinking contest. Here, in the guise of a bull, he was married to his queen, representing a heifer goddess or cow-eyed Hera. The Romans called her Anna Perenina (ever virgin Anna), and it may be that she was the original Queen Anne of Chalvey Well. "Anner" means heifer in Welsh, the pre-English language a form of which, Mr.Bayley believed may have survived in the area into comparatively recent times. He considered that perhaps "Monk" may in fact be derived from the archaic Welsh "muner" meaning lord or possibly "myncig" meaning young kid's flesh. The drinking contest is paralleled by the Mayor of Chalvey's organising of beer drinking in the village green. The image of the infant god was afterwards carried back to Athens, reborn for another year, and this again is similar to the bearing back of the Stab Monk from its grave.

d) The birth, death, burial and resurrection of Dionysus were also ritually enacted in the Greater Mysteries of the goddess Demeter at Eleusis in Greece. One element consisted of a procession which involved obscene horseplay on a river crossing near a bridge, whose parallel here is the ducking which Chalvey's mayor had by the Brook Street bridge.

e) The women devotees of the Dionysian cult, the Maenads or wild women, were prone to indulge in wild orgiastic frenzies out in the open, often on hilltops. At midwinter they went out onto Mount Parnassus at midnight and in their excitement where their own personality became merged with that of the god they caught, tore to pieces a bull calf and ate it raw. The calf is of course the representative of the god, as is the Stab Monk whose fate is so similar.

Thus the monkey, or calf, can be seen as the surrogate sacrifice for the tribal king, or Mayor of Chalvey, killed and buried for the good of the tribe. The Mayor's custom of lying down in the grave seems to add a touch of authenticity to the hypothesis. Perhaps the original sacrificial victims of the Chalvey area also wore calf-head masks.

This, then, is the hypothesis even it is somewhat controversial. However, there is no doubt that there is a strong element of death and rebirth reminiscent of practices which took place within early religions. The concept also was later incorporated into Christianity.

There are one or two further points which, support the fertility aspect of the Stab Monk. It appears that a visitor to Windsor in the 16th century reported that the local people who lived just across the river Thames carried out an annual harvest festival, which resembled a fertility rite. At the end of the harvest each year it was the custom to carry back to the barns the figure of a woman dressed in a highly decorative manner. Furthermore, annual competitions still took place up until the 1930s at nearby Cippenham Court Farm to find the best corn dolly.

From early times, it was believed that the harvest spirit dwelt in the fields, specifically in the corn, and that as the reapers cut the corn the spirit was forced to remain in a smaller remnant, which dwindled as the reaping continued. The last stand of corn was then plaited into the shape of a woman and this corn dolly had place of honour at the harvest supper, before being buried in the post-harvest ploughing. An associated theme is that of John Barleycorn whose annual death determined that the fertility of the following year's crops would be ensured.

There remains one problem, however, and that is how did such a foreign cult of Dionysus find its way to Britain? Mr. Bayley had two suggestions. The first is via the legendary figure of Brutus, a prince of Troy, who came to Britain and gave his name to it, Albion being its former name. He and his companions drove away the giants who inhabited our islands at this time and set about settling and cultivating the land. He eventually sailed up the Thames and founded his capital along its banks, calling it Troia Nova, or New Troy. However, this story is mythical, coming from the pen of Geoffrey of Monmouth whose *History of the Kings of Britain* (1136) is largely a matter of romantic embellishment of the stories told by earlier chroniclers.

The second theory is that the cult reached our shores with the arrival of the Picts or the Danaans. The latter known as Tuatha de Danaan (People of the Goddess Danu), came to Britain from the eastern Mediterranean in Mycenaean times, somewhere around the 15th century BCE. Later known as Buan Anner, Danu was a cow goddess like Hera of the Greeks and Anna Perenina of the Romans, and she was associated with corn, particularly barley which was used in brewing. The story of the Danaans' arrival in these islands is recorded in Irish mythology, and its relevancy to the Stab Monk has a certain ring of plausibility about it, but dealing with such remote periods, it is difficult to reach firm conclusions. The second millennium BCE does seem to be a likely period, however, since it was a time of invasion, and there were contacts with places as far away as Egypt.

We now come to the final clues as to the nature of the Stab Monk ceremony, and we turn to Anglo-Saxon times. From this period, and for many centuries after, the parish of Upton-cum-Chalvey was more important than the small village of Slough, which only really grew after the First World War. The origin of the name Chalvey is very interesting, since it comes from the Anglo-Saxon meaning "calf island", and it is probable that the area at that time was not actually inhabited but was the pastureland of the villagers of nearby Upton. But it may also be an acknowledgement of the sacred nature of the area and of the calf rites that had taken place there from time immemorial. Chalvey, therefore, has an interesting history, although the urban community of today is very different from earlier times.

Who Hung the Monkey?

There is another folklore story of killing of a monkey, which was said to have occurred in Hartlepool during Napoleonic times. The story goes that a monkey was washed up on the seashore and was, strangely, mistaken for a French spy. It was said that it was dressed in a military uniform, a common practice for pets in those days, but it was decided that it should be hanged just to make sure. Apparently, there is a very similar legend from Greenock in Scotland dating from about 1760, except that instead of being washed ashore, the monkey was found wandering around the nearby hills. The Stab Monk tradition is quite a bit different from these other two legends, but why are there such peculiar British tales about killing monkeys?

Epilogue

Thus, we have reached the end of the story, except to tie up one or two loose ends. A question which comes to mind is how the plaster cast of the monkey could have been made if the animal had been dead for a year. There are two versions of how it was made.

One is that stonemason from Chalvey Grove fashioned it from plaster, and the other was suggested by antiquarians who examined it in 1937. Their view was that it was probably made 200-300 years ago by a tradesman plasterer engaged on work at either Windsor or Eton College. If it is accepted that the Stab Monk is this old, as it seems to be, then it seems likely that the cast was made from an earlier version. This may have been carved from wood, which perhaps had deteriorated or had even been broken up by idol-smashing Puritans.

However, reminiscences from local residents point to the plaster cast being made in Victorian or early Edwardian times, one lady stating that her father was a plasterer at Windsor Castle and it was he who made the cast of the original Stab Monk. The shape of the Stab Monk changed over the years, with local residents recalling their grandparents saying that in the mid 19th century it had no "teddy bear eyes", having no fig leaf and with a shorter stubbier tail. It is apparent that the plaster cast has been altered a number of times over the years.

And finally, there was once a recollection by a Chalvey resident that at the aforementioned St Anne's Well there was an inscription on the stonework which once adorned the well saying: "The two monkeys, Romeo and Juliet". Could it be that this has some connection with the Stab Monk tradition? Alas we shall never know. So, organ-grinder's monkey or sacrificial calf-god? Whichever you choose, it was a strange, unique custom.

Works Consulted:

The True History of the Stab Monkey, by independent thinker Michael Bayley (in the Journal of the Middle Thames Archaeological & History Society, vol 1 nos 3 and 4   1963/4)
The Chalvey Stab Monk, by Michael Bayley (in Berkshire Old & New journal, No. 9, 1992)
A History of Slough, by Maxwell Fraser (1973)
The Greek Myths, by Robert Graves (1955)
The White Goddess, by Robert Graves (1952)
The Golden Bough, by James Frazer (1922)
Slough Observer (various), Slough Express (various)

This chapter was first published in Strange Berkshire (1985), edited by Alan Cleaver. It has been revised and expanded for this volume.

Addenda

1. *The plaster cast of the monkey, now renovated, can be seen in Slough Museum.*
2. *A play entitled "The Mayor & The Monkey: A Short Radio Play Based on Slough Folklore" by William Olson Campbell has had a performance radio-reading at Waterstones in Slough by Total Theatre Workshop Company. A copy of the script can be found at:www.sloughcentrestage.co.uk/pdffiles/mayormonkey.pdf (Campbell also has his own website).*
3. *Chalvey residents call themselves Stabmonks, but only if they were born in the village, and of family who have resided there as long as anyone can remember.*

FOLKLORE

10 - The Raven: The Bird, Its Folklore & Legends

Figure 1Jubilee and Munin, Tower of London ravens (Colin / Wikimedia Commons / CC BY-SA 4.0/Greyscaled for publication)

Introduction

The crow family (Corvids), along with that of the parrot, shows clear signs of an intelligence over and above that of most other avian species, the raven especially so, which has been confirmed with observations in the wild and with experiments (harmless ones I can assure you). In fact recent research has suggested that ravens are one of only four animal species that can communicate about things that are not happening at the present moment or are happening elsewhere (the other three are ants, bees and humans). The common raven has a brain that is amongst the largest of any bird, which allows it to solve problems, steal, play and even practise deception. Recent research has discovered that ravens can plan ahead better than four-year old children, chimpanzees and orang-utans, with some claims that they have the intelligence of a nine year old child. They can even barter with humans and select tools for use sometime in the future, as well as expressing self-control involving ignoring lesser rewards so that they could receive one of more worth the following day.

There are several species of raven around the world, the common raven being the most widespread and that found in Britain. Its Latin name is *corvus corax*, and is the largest raven species. In the wild they can live up to 40 years, mate for life and they are, like humans, omnivores, feeding mainly off carrion and anything else they come across from insects to fruit and small animals to food waste. Their cleverness leads them to not only seek out carcasses, but also to anticipate them by following hunters and the results of battles. The eating of carrion led to people associating the bird with death, forlorn souls and ill omens, themes that will crop up again later.

However ravens seem also to have a soft side, couples often being observed rubbing their beaks together and even to "talk" to each other, as they have a wide range of vocalisation, as a report in the i newspaper on 15th August 2018 reveals. Igraine Skelton is Her Majesty's Keeper of Castle Ravens at Knaresborough Castle in Yorkshire. Apparently, one of her birds named Mourdour can often be heard saying "Y'alright love" by visitors walking around the grounds, and all of them can say "hello". But there is one raven going by the name of Izabella who is quite brazen in her utterances. She has the habit of feigning injury by lying down on the grass, and when someone walks over to her to see if she needs help, she squawks "What the f**k you looking at?", after which she flies off, whilst once picking up a tourist's camera and promptly alighting on the castle roof and leaving it there. And to add to these verbal feats, they are all made in a Yorkshire accent!

Ravens can also be seen indulging in aerial acrobatics, especially during courtship, but this activity takes place at other times, seemingly carried out merely for the joy of it. Juvenile ravens are very playful and have been observed joyfully sliding down snow slopes. Ravens have even being seen to engage in games with other species, and they even make toys by snapping off twigs to use for playing with each other. Such is the wonder of the raven.

Now to move on to the raven's story from the ancient past onwards. In general I shall be limiting the scope to Europe and the Bible region.

Myths and Legends

Perhaps the most familiar event involving a raven, to those of Judaeo-Christian culture anyhow, was its appearance in the Great Flood story in Genesis. Having been floating in the Ark for forty days, Noah was keen to find dry land so that the Earth could be repopulated. He therefore decided to make use of his animal menagerie and selected a raven, the first avian species to appear in the Bible, which he set free in order that it could find somewhere to land. But the bird did not return to the Ark, and it was the second bird, the dove, which he sent out that returned with an olive branch, indicating land was near. This led to the two species becoming representative of hope and peace, the dove, and evil, the raven.

There is another ancient flood story parallel, the Sumerian Gilgamesh Epic that predates the Biblical account by several centuries. The Noah equivalent is named Utnapishtim, who is warned that the creator god Enlil is planning a worldwide deluge and that he must build an ark. Utnapishtim gathers together his family, other folk and numerous animals into the ark, which floats upon the waters for a fortnight. He then sends out a dove and then a swallow, both of which return to the ark, finding no other landing place. Utnapishtim finally sends out a raven, which does not return because it has found carrion to eat on land now appearing again, the reverse of the Biblical narrative. (Incidentally, in the Greek flood account where Deucalion, the Greek Noah, sends out only a dove. See also note below.)

Biblical folklore reveals that the Hebrews were in two minds about ravens. They were venerated in Job 27.41 as well as in Psalm CXLVII.9, where Yahweh seems to have taken special care of them. However, in Deuteronomy 14.14 in a list of clean and unclean animals, ravens were included amongst the unclean birds, which must not be consumed. Hebrew folklore told that once upon a time the raven was not black, but white, and the colour change was brought about by God because of its failure to fly back to the Ark. Ravens appear eleven times in the Bible, ten times in the Old Testament and once in the New Testament (see Luke 12.24).

On the other hand, Christian art often portrays the raven as an emblem of God's providence, because of the ravens, which fed Elijah, ordered by God himself to provide sustenance to the prophet whilst he stayed in the ravine of Kerith (see 1 Kings 17.4-6). King Solomon apparently had hair as black as a raven, and one of the Kings of the Midianites who was defeated by Gideon was named Orev, meaning "raven". Turning to a saint, St. Oswald is often portrayed holding a raven in his hand, which holds a ring in its beak. Moving on a few centuries St. Benedict (circa 480-553) was said to have been protected by a raven, which flew off with a loaf of bread that had been poisoned by jealous monks after having been blessed by the saint. In art he is shown accompanied by a raven with the loaf of bread.

St Cuthbert (circa 634-687) also had an experience with ravens. Whilst he was on one of the Farne Island, two of the birds turned up and began to peck away at a hay roof belonging to one of the saint's buildings until it was totally destroyed. Cuthbert reprimanded them, after which they flew off only to return begging forgiveness with a piece of lard from a pig, which they presented to the saint as reparation for their bad deed. Indeed a winning tale from our Anglo-Saxon past.

Another few centuries again, but remaining in Christendom, brings us to the reign of the Holy Roman Emperor Frederick Barbarossa (circa 1123-1190) who, like King Arthur, was said to lie sleeping along with his knights in a cave in Bavaria. Here he lay waiting for an unkindness of ravens to stop flying around the mountain when he would wake from his slumber and restore Germany to its earlier glory. He kept his eye half closed, but sometimes lifted a hand and asked a boy to look to observe if the ravens have ceased to fly. And finally in their carrion capacity, Christian tradition has it that ravens had a particular liking for criminals, and savoured the plucking out of sinners' eyes in order to reach the brain. Nice.

And now another colour change. In ancient Greece it was believed that ravens were originally as white as swans, but all that changed after a raven got on the wrong side of Apollo, the god of music, poetry, healing and prophecy amongst other things. Up until this point, ravens were a symbol of good luck, and they acted as the messengers of the gods when they were in the world of humankind. However, one day Apollo sent a raven to his lover the nymph Coronis, a Thessalian princess, to see if she was being unfaithful. The raven reported back that she had indeed been unfaithful, at which Apollo arranged for his sister, the goddess Artemis, to shoot the nymph with an arrow. In a rage, he scorched the raven's feathers black, which colour the bird has kept ever since. And finally Coronis was placed amongst the stars that make up the constellation Corvus, the crow.

When Alexander the Great (see also chapter 7) was on his way with his army to the oracle at Siwa in Libya, they were hindered by a sandstorm, which obliterated the route. However, they were saved when a number of ravens flew into view, upon which Alexander ordered his men to follow them, as he assumed that they would be aiming for an oasis. This proved to be the case and they all reached Siwa without any more adverse incidents.

As mentioned above, ravens have the ability to talk to some degree, and in the time of the Roman Emperor Tiberius, who ruled at the time of Jesus's crucifixion, there was a raven with amazing vocal abilities. The Roman writer Pliny the Elder (circa 23-79 CE) tells of a young raven which emanated from a nest positioned on the top of the Temple of Castor and Pollux in Rome. It apparently flew down and made its home in a cobbler's shop, the owner of which was quite happy with the situation. It wasn't long before it learnt how to imitate human speech, and every morning it greeted the Emperor by name, and after Tiberius died it did the same to the ordinary people as they passed by, and this continued for several years. Unfortunately, the next tenant of the cobblers shop took a dislike to the bird and he killed it, much to the displeasure of the public. However, the cobbler was executed and the deceased raven was given a grand funeral, with floral tributes and a processional bier preceded by a flautist, so much was he missed.

Reaching back to the Republic in the 3rd century BCE, the Roman General Marcus Valerius Corvus earned his last name as a nickname after a raven landed on his helmet during a fight with a huge Gaul, whereupon the bird promptly flew into the Gaul's face, thereby allowing the general to kill him. Corvus lived to the ripe old age of 100, dying in 270 BCE, having been saved by a stray raven just when he needed it.

Apparently, the Roman writer and orator Cicero was forewarned of his demise after hearing the fluttering of ravens' wings, the legend going on to say that a raven came into his room on the day he was murdered, went over to his bed and tugged off the bedclothes.

The Roman naturalist Pliny the Elder was impressed by the raven's intelligence and wrote about an incident, which he himself observed. Apparently, he caught sight of a raven which was obviously very thirsty and which quenched its thirst by clever means. It was perched on a memorial urn that contained rainwater, but it could not reach the water because it was too far down inside the urn. It then had a brilliant idea. It started picking up stones and throwing them one by one into the urn until the water level had reached the urn's top, whereupon it was able to drink as much as it needed.

The raven was also an important feature of the cult of Mithras. Originating in the Middle East, Mithraism became very popular, especially amongst the Romans and in particular with Roman soldiers. It became a rival to Christianity as it shared some features with the other faith, including a sacred meal, salvation and compassion, and it was open to anyone, so it appealed to the poor and slaves as well as to the rich.

The devotees of Mithraism worked their way up a seven-step hierarchical structure, each level associated with an emblem, the lowest being Corax (the Raven), the rest being Nymphus, Miles, Leo, Perses, Heliodromus and culminating with Pater. Corax initiates were taught to serve those in the higher levels, and in their rituals, they wore a raven headdress and carried a caduceus or staff with two snakes entwined around it, linking the initiates with the god Mercury who also carried such a rod as psychopomp and messenger of the gods. Mithraism finally gave way to the faith that was adopted by the Roman Empire as its official religion, leaving iconoclastic Christians sacking and burning Mithraic temples, burning their books and even attacking the adherents of the defeated cult, but that is another story. (The Temple of Mithras in London has now been restored and opened anew to the public.)

Now perhaps the most well known ravens in Norse mythology were the two who accompanied the god Odin whilst travelling on his eight-legged horse Sleipnir. They were named Huginn, which represented Thought, and Muninn, representing Memory. They acted as messengers flying between the world of men, Midgard, and the world of the gods, Asgard. The latter was a kind of celestial dwelling similar to where the Greek gods lived on Mount Olympus. It was accessible via the rainbow bridge Bifrost, and included the eternal abode of Odin's warriors slain in battle, Valhalla. The ravens reported to Odin in particular, telling him about the deeds of men. One of Odin's names was Hrafnagud, meaning "Raven God", whilst his daughters the Valkyries were able to transform themselves into ravens, accompanying the souls of dead warriors into Valhalla. The 19th century engraver Joseph Swain produced a work entitled Valkyrie and Raven in 1862 to accompany an edition of the Norse poem Hrafnsmal (Old Norse for "Raven Song"), written in the 9th century Norwegian skald Thobjorn Hornklofi, portraying a conversation between a Valkyrie and a raven.

The Vikings often used the symbol of the raven and Ragnar Lodbrok, a legendary Norse King whose second name means "Hairy Breeches", possessed a banner called Reafan, which was embroidered with the figure of a raven. The legend that accompanied this banner was that in battle, if it flapped, then he would be the victor, but if it just flopped he would lose.

The raven was also important to the Celts, the name of the Irish god Bran, translating as "raven". In Celtic mythology Bran's head came to be buried near the Tower of London, a protection from any invading force (see also below). Ravens were also associated with the goddess Rhiannon who appears in the Welsh Mabinogion as well as Badb and the Morrigan, both of whom could transform themselves into ravens or crows, each being referred to as Battle Raven. The latter two, both war goddesses, could also foretell the outcomes of battles. The connection between the female and raven is enhanced by the latter's call which sounds like a human voice mimicking human speech. Also a number of Celtic Breton coins have been discovered which depict on them a large raven perched on the back of a horse, probably in deference to the horse-goddess Epona, and in Romano-Celtic Gaul there are references to a raven-goddess called Cathubodua.

The war-god Lugh was informed of the oncoming of an enemy by his raven familiars, much like Odin's, and it is probably not a coincidence that the Celtic word "lugos" translates as raven, indeed there was a Celtic tribe named the Lugi in Sutherland, Scotland, which translates as People of the Raven. Also the Irish hero Cu Chulainn's escapades often involved ravens in their otherworldly malevolent roles, one tale recounting when he destroys an entire flock of huge ravens with his sling. After this he takes the last bird to be killed, cuts off its head, washes his hands in the raven's blood, and places its head on a rock. This strange ritual could be the acquiring by Owein of supernatural powers from the magical bird. In the 13th century *Dream of Rhonabwy* the Welsh figure of Owein ap Urien was depicted as having a raven army, a legend which was rife in the Middle Ages.

Skeletons of the birds have been discovered in archaeological contexts. For instance at the Celtic (Iron Age) hill-fort of Danebury in Hampshire a large number of raven and crow bones were identified, which appear to have been deliberately interred as ritual acts. At Winklebury hill-fort in Basingstoke a bizarre burial of a raven was excavated with its limbs and wings spread out at the bottom of a pit, surely ritualistic. More raven burials have been excavated at Iron Age archaeological digs in Hampshire, and it could well be that they were offerings to the gods to gain some sort of favour from them, perhaps good fortune or some other wish.

A unique discovery was made at a well connected with a Romano-British temple at Jordan Hill in Dorset, where sixteen pairs of tiles were excavated, each of which contained a coin and a raven skeleton. This may have indicated a connection of ravens with chthonic symbolism, ritual shafts acting as means of communication between the Underworld and the world of men. Corvid burials are not uncommon in the Celtic/Roman-British periods, dating approximately between about 1000 BCE and 500 CE, all appearing to be of a religious/cultic nature. On the one hand the raven acts as an oracle with the themes of the dead, but on the other hand it sometimes appears as a friendly bird which warns humans and protects them, and were often used by Irish Druids in divination. Their reputation for their prophetic powers apparently continued up until at least the 17th century when a pamphlet written in 1694 referred to the county of Herefordshire, where a local raven thrice voiced a prophecy.

There are a number of Raven place-names, which go to emphasise the importance of the bird to the Celts, Anglo-Saxons and Vikings. The Celts tended to name places according to their topographical features, such as hills, valleys and woods etc, whereas the Germanic peoples were more used to naming places after the people or person who lived there, although this is not a hard and fast rule. Raven examples are listed in Eilert Ekwall's The Concise Oxford Dictionary of English Place-Names (4th ed 1960), using old county names (OE=Old English):

Raveley (Huntingdonshire)	*Raven Wood (OE)*
Ravendale (Lincolnshire)	*Raven Valley (earliest recorded 12c)*
Ravenfield (Yorkshire)	*Ravens' Field (earliest recorded 12c)*
Ravenscar (Yorkshire)	*Ravens' Rock (scar = rock - Viking)*
Ravensdale (Derbyshire)	*Ravens' Dale (OE)*
Ravensden (Bedfordshire)	*Raven's Valley (earliest recorded 12c)*
Ravenstonedale (Westmoreland)	*Ravens' Stone Valley (earliest recorded 13c)*

There is also a cluster of Raven names west of Holmfirth in the South Pennines, which may have some Celtic significance, as suggested by Guy Ragland Phillips, author of Brigantia, published in 1976. Here in Cross Fell, the highest point in the Pennine Hills, are a few topographical features with raven names: Raven Stones, Ravenstone Rocks, Raven Rocks and Ravenstone Brow. Phillips' theory was that these appellations and their position might have indicated boundary markers of the ancient Celtic kingdom of Rheged, keeping it separate from Celtic Elmet and later the Angle kingdom of Northumbria, until the two merged sometime before 730 CE. There are other raven names in Cumbria such as Raven's Edge, Raven Crag and Raven's Barrow, all of which could mark more Rheged boundary features.

As we have seen, ravens played an important role in Celtic mythology, and the people of Rheged, who spoke a Celtic language allied to Welsh, may well have seen ravens as perhaps "guardians" of their land. The kingdom would wish to maintain its distinctness from neighbouring Elmet and the later Northumbria, perhaps by controlling the routes through the Pennines. Ultimately, of course Angles and then Vikings made their mark on the region, and the Celtic kingdoms gradually fell to the invaders and, as they say, the rest is history.

Folklore & Superstitions

Although ravens were sometimes seen as good birds, more often or not they were seen as evil, and in folklore they became witches' familiars, along with toads, cats and the like. For instance if one were to hear a raven croaking on one's left side, then that would be a sign that something bad was going to happen, particularly if this occurs in the early morning. And even worse if one croaks near a house with an ill person inside, or flies over it, then that unfortunate individual will die (prematurely I assume!). If two ravens are seen together that would be a grim omen, and to see three would prove to be even grimmer. By the way, a flock of ravens was known as an "unkindness" or a "conspiracy", probably due to their ploy of scaring off other birds that had the same predatory nature, and their "cruelty" in scavenging on corpses. However, these peculiar terms are now obsolete.

In the Celtic countries the raven is especially auspicious. For example in Scotland when a fishing fleet is about to set out, the trip will be unlucky if a raven croaks at the point of departure. On the other hand in Wales, if a blind person carries out a kind action regarding a raven, then the sight of that person will be restored. Ireland has the saying "the raven told it, the grey crow told it", which indicates that when news is reported, that news is considered to be true. In Cornwall, whose Celtic heritage is nowadays being lauded, there is a legend that the raven, or more commonly the chough, houses the soul of King Arthur. The Cornish have a motto "He is not dead, King Arthur" and one of the old Cornish songs is called "He shall come again", which shows the importance of both King Arthur and the raven/chough to the Cornish people.

Returning to Scotland, the Second Sight possessed by some of the Highlanders was a key feature of their society, and two instances can be mentioned here. There was once a 19th century seer named Angus MacInnes who prophesied that certain troubles would begin when a white raven and then a white crow were observed. Apparently the interesting named Aonghus Òg of Arivullain saw the white raven and immediately killed the bird, but not long after the event he was drowned in Loch Eynort, ending his family line. MacInnes himself caught sight of a white crow at Kilbride on the Isle of Skye, after which the place was lost to the family who owned it.

In the 17th century lived the Brahan Seer, named Coinneach Odhar, who was aided in his abilities by the possession of an adder stone or a stone with a hole in the middle into which he would see visions. Ravens featured in many of his prophecies, but to the Gaels the bird was a harbinger of death, whilst to the Vikings, who settled in Scotland, it was treated with respect. Odhar was eventually found guilty of false accusations and, after a hasty trial his punishment was to be thrown head first into a tar barrel studded with spikes, which was set alight. Lady Isabella Seaforth, wife of the local laird, taunted him saying he would never enter heaven. He replied that he would but she would not, telling her of a sign to prove it. He prophesied that after his death, a raven and a dove would circle over his ashes, and if the raven alighted first then she had spoken truly. However if it was the dove, then his words will have turned out to be truthful. It transpired that the dove alighted first, while the raven flew away, sealing the Brahan Seer's destiny and his entry into heaven.

We now travel down to the south of England where ravens have a guardian role, beginning with Sinnoden Hill in Oxfordshire. The hill has a legend that treasure was hidden there during the Roman occupation in a spot called the Money Pit. This is where the raven comes in, as it is said that one of these birds guards the buried treasure from being discovered and stolen. Folk tradition has it that a local man once tried to find the treasure, began digging at the Pit and came across a sturdy iron chest. He immediately attempted to open the chest when a large raven appeared, which soared down to the man, interrupting his activities. The raven then, to the perpetrator's surprise, began to speak the words "One is not born as yet". The man, frightened out of his wits, quickly abandoned his mission, reburying the chest and hastening back to his house. Such is the fate or bad luck meted out to those who meddle with ancient forces!

Now we come to the most well known ravens in Britain, those at the Tower of London. The story, traditionally dating from the time of Charles II, tells that when the ravens at that historic structure disappear, then Britain will be doomed. This legend has the feel of being very ancient, but modern research cannot find any mention of it before the 19th century. It could be that some Victorian antiquary came across the story of Bran (see above), saw that his name meant raven and put two and two together. Who knows?

Ravens are protected birds in Britain and at the Tower they are looked after by one of the Beefeaters called the Ravenmaster, although they cannot fly off because one of their wings is clipped. Apparently it is not uncommon that when one of the ravens dies the rest of the flock come together for a "raven funeral", which is a noisy affair lasting for a whole day. The dead bird is then buried by the Ravenmaster in the Raven Cemetery near the St Thomas Tower. Each raven interred there is recorded on the Raven Memorial Headstone, a custom that has been carried out since 1956.

Six ravens, although there is always one "spare", are kept at the Tower, being named Erin, Gripp, Harris, Jubilee, Merlina, Rocky and Poppy. At the end of the Second World War, only one bird remained, but when the Tower was opened again on 1st January 1946, the decreed quota of six ravens was re-established. The flock is known as the "constable" of ravens, as they are responsible for protecting the monarch of the realm. In 2012, two new ravens began their life at the Tower. Named Grip and Jubilee (for obvious reasons) they were subsequently killed and eaten by a fox; however two new birds were introduced and were given the same names. However, not all of the ravens at the Tower have lived up to expectations. Some of them have been "dismissed", one being George who had a habit of eating TV aerials, while others have been "absent without leave", such as Grog was who last spotted outside an East End pub.

There was once a rogue raven who would imitate the barking of a dog behind groups of people. When they looked round for the annoying canine, the raven would run away cackling, which must have meant that he had a sense of humour, at which I am not surprised, as they seem to possess something extra over and above other birds. There is also evidence that they show emotion, as the Ravenmasters will attest. At night the ravens are caged, mainly because of attacks by foxes or cats, although the odd fight that does occur usually ends up with the attacker being the loser. Hats off to the defenders of our shores!

There is much more folklore surrounding ravens, but readers will be able to follow up these themselves, and I shall finish here.

A Tale and a Ballad

There is a fairy tale, too long to reproduce here, which goes by the name of "The King of the Ravens", which concerns a king who has been cursed by some diabolic individual, causing him to being a raven by day and a human by night, when he must not be seen. It also involves the King marrying the youngest of three daughters of someone called the Green Man (not the fertility figure of the 20th century invented by Lady Raglan in 1939), his imprisonment, and his release involving a magical herb recommended by a fairy washerwoman. This story has common features with the Classical tale of "Cupid & Psyche" and the French tale of "Beauty & the Beast", demonstrating the many similarities there are in fairy tales of different countries, which have been catalogued by folklorists into "motifs", this one being Type 425 "The Search for the Lost Husband".

Now browsing in second-hand book shops is a favourite pastime of mine, and occasionally I come across a book which is unusual and pleasing. Some time ago, I discovered a book entitled *The Oxford Book of Ballads*, which was published in 1910. The following ballad from this tome is entitled "The Three Ravens":

There were three ravens sat on a tree,

They were as black as they might be.

The one of them said to his make, '

Where shall we our breakfast take?'

'Down in yonder greene field

There lies a knight slain under his shield;

'His hounds they lie down at his feet,

So well do they their master keep;

'His hawks they flie so eagerly,

There's no fowl dare come him nigh.

'Down there comes a fallow doe

As great with young as she might goe.

'She lift up his bloody head

And kist his wounds that were so red.

'She gat him up upon her back

And carried him to earthen lake.

'She buried him before the prime,

She was dead herself ere evensong time.

'God send every gentleman

Such hounds, such hawks, and such a leman!'

Notes - In verse 2, 'make' is an early form of 'mate', in verse 9, 'prime' refers to an early morning church service, and   In verse 10, a 'leman' is a sweetheart or beloved one.

An unusual little piece, I think you will agree.

Poe, Tolkien & Jung

I am not an ardent reader of poetry, but Edgar Allan Poe's poem "The Raven" really captures my imagination. In the poem a forlorn young man is sitting in a room bewailing the loss of his loved one, Lenore, by trying to take his mind off her. Perhaps the first verse will give the tenor of the poem:

*Once upon a midnight dreary, while I pondered,
weak and weary,*

*Over many a quaint and curious volume of forgotten
lore-*

*While I nodded, neatly napping, suddenly there
came a tapping,*

*As of some one gently rapping, rapping at my
chamber door.*

*" 'Tis some visitor," I muttered, "tapping at my
chamber door-*

Only this and nothing more."

When he hears the tapping he opens the door, but sees nothing but darkness and he whispers "Lenore", in the vain hope that she will return, but all he hears is an echo. As he steps back into his chamber he again hears a tapping, but this time it is at the window, which he flings open. Immediately in steps a "stately raven", which perches itself on a bust of Pallas, the Greek goddess of wisdom, which stands above the door. The man asks the raven what his name is and it answers "Nevermore". After this, he asks the bird several other questions, to all of which it answers "Nevermore". Here are the last two verses:

*"Be that word our sign of parting, bird or fiend!" I
shrieked, upstarting-*

*"Get thee back into the tempest and the Night's
Plutonian shore!*

*Leave no black plume as a token of that lie thy soul
hath spoken!*

*Leave my loneliness unbroken! - quit the bust above
my door!*

*Take thy beak from out my heart, and take thy form
from off my door!"*

Quoth the Raven, "Nevermore."

*And the Raven, never flitting, still is sitting, still is
sitting*

*On the pallid bust of Pallas just above my chamber
door;*

*And his eyes have all the seeming of a demon's that
is dreaming,*

*And the lamp-light o'er him streaming throws his
shadow on the floor;*

*And my soul from out that shadow that lies floating
on the floor*

Shall be lifted - Nevermore!

Published in 1845, the theme of the raven which Poe used reflects the association of this jet black bird not only with battle scenes but with melancholia in general, the repeated term "nevermore" lending itself to the overbearing atmosphere of despair.

Poe wrote a number of morbid verses and prose about lost loves, probably because he lost so many women whom he had encountered through his short life. The raven symbolised for him the fleetingness of human existence and ultimately death itself, which came to him at the early age of 40. Poe's poem has been the basis for four films:

(i)   The Raven (1915) - a silent biographical film of Poe's life. It includes a hallucinatory scene, which recreates his poem, including a raven uttering the word "Nevermore".

(ii) The Raven (1935) - b/w film starring Boris Karloff and Bela Lugosi. The story only indirectly associated with the poem, but worth viewing for the interplay between the two characters.

(iii) The Raven (1963) - colour film starring Boris Karloff, Vincent Price and Peter Lorre. The story is again only indirectly associated with the poem, but definitely worth a view nevertheless, in particular the magic contest between Karloff and Price.

(iv)   The Raven (2012) - colour film starring John Cusack as Poe, depicting a fictionalised account of the last days of his life. Poe helps out solving murders based on some of his stories

Turning now to J.R.R. Tolkien (see also chapter 1), ravens make an appearance in the stories of Middle Earth, where they are portrayed as birds with great strength and long life. In the tale of the killing of the dragon Smaug the Golden, the Ravens of Erebor were portrayed as wise counsellors and speedy messengers of the Dwarves, being fluent in many languages, and they were ruled by The Lord of the Ravens, the ancient and knowing Roac.

The Dwarves of Erebor, workers in metal and stone, lived in the Kingdom under the Mountain, where they constructed fortifications at the top of the mountain itself. They named this Ravenhill, as this was home to the Ravens of Erebor, and it was to this place that Roac delivered the news of the death of Smaug to the Dwarf Thorin Oakenshield. It was also the place where the Hobbit Bilbo Baggins, Gandalf the Wizard and the Elves made their stand at the Battle of Five Armies. The Ravens of Erebor are just one of the many inhabitants of Middle Earth, and there is now a prodigious body of literature to be explored by those who wish to delve into the awesome world of Tolkien.

And finally the psychologist Carl Jung. He saw the raven as symbolising the Shadow Self or the dark side of the psyche, the traits of ourselves that we would like to ignore. He felt that it was a type of bad complex, but that it had an important role in balancing the overall psyche, the dark with the light necessary for a sound mind. So there we are.

Thus Quoth The Raven.

Works Consulted:

Brigantia: A Mysteriography, by Guy Ragland Phillips (1976)
Ravens & Black Rain: The Story of Highland Second Sight, by Elizabeth Sutherland (1985)   *Three Ravens to the West, by Steve Sneyd in Northern Earth No. 76 (Winter 1998)*
The Wordsworth Dictionary of Phrase & Fable, revised by Ivor H Evans (1970)
Animals in Celtic Life and Myth, by Miranda Green (1992)
Dictionary of Celtic Myth & Legend, by Miranda Green (1992)
The Oxford Book of Ballads, edited by Arthur Quiller-Couch (1910)
A Guide to Tolkien, by David Day (1993)

knaresboroughcastleravens.webs.com/
Experience the Tower of London, Historic Royal Palaces (2009)

I can recommend the 1999 album Ravenchild performed by Maddy Prior, which includes a suite of six songs entitled "In the Company of Ravens".

Additional Note:

I understand that the robin has been designated as Britain's national bird, but I have a problem with this. In all my archaeological, historical and folklore researches into early and historic Britain, as far as I can recall I have never come across a mention of the robin. However, for me the raven should have this honour, as it occurs frequently in British myths, legends and folklore, and notably it is ravens at the Tower of London which guard this island of ours.

11 - Ghosts & Burial Mounds: Spectral Occurrences At Ancient Barrows

Burial mound or barrow

Ancient sites abound throughout the British Isles, and such sites include stone circles, standing stones, burial mounds, hill-figures and hill-forts, ranging from the Neolithic, Bronze Age, Celtic Iron Age and Roman periods, i.e. from about 3600 BCE to the fourth century CE. Britain also has a treasure trove of folk-tales, many of which are associated with ancient structures, and to certain of these are attached stories of ghostly apparitions. This chapter deals with prehistoric burial mounds, or as they are also known, barrows, tumuli or cairns.

Burial mounds have a folklore all of their own, with tales of hidden treasure guarded by dragons, of fairy and goblin dwellings, of giants' graves and meeting places for witches' Sabbaths. They were also held to be sacred and were respected by both the Celts and Anglo-Saxons. Perhaps one of the most noteworthy is a cairn situated near Mold in Wales, known as Bryn-Yr-Ellyllon, which translates as "hill of the goblins" (see also chapter 14). Traditionally regarded as the burial place of a Celtic chieftain named Benlli Gawr, it was excavated in 1833 and was found to contain a male skeleton together with amber beads, remains of cloth and pottery and, most importantly, a gold cape. It also had a tradition of being haunted by a figure described as a golden spectre of a gigantic man.

The story behind this apparition is that once upon a time a woman was walking home near the cairn with her drunken husband, when they saw the gigantic, golden phantom standing on top of the cairn, which caused the woman to have a spate of fits and the man to suddenly sober up! After that, others saw the ghost over the years and women and children were scared to walk through the field at night where the mound was situated. Does the link of the gold found in the mound and the subsequent "golden" spectre tell of an ancient folk memory of the chieftain's burial? Who knows?

Headless ghosts are a well known phenomenon, appearing at many haunted sites throughout our country and burial mounds are no exception. A headless horseman is said to appear at Barrow Hills near Newquay in Cornwall where, at midnight, he is said to be seen galloping through the air with his head under his arm. The sound of rushing horses has also been heard in the vicinity.

At Angledown Copse Barrow near Litchfield, Hampshire, a frightening ghost appeared when certain individuals tried at night to dig for a golden image said to have been buried in the barrow. However, on this moonlit night after the digging had commenced, again the figure of a headless horseman with his head tucked under his arm suddenly manifested, at which the diggers, terrified, ran away as fast as they could!

Tumuli are often to be found in remote, eerie places which are accessible only by an invigorating walk. An example is Broken Barrow near Challacombe on Exmoor where there is a story of a man who attempted to dig into the mound. He apparently came upon an earthen pot, which he immediately assumed contained treasure. However, suddenly he heard the sound of horses coming towards him but, as he could see neither horse nor rider, he became so frightened that he went blind and deaf and died less than three months later. A warning to anyone daring to dig such a mound!

Headless, pedestrian ghosts are associated with a number of prehistoric barrows. For example, Roundway Hill barrow near the village of Roundway in Wiltshire used to be haunted by a wraith with his head under his arm. However, after the mound was dug into in 1855 he was seen no more. Again, at Sadler's Farm round barrow near Inkpen in Berkshire there is a tradition of it being haunted by some form of a headless being. More such headless figures have been reported at Giant's Stone long barrow near Bisley-with-Lypiatt in Gloucestershire, where the ghosts used to terrify people walking nearby. However, by 1931 it was reported that the sight of such spectres had suddenly ceased.

Also not far from the last site is a round barrow called Money Tump, its name probably indicating that it was thought to contain buried treasure, has an interesting tale attached to it. Apparently, two Chalford men were returning from a local festivity called the Bisley Feast along a track, which passed the barrow, when they saw some people ahead. They assumed that they were friends who had also attended the festivities and who had left before them. So they hurried on to catch up with them, but to their horror they found them not to be their friends, but a group of headless ghosts. Evidently this encounter "had an abiding effect on the men"!

Turning to Dorset, strange happenings used to occur at the now destroyed round barrow near Ashmore. Here it was formerly haunted by the "gabbygammies", who would fill the air with weird noises, which ceased when the barrow was excavated and the bones contained within were reburied in the local churchyard. A similar tale occurred at Buggane Celtic Fort on the Isle of Man, where there was a belief that the site was haunted by "bugganes" or spirits. Further south near Llansannan in Wales is a cairn called Bedd Robin Hood (Robin Hood's Grave), which by 1915 had almost been destroyed, but a tradition persisted that a ghost haunted the site, and this was confirmed by locals who still dared not pass it at night, (folklore recorded in 1929).

We now turn to Scotland, which as a Celtic land is full of folklore, myths and legends and where the "Second Sight" is common. An entertaining tale attached to a cairn near Largo in Fife called Norrie's Law (law meaning mound), which was reputedly made by demons, servants of the notorious 12th century wizard Michael Scot. This cairn was also supposed to contain a mine of gold so great that, when sheep lay on it, their fleeces turned yellow. One night near the mound, a shepherd encountered not demons but a ghost, and asked it why it had appeared, to which the ghost replied:

"If Auchindownie cock disna craw,

And Balmain horn disna blaw,

I'll tell ye where the gowd mine is in Largo Law."

The shepherd then made sure that none of these things came to pass so he could gain possession of the gold. At the allotted time, the ghost reappeared. The shepherd had been careful and successful in his aims, except for the fact that the forgetful Balmain cowherd, Tammie Norrie, went and blew his horn. The ghost then uttered these words:

"Woe to the man that blew the horn,

For out of the spot he shall ne'er be borne!"

At which it disappeared. The cowherd was struck dead on the spot, but it was discovered that his body could not be moved, so the cairn was built over him, which from then on was referred to as Norrie's Law.

On the Scottish island of Bute a cairn called Carn Ban (white cairn) was said by a farmer in 1893 to be haunted by apparitions, which were sometimes seen about it. And in 1895 in Ayrshire, at Knockrevoch Mound near Ardrossan a man was disturbed by an "apparition" when he attempted to dig into the barrow, another example of dire results when the spirits are disturbed.

Returning to southern England, a round barrow at Bottlebrush Down near Wimborne St Giles in Dorset is the scene of a ghostly warrior seen by an eminent archaeologist during the winter of 1927-8. He was driving homewards one night when he saw a phantom horseman dressed in skins, who rode up beside him, passed him and promptly disappeared into the side of the barrow. Apparently this apparition has also been seen by others, who have been terrified at the sight of this spectral appearance, but whether there have been recent sightings is not known.

A strange old tale concerns a megalithic chambered long barrow, dating to about 3600 BCE, by the ancient Ridgeway track near the Uffington White Horse hill figure in Oxfordshire. It is called Wayland's Smithy, Wayland being the godlike blacksmith of Norse mythology. Here there is a tradition that, if a coin is left overnight on the mound's capstone, the ghostlike, invisible smith will shoe a traveller's horse by morning. However, after an excavation at the site in the early 1970s, scarcely any coins were discovered which might have backed up the superstition. Thomas Hughes, in his 1859 book *The Scouring of the White Horse*, features this little rhyme about the tale:

They say that in this cave did dwell

A smith who was invisible;

At last he was found out, they say,

He blew up the place and flew away.

The blowing up of the barrow presumably refers to its ruinous state before it was excavated and restored in the 20th century.

Thus, we come to the end of our ghostly tour around the ancient burial mounds of Britain, which, as we have seen, abound with spectral appearances, contributing to the rich folklore of our land. However, do not be tempted to dig for treasure in ancient mounds, for, apart from being illegal, you could bring retribution on yourself. There are many reports of terrific storms and torrential rain or even tornadoes occurring if such sites are desecrated, causing the diggers to flee pretty sharply! There are even tales of the perpetrator's house becoming haunted or even being blown up, and it could even result in the death of the culprit, as we saw in the case of Broken Barrow on Exmoor. A superb literary adaptation of this theme can be experienced in the classic M.R. James's ghost story A Warning to the Curious (see also chapter 25).

So, by all means visit these mysterious mounds, and perhaps you may have a ghostly experience, but if you interfere with the monuments, then beware!

Works Consulted:

Folklore, Myths & Legends of Britain- Reader's Digest (1973)
The Folklore of Prehistoric Sites in Britain- Leslie V Grinsell (1976)
Albion : A Guide to Legendary Britain - Jennifer Westwood (1985)
The Lore of the Land : England's Legends- Westwood & Simpson (2005)
themodernantiquarian.com

This chapter first appeared in Ghost Voices Magazine no. 17 October/November 2011.

12 - Ghosts & Other Ancient Sites: Hauntings at Prehistoric Locations

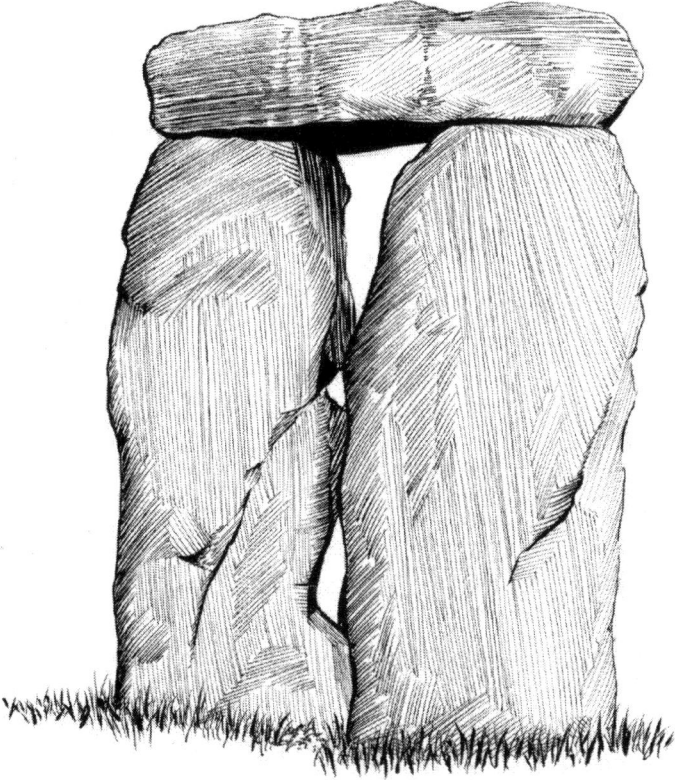

Stone monument (Mark Hetherington)

In Chapter 11 on the hauntings of the ancient sites of Britain, I looked at burial mounds. This second chapter takes a look at other kinds of ancient monuments such as stone circles, Celtic hill forts and Roman sites.

Perhaps the most well known stone circle after Stonehenge is the massive circle at the village of Avebury in Wiltshire. Here, along with nearby Silbury Hill and the West Kennet Long Barrow, can be found a breath-taking prehistoric landscape. The Avebury circle has its own folklore including hauntings. Apparently, there is a history of people seeing eerie phantoms and strange lights at night as well as hearing ghostly chanting. The figures seem to scurry about hither and thither, as though in haste to prepare for some kind of special event, although could these incidents be modern day pagans performing their rituals?

The Avebury stones have had a chequered history, the original number being around two hundred arranged in various circles and rows. In the Middle Ages they were seen as the works of the Devil and, sadly, many were dug up and destroyed. Some remained in situ and others were restored to their stone-holes in the 1930s. It is said that Avebury village buildings, such as cottages, which have been constructed using the ancient stones from the circle are prone to poltergeist incidents known locally as "The Haunt". There are also stories of spectral horsemen on small palfreys being glimpsed in the locale of the circle, galloping wildly over the ancient terrain.

Although not a report of an actual haunting, an interesting event happened at the aptly named Ghosts' Hillock near Fearn in Ross & Cromarty, Scotland. In 1937, a housing development was planned here and an excavation was carried out beforehand on what was probably a Bronze Age cemetery. However, the fact that the locals believed that the site was haunted had to be hushed up in order that future occupiers were not put off moving into the area. This is a prime example of old superstitions lasting well into modern times.

Phantom armies are a common manifestation, perhaps the most well known one is that which appeared after the civil war Battle of Edge Hill in Warwickshire in 1642. However, the spectral army which concerns us materialised at the Celtic promontory fort of Flower's Barrow Camp near East Lulworth in Dorset. One evening in December 1678 it was seen marching from the camp making a "great noise and clashing of arms". Apparently after this appearance the locals began to make preparations to defend themselves, but whether the phantom army was seen again is not recorded.

Several hauntings also occurred in Dorset at the site of the Celtic hill fort of Badbury Rings, which has been a suggested site of the Battle of Mount Badon where King Arthur defeated the Saxons. The story goes that a group of archaeology students were camped here when they heard the sound of a marching army, the clashing of metal and a soldier barking out orders in an incomprehensible language. Apparently, the students hurriedly abandoned their camp and ran off, one of them having a nervous breakdown. Who knows, these hauntings may be a recording in the landscape of King Arthur and his knights fighting the attacking Saxons, the sounds of battle being played back when the psychic conditions are right. Evidently one of these spectral soldiers is said to creep up on people after sundown, especially courting couples. His has an old appearance with a leathern face and ghastly wounds, a sight to terrify anyone in such an eerie place at night.

We haven't finished with Badbury Rings, however, since there have been reports of "an old lady" being seen, who was not of this world. This was reported by a woman who was visiting the hill fort one afternoon with her husband sometime in the 1970s. She suddenly saw an old lady standing on one of the fort's banks who was dressed in what looked like old-fashioned clothes, including a long, dark coat and a hat "like Queen Mary used to wear". The woman's husband turned, saw the old lady and suggested that they went over to help her down the slope. However, when they arrived at the spot where the lady had appeared, she had vanished. Badbury Rings certainly has a contrasting set of hauntings!

We now turn to Chanctonbury Rings hill fort in Sussex, which was later occupied by the Romans, a Roman temple being recognised at the centre of the fort. This site has much folklore attached to it, including its building by the Devil, being a local haunt of fairies, a gathering place for witches and an excellent site for seeing UFOs. Our interest here, however, is its ghosts, beginning with sightings of another spectral horseman. On other occasions, though, only the sounds of invisible horses are heard galloping across the fort.

Like Badbury Rings, Chanctonbury has a quite different ghost as well, this time being an old man with a white beard. Local legend has it that he is either a Druid seeking buried treasure or a Saxon warrior slain at the Battle of Hastings. It may be that this tale appeared after a hoard of Saxon coins was discovered at a nearby farm in 1966, although it is said that a ghost of someone searching for something was current at the farm before the excavation of the coins. Folklore is sometimes a perplexing subject, often with variations on stories from different sources, but that adds to the richness of Britain's legends and folk-tales.

Another Celtic hill fort with supernatural associations is Caesar's Camp near Bracknell in Berkshire, a wooded site that is situated about half a mile from a Roman road called the Devil's Highway. It was a northern outpost of the tribe called the Atrebates, who also occupied Silchester, which later became a Roman town, Latin *Calleva Atrebatum*. Here, during the Second World War, two women staying in a nearby house heard one night the sound of phantom footsteps marching along the Camp, together with accompanying voices, but upon looking out could see nothing. Were these the ghosts of Roman soldiers on an eternal march along the Devil's Highway and around the hill fort, who knows?

Staying with the Romans, there is a tale relating to the Roman fort of Richborough (Latin *Rutupiae*) in Kent. Here, during the Second World War, soldiers posted along the coastal defences described seeing entire cohorts of legionaries marching into the sea. And there are also persistent accounts of two figures fighting on the misty beach, one a Roman soldier, the other a Saxon warrior, re-enacting historic clashes which took place towards the end of Roman rule in our islands.

The Roman town of Chester (Latin *Deva*) not surprisingly has its own spectral Roman, here haunting the George & Dragon Inn, which was built on the site of a Roman cemetery. The tradition is that the ghostly footsteps of a Roman legionary can be heard in the early morning pacing the inn's upper floor going one way, and twenty minutes later, they are heard coming back, whilst walking through a brick wall on his unending sentry duty.

And finally we come to the legendary King Arthur, whose name is associated with many ancient sites up and down our legendary landscape. However, there is only one place where his ghost is allegedly seen, and that is Cadbury Castle in Somerset. This Celtic hill-fort has been claimed to be the site of Camelot since 1542, when the antiquarian John Leland reported this tradition. In the 1960s, the fort was excavated and was found to have been re-occupied in the post-Roman period, just when Arthur is supposed to have lived. Here inside the hill Arthur and his knights are said to be sleeping in a cavern closed with iron or golden gates, waiting for the time when Britain has need of them in troubled times.

Leading from the castle towards Glastonbury, that mystical town associated with Arthur and Joseph of Arimathea, is Arthur's Causeway. It is said that on the nights of the full moon, Arthur and his ghostly knights emerge from their cavernous abode and gallop round the hill on horses shod with silver. They stop for water at Arthur's Well on the side of the hill and then proceed along the causeway. However, on Midsummer Eve the gates of the cave are meant to open for an instant, when one can then briefly catch a glimpse of the sleeping Arthur and his entourage of knights.

So, how fitting we end our tour of ghostly happenings at our ancient monuments with Arthur, the once and future king, whose rule occurred at a time when myths and legends overlap with history. For those interested, there are many ancient sites associated with Arthur from Scotland down to Cornwall, which can lead to many an interesting trip into the countryside searching out Arthurian sites, folklore and, of course, ghosts!

Works Consulted:

Myths & Legends of Britain, Reader's Digest (1973)
The Folklore of Prehistoric Sites in Britain, Leslie V Grinsell (1976)
Albion : A Guide to Legendary Britain, Jennifer Westwood (1985)
The Lore of the Land : England's Legends, Westwood & Simpson (2005)

themodernantiquarian.com

This chapter first appeared in Ghost Voices Magazine no.18 December 2011/January 2012.

13 - Hairy Stars & Shooting Stars: Folklore Of Comets & Meteors

The title of this chapter refers to two celestial phenomena which were known formerly as hairy stars (comets) and shooting stars (meteors) for reasons which will become clear in each of their separate sections. The emphasis is on the folklore and legends attached to these heavenly spectacles.

Comets

To begin with the name, comets were known as "hairy stars" as that is how they appeared to those who lived in the times before telescopes. Relying on naked-eye vision only, the tails of comets appeared to be a hairy appendage to what looked like an ordinary star, the word being derived from the Latin *cometa* from the Greek word *kometes*, which means "long-haired (star)". However the Chinese saw them as "broom stars", the Aztecs as "smoking stars" and other peoples referred to them as "feather stars" or "dust stars". The earliest record of observing a comet was by the Chinese in the 15th century BCE, and they recorded well over 300 comets from then until 1600 CE.

It was not until the 20th century that the nature of comets was finally understood. The most famous one is Halley's Comet, which orbits the sun about every 75 years and, even though it was not spectacular when it arrived in 1986, at least I managed to see it myself through a telescope at a public viewing arranged by a local astronomy society. My son, who was five at the time, also viewed it, and hopefully he will be able to see it again in the year 2061 when he is 80. Nowadays we have even sent probes to comets, which have sent back photographic details of their surface, as well as other scientific information, and they are thought to be survivors of the early days of the solar system's formation.

Comets are icy/rocky objects, colloquially referred to as icy dirtballs[7], which live right at the edge of our solar system in what is termed the Oort Cloud, after the name of the Dutch astronomer Jan Oort (1900-1992) who formulated the idea. We see them because, for reasons not quite understood yet, occasionally one is "knocked" out of the cloud and is propelled into an eccentric orbit around the sun. As they approach nearer the Earth's orbit they appear in the sky, mostly quite faintly, but sometimes they are such a glorious sight that they can be seen in daylight. Of course it is their tails that mark them out as wonderful objects to view, but it is interesting to consider that even though the tails trail for millions of miles, they are so nebulous they are the closest to being a vacuum without actually being a vacuum.

The lore surrounding comets is almost all about portents, mainly of tragic events to come including crop failure, war, plague, hunger, drought, floods, heat waves and insurrection, to name but a few. A book discovered in a Chinese tomb dating to about 300 BCE, portrayed 29 comets as well as other celestial phenomena, where they were described according to their appearance, and by the terrible, or sometimes favourable, events they portended. Up until the 20th century, it was said that comets were associated with cold weather, but in France they greeted the arrival of comets with glee, as they were considered to point to a fruitful grape harvest, leading to what became known as comet wine.

Aristotle (384-322 BCE) was of the opinion that comets were caused by sparks in the Earth's upper atmosphere igniting gases which then burned slowly until eventually fizzling out. The reason for thinking that they were essentially atmospheric was due to Aristotle's belief that they could not emanate above the atmosphere, as this was the realm of the heavens, whose perfect domain could not be polluted by anything mundane.

Turning to the Roman Empire, the philosopher and playwright Seneca (4 BCE-65 CE) had a better stab at the nature of comets which was, that like the planets, they were in orbit within the solar system and that future generations would recognise that they would come round again. Apparently, this view did not go down well with astrologers and fortune tellers, as it affected their businesses!

---

7 Since the Rosetta space probe visited and orbited around Comet 67P/Churyumov-Gerasimenko, and which completed its work in September 2016 when it was crash landed onto the comet, its findings were such that comets should now be referred to as "dirty iceballs".

The writer Pliny the Elder (23-79 CE) had his own view on comets, his book *Natural Selection* written in 77 CE featuring a number of them. He wrote of the Greeks calling comets "bearded stars" or "javelin stars", the latter quivering like a spear, which always foretold a calamitous event. He mentions a specific comet, which was observed by the Ethiopians and Egyptians, which apparently appeared to be very fiery, twisted and generally of a disordered nature.

Pliny described different types of comets, according to how they manifested themselves. If they resembled a flute, then they were a portent connected with music, but if they appeared to form a square or triangle with a fixed star, this indicated a connection with learned men or men of genius. He also recorded a comet, which foretold the end of the reign of the Emperor Claudius in 54 CE, portending his imminent death by poison. In 66 CE the Jewish historian Josephus recorded that what became known as Halley's Comet was, seen hanging over Jerusalem for over a year, which foretold the destruction of that city under the rule of the Emperor Vespasian, whose own death was later portended by the appearance of another comet in 79 CE.

Just about 79 years prior to this, a comet has been suggested to have been the Star of Bethlehem and which appears in a painting of The Nativity by Giotto (1270-1337). But there are so many other suggestions as to what the Star was, including a planetary conjunction or a fireball (the late Patrick Moore's solution), that there is no consensus. (My personal view is that the story of the Magi and the Star is almost certainly fictitious and mythical in nature, but that is another story.)

Jumping forward to Anglo-Saxon times, the Venerable Bede (672-735 CE) makes mention of comets, only to point out that they presage events such as war, winds, floods, plague or a change of ruler. The Anglo-Saxons did, however, have a belief in one beneficial effect of a comet, and that was its portent of a good crop yield. But another was seen as a warning of the calamitous defeat of the last Saxon King Harold II (1022-1066) at the Battle of Hastings. The resultant Norman invasion of England was foretold, as shown on the Bayeux Tapestry (actually an embroidery) which depicts Halley's Comet as it appeared that year.

So now, we can consider the appearance and reaction to this most famous of comets. The reason for its name is that the astronomer Edmond Halley (1656-1742) observed his comet and realised that it would reappear 75 years later, which it did long after his death in 1758, thus proving that comets orbited the sun. Halley was influenced as a boy by observing two particularly prominent comets, one in 1664 when it was popularly associated with the Great Plague of London, and the other the following year when it was associated with the Great Fire of London.

Its appearance in 218 CE was said to have presaged the death of the Roman Emperor Macrinus (165-218 CE), and in 451 CE it was the only recorded defeat in battle of Attila the Hun (406-453 CE). The Comet was apparently accused of bringing the Black Death to England, and unbelievably Pope Calixtus III in the early 15th century actually excommunicated the Comet as he regarded it as emanating from the Devil.

The return of the comet in 1910 caused some interesting reactions, especially taking into account that it was suggested that the Earth was to pass through its tail. The rumour that the gas in the tail was poisonous took hold, with people fearing that they would die a gasping death. In fact this did not turn out to be the case and all was well, not that anything disastrous would have happened if our planet had indeed passed through the tail.

However, this was not what H.G. Wells (see also chapter 26), the father of science fiction, depicted in his novel *In the Days of the Comet*, which was published four years earlier in 1906. He describes the arrival of a comet through which planet Earth passes, but here the consequences are quite unexpected. Green vapours descend, making everyone unconscious for several hours, and after awakening find themselves changed. The vapours made them amend their old ways and becoming kind, altruistic, and generally leaving behind their previous petty jealousies, arguments and violence. The end result is that humankind's minds expand and have a higher level of understanding, resulting in the reorganisation society along Utopian lines with crime eliminated. If only! The book also advocated free love, which upset many who saw this as leading to general promiscuity, but again that is another story. Now back to Comet Halley.

The Comet produced a range of reactions. In the case of music two pieces of music were composed, "Halley's Comet Rag" and "The Comet March", and products such as custard, scent, soap and even corsets were advertised in connection with the Comet to boost sales. Earlier in 1910, there had been the appearance of what came to be called The Great Daylight Comet, which speaks for itself as to its nature, and the two were often confused. Returning to Patrick Moore, he was also a musician and composer with perfect pitch, and one of his works was entitled "Halley's Comet". I well remember attending a concert by him when he played his xylophone.

During the centuries before the Enlightenment, soothsayers were well occupied with interpreting the meanings of cometary arrivals, and in the Middle Ages even the Catholic Church regarded them as signs from God. We have come a long way since then.

To round off this section I shall leave you with the words of the late Carl Sagan on these celestial denizens:

When the rest of the solar system is dead,

*and the descendants of humans long ago emigrated
or extinct,*

the comets will still be soaring.

Meteors

Meteors and shooting stars

To begin with, shooting stars are particles of debris left behind by a comet and which continue to orbit in the same plane as their parent. The Earth passes through meteor showers several times a year, but odd meteors can be observed on any night. Typically, they are very small, no more than a grain of sand, but the speed they are travelling at, approx. 40,000 mph when they enter the Earth's atmosphere, this causes them to "shoot" across the sky with varying degrees of brightness. The major regular meteor showers are the Perseids (August), the Orionids (October), the Leonids (November) and the Geminids (December), but to see them at their peak it is best to observe them in the early hours past midnight. In November 1833, the Leonid shower was so great that it was estimated that 100,000-200,000 meteors an hour were observed, but such dramatic showers occur only infrequently.

Larger meteors sometimes appear as what are termed fireballs, which occasionally hit the Earth's surface itself, potentially causing much damage, but most fall harmlessly into the oceans. Such meteors as these are called meteorites. One memorable fireball was the Great Daylight Fireball, which occurred over Utah on August 10th 1972. It size was about 10 to 45 feet in diameter, and its trail of smoke remained in the sky for several minutes.

It should be noted, however, that it took modern science until the early 19th century to recognise officially that meteorites emanated from outer space; before this, the idea that rocks fell from the sky was looked upon as preposterous. It is thought that the Black Stone which is held in the Kaaba at Mecca is of meteoric origin, and it has also been mooted that a sacred stone which was kept in the Temple of Artemis at Ephesus, one of the Seven Wonders of the ancient world, could well have been a meteorite.

Meteor Crater in Arizona, or Barringer Crater as scientists call it, was formed about 50,000 years ago by a meteorite about 160 feet across, and the Chicxulub Crater in the Yucatan Peninsula in Mexico, 110 miles in diameter, was formed by a body much larger than most meteorites, perhaps an asteroid or comet. It was about six miles in diameter, whose impact led to the extinction of many forms of life, including the demise of the dinosaurs, 66 million years ago. Of course, a large extra-terrestrial body could hit the Earth at any time, but it is not worth worrying about it, as, on average, bodies of this size do not occur for millions of years between each one.

The fireball, which fell and broke up over the Russian town of Chelyabinsk on 15th February 2013, was a deadly example however. 112 people were injured and hospitalised, two seriously, while some were hurt by the blinding light, which was produced, and others received ultraviolet burns. Over 7,000 buildings were damaged by varying degrees and about 100,000 homeowners were affected. Fortunately, this kind of event is rare, but it could happen anywhere on our planet at any time, potentially causing untold destruction.

Of course, the most well-known custom that is recommended when catching sight of one of these fleeting entities is to make a wish. But much of their lore is similar to that of comets, especially that of portents. Again the ancient Chinese kept detailed records of meteor showers, the earliest known being a description of one that occurred on 23rd March 687 BCE when "stars fell like a shower". However in ancient and historic Western countries, there were practically no records made of meteor showers, which seems a little strange, but the odd fireball was noted.

For instance in the year 1000 CE, when many thought that the world would end, the following account was made of a bright fireball. It was described as falling through a gap in the heavens, "a kind of flaming torch" leaving "a long track of light", its brightness so startling that it frightened people both in towns as well as the countryside. And as the gap in the sky gradually began to close, "men saw with horror the figure of a dragon whose feet were blue and whose head seemed to grow larger and larger". Certainly an extraordinary sight!

Now turning to beliefs about meteors, some cultures saw them as souls being reincarnated and falling down to Earth in order to be born again, or alternatively as heralds of the arrival of God, as believed by tribes from West Africa. In the case of the Jukun tribe, they considered a meteor as a gift of food being transferred from one star to another. The Kamba, on the other hand, saw a meteor as a royal ensign, indicating that those who lived up amongst the stars were about to make a visit to our world. In other parts of Africa, particularly where Islam is the religion, meteors were seen as daggers hurled by angels in order to prevent such beings as genies from finding their way to the heavenly realms.

The Native Americans had their own lore concerning meteors, considering them as bad or good portents depending on the tribe's point of view. For instance the Pawnees saw them as beneficial, as their belief was that they were souls coming down to be reincarnated. However, the Shawnees' view was that they were ominous because they were a warning that something was about to happen, particularly that they were spirits fleeing from danger.

We must not forget the ancient Greeks, as they had another angle on the phenomenon. They also had the tradition of making a wish, but with added features. The astronomer Ptolemy in the 2nd century CE came up with the notion that the gods needed to keep an eye on humanity, and that to do this they created an opening in the sky, which enabled them to look down onto the world from their lofty abode. This action created a space whereby the stars fell through the opening, thus becoming shooting stars.

When the people saw these "stars" they made their wishes, as it was a sign that the gods were monitoring their thoughts and behaviour. The Greek playwright Aristophanes (c446-c386 BCE), however, was of the view that shooting stars were the souls of the poor walking homewards quite drunk, having dined at a rich star. Quite differently from the ancient Greeks though, Jews and the early Christians regarded them as fallen demons or even angels, which resonates with their connected religious beliefs.

Some superstitions have survived into modern times, of which two are worth recording. When people make a wish upon seeing a meteor, in the Philippines one should tie a knot in one's handkerchief, whilst in Chile the tradition is that one should immediately pick up a stone.

Thus to conclude, even if you do not accept some of these various points of view, then perhaps when you do catch sight of a shooting star, at least you could make a wish - why not?

Works Consulted:

Comet, by Carl Sagan & Ann Druyan (1985)
Weather Lore, by Ruth Binney (2010)
ianridpath.com

14 - Goblins, The British Scene - Folklore Of These Little Creatures

Goblin

In a sense goblins are not native to Britain, since their origins lie on the Continent. The word goblin does not appear in the English language until the 14th century, borrowed from the Old French *gobelin*, and the creature was originally connected to the region called Evreux in Normandy, until it expanded into the rest of Europe including Britain. This theme was taken up by Wirt Sykes (1836-1883) who wrote the tome *British Goblins; Welsh Folklore, Fairy Mythology, Legends & Traditions*, published in 1880, but it seems that he used this term to encapsulate all creatures such as fairies, pixies, imps and the like.

Goblins are a general term covering malicious spirits who are up to no good, their appearance normally being that of small individuals with grotesque features such as pointed ears, and usually they sported beards and had grey hair. They are wanderers, preferring to make their abodes amongst the roots of ancient trees or in nooks and crannies of rock formations. However, they occasionally attach themselves to a homestead, where they have the habit of rattling pots and pans, knocking on doors and walls, moving furniture around in the middle of the night, and pulling off the bedclothes of people whilst they are asleep. Other than the above, there is not much to tell about goblins, especially British ones. Nevertheless, there are stories, including two from the mining area of Northumberland related in 1863, featuring two goblins named Cutty Soames and Shilbottle Bluecap.

Cutty Soames was known as a spiteful elf who would cut the rope-traces, or soams, which were connected to a tub, an open-topped wheeled truck, within the mine. Even though everything in the mine was checked each evening before it shut for the night, known as "kenner-time", the following morning the rope was found to have been cut in half. All the miners could say was "Cutty Soames" has been at work.

Associated with the Shilbottle Colliery, situated three miles south east of Alnwick, Bluecap was quite different however, in that he was considered to be hard-working and honest, more like the Scottish brownie, sometimes leading the miners to rich mineral seams. Reputed to have inhabited the colliery in the 18th century, he would appear to miners who would see a flickering light blue flame, which would settle on the top of a packed truck of coal. This would then proceed along the mine as though it was being propelled by some strong force, which was said to be the work of Bluecap.

The miners considered that he should be rewarded for his assistance, in the form of the equivalent wages paid to a putter, or a miner who pushes the trucks of coal. Once a fortnight they would secrete his earnings in a secluded corner somewhere in the mine. However, if Bluecap was underpaid by as little as a farthing, he was indignantly wont to reject the payment altogether, but if he were to be overpaid by a farthing or more than he considered was what he was owed, he left behind the extra he had been overpaid. It could be that the miners mistook a natural phenomenon for a goblin, the blue flame being seen as his blue bonnet. Despite the danger of a naked flame appearing in a mine, where such an occurrence could lead to natural gas exploding, the miners deemed the blue flame to be harmless and were not worried about it. Apparently Bluecap abandoned the colliery in the 1840s.

There is also another Northumbrian goblin legend, which emanates from Tynemouth, about 34 miles from Shilbottle. A cavern formerly named Jingling Man's Hole, but now referred to as Jingling Geordie's Hole, close to Tynemouth Castle, is reputed to being the resting place of the lost treasure once belonging to Jingling Geordie. This character was a 17th century pirate who plundered shipwrecks and hid his booty in the maze of tunnels beneath the castle. The legend has it that he had fetters on his legs, the chains of which would rattle, thus resulting in his nickname, as he ambulated around, and his ghost is still said to haunt the castle walls. Local folklore tells that the immense hoard of treasure lies deep down into the cavern, and is protected by three guardians - a dragon, a pack of hellhounds and, to bring us back to the main subject, a host of goblins. Apparently, there is no access now to the cavern, only a slit just over a foot long, which allows one to peep just a little into its murky bowels.

From goblins in northern England, we now turn to the south where there are two goblin place names, Pook's Hill in Sussex meaning "hill haunted by a goblin", and Goblin Combe near Cleeve in Somerset, which is a nature reserve looked after by Avon Wildlife Trust. This reserve has two contrasting terrains, one described as "airy grasslands" and another a "dark combe", the latter conjuring up visions of gnarled old trees, goblins and fairy folk. A quote from an old tome by H. Hay Wilson dated 1912 which appears on the Faery Folklorist website describes a visit to the combe thus:

That lane to Goblin Combe, one June morning, promised to be unending, and nothing happened for all its turns and twists until suddenly a small boy-thing came walking around the next corner. He had very large ears like jug-handles, and an expressionless freckled face; and when he was asked where the road led he only smiled and would not answer.

Whether this was a true tale or not is irrelevant, as it brings up a vision that one would almost expect to experience in such an atmospheric place.

Although not a goblin story, a fairy sighting in Goblin Combe was retold in a 1965 book entitled *Folktales of England by Katherine Briggs and Ruth Tongue*, which related the following tale. One day a group of children were out picking primroses, when one girl strayed from the others and ended up in Goblin Combe. She was obviously lost and began to cry, and flung herself down against a rock, which opened up. Out of the hollow trooped a band of fairies who arrived to give her comfort and gave her a golden ball, after which they led her back home safely, as she had the primroses. The ball became an object of wonder in the village and a local wizard decided he wanted get his hands on several balls when the fairies next opened up the rock. He proceeded to pick some primroses and went off to Goblin Combe. He found the rock, but it was not the right day, he did not have the correct number of primroses, nor was he a sweet little soul, so the fairies snatched him away, so he got his comeuppance!

In East Lothian in Scotland the ruined Yester Castle has a goblin connection. Although there is not much left of the structure, the most complete part is a subterranean undercroft known as Goblin Ha', or Goblin Hall, which was thought to have been formed by magic. Connected to this is an interesting story concerning Sir Hugo de Giffard, or the Wizard of

Yester, who is regarded as the builder of the original keep in the 13th century. He was believed by the locals to be a necromancer and a warlock, and it was in the Hall that he was deemed to engage in his occult practices. The legend goes that, having agreed a pact with the Devil himself, he could raise an army of goblins and train them to carry out whatever nefarious deed he wanted. In fact local lore had it that this goblin host that constructed the castle itself. Today there is a hotel in Gifford called The Goblin Ha', the latter word normally pronounced as Haw. The castle is difficult to find, but directions can be found on the internet.

From one Celtic land to another - Cornwall. The Cornish are proud of their Celtic past, just as the Scottish, Irish and Welsh are. Centuries ago, Cornwall was referred to as West Wales, whilst Wales was known as North Wales. The Cornish language was related to Welsh and Breton, the last natural speakers dying out in the eighteenth century, although there is a revival movement, and it is now being taught in some Cornish schools [8].

This last goblin story involves the Cornish language. Cornish folklore tells of a water spirit called a *bucca*, which appears in a mid-16th century tome entitled *Gwreans an Bys* or *The Creation of the World*, and the word is translated as goblin. A verse from this book translates as follows:

> *Hairy, quaint he is and ugly;*
>
> *I know not what beast it can be:*
>
> *It should seem by his favour*
>
> *That he is some goblin of night,*
>
> *And that shall be proved.*

In olden times it was the practice to propitiate the *bucca*, with fishermen leaving a fish on a beach, and at the time of harvest bread was cast over the left shoulder, whilst drops of beer were spilt on the ground for good luck. There is also a story that a *bucca* haunted moors near Bolenowe up until the 19th century, when a young boy once got lost there. When he was eventually found by his parents, he told them that he had been alone there apart from the *bucca*. Belief in the goblin lasted at least into the 19th

---

8 Incidentally, when the Saxons came over to Britain after the Romans had left, many people from Cornwall crossed the Channel to what became Brittany. Before the area came to be called this name, it was referred to as Little Britain, and the British mainland became Great Britain, to distinguish the two. The name Great Britain has nothing to do with the land being "great" in the monumental sense.

century, when a road between Penzance and Land's End and the River Tolcarne bridged, the area became known as Bucca's Pass.

Prehistoric sites often have names that are associated with the Devil, giants, fairies and the like. As a follow-up to chapter 11 on ghosts and burial mounds, there are three mounds, which are associated with goblins. Near Little Horwood in Buckinghamshire is Shucklow Warren, the site of a now disappeared tumulus, whose name derives from the Anglo-Saxon *scuccan hlaew*, which translates as the Goblin's Hill, indicating that the mound was once haunted by one of these creatures. Another now vanished mound, this time in Wales, was situated on a hill called Bryn-Yr-Ellyllon, in English "The Hill of the Goblins", and the field in which it was actually placed, Cae'r Ellyllon, translates as The Field of the Goblins.

The term hobgoblin has its own associations with ancient sites. Obtrush Rook in Yorkshire has a still existing cairn whose name derives from "hob" and "rook", the latter denoting a heap, and the former an alternative form of goblin who traditionally haunts the site. Other Hobs to be found in England are Hob on the Hill near Guisborough in Yorkshire, Hob Hurst's House near Beeley in Derbyshire and Hardhurst Howes near Harwood Dale in Yorkshire, a group of round barrows.

Hobgoblins are more of a friendly type of creature, not unlike the brownie, and as such they are genial and willing to help humans, but they are prone to play practical jokes. At one time they were considered to be of a miscreant nature, as seen in Shakespeare's play *A Midsummer Night's Dream*, when a fairy says to Puck:

Those that Hobgoblin call you, and sweet Puck,

You do their work, and they shall have good luck:

Are you not he?

The Bard was obviously aware that if one calls a person a bad name, they will slowly take on those adverse characteristics. Nevertheless, Hobgoblins were normally attached to a homestead, carrying out odd jobs around the house while the family is asleep, and their only reward is to be given some food.

There are traditional rhymes concerning goblins, such as this one:

Laughed every goblin

When they spied her peeping:

Came towards her hobbling'

Flying, running, leaping,

Puffing and blowing,

Chuckling, clapping, crowing,

Clucking and gobbling,

Mopping and mowing.

One poem in particular concerns goblin markets. These are entirely different from the traditional fairy markets which involve activity amongst the fairies themselves, however if any human being approaches them good naturedly, then they are sometimes allowed to trade with the fairies themselves. *The Goblin Market* (1862) is a long poem by Christina Rossetti, sister of the Pre-Raphaelite artist Dante Rossetti, and is another matter altogether. The first stanza sets the scene:

Morning and evening

Maids heard the goblins cry:

'Come buy our orchard fruits,

Come buy, come buy:

Apples and quinces,

Lemons and oranges,

Plump unpeck'd cherries,

Melons and raspberries,

Bloom-down-cheek'd peaches,

Swart-headed mulberries,

Wild free-born cranberries,

Crab-apples, dewberries,

Pine-apples, blackberries,

Apricots, strawberries; -

All ripe together

In summer weather, -

Morns that pass by,

Fair eves that fly;

Come buy, come buy:

Our grapes fresh from the vine,

Pomegranates full and fine,

Dates and sharp bullaces,

Rare pears and greengages,

Damsons and bilberries,

Taste them and try:

Currants and gooseberries,

Bright-fire-like barberries,

Figs to fill your mouth,

Citrons from the South,

Sweet to tongue and sound to eye;

Come buy, come buy.'

The goblins here aim to entice humans to buy and eat their food, a deed ending in death, as is the traditional danger of consuming any fairy food. The poem tells the tale of two sisters, Lizzie and Laura, who hear the goblins calling out advertising their wares, but Laura succumbs, buying some fruit and eagerly eating it. Eventually, having consumed the fruit and not having the opportunity of obtaining any more, she wastes away and approaches death. Fortunately, she is saved by the love of her sister which overcomes the evil perpetration of the goblins. There are varying interpretations of the poem from the idea of Christian sacrifice/redemption to an incestuous lesbian theme, but Christina herself claimed that she wrote it as a fairy tale with no deeper meaning.

Ten years later in 1872 the author George MacDonald published his children's story *The Princess and the Goblin*, involving eight year old Princess Irene, and a goblin castle whose inhabitants are particularly nasty, but who eventually come to a watery end. MacDonald published a sequel entitled *The Princess and Curdie* in 1883.

Turning to adult fantasy, Tolkien is well known for his otherworldly creatures, not least his goblins as they are referred to in *The Hobbit*, but known in *The Lord of the Rings* as Orcs. They resided in dark places, were red-eyed, black-blooded and were notorious for their evil nature. Apparently Tolkien chose the word Orc over Goblin, as it is Germanic and appears in the Anglo-Saxon epic poem *Beowulf*, whereas the former originated in the Romance languages which Tolkien considered inappropriate. (Also see Tolkien in chapter 1.)

To finish, I acknowledge the importance of goblins to computer games, but this is beyond the remit of this chapter!

Works Consulted:

Folklore of Prehistoric Sites in Britain, by Leslie V. Grinsell (1976)
The Encyclopedia of Magical Creatures, by John and Caitlin Matthews (2004)
A Dictionary of Fairies, by Katharine Briggs (1976)
"A Fishy Tale of a Lost God", by Andy Norfolk in Meyn Mamvro: Ancient Stones and Sacred Sites in Cornwall, no. 95 (2018)
A Guide to Tolkien, by David Day (1993)
http://faeryfolklorist.blogspot.co.uk/

15 - Herne The Hunter Revisited: Follow-Up To The Author's Book *In Search Of Herne The Hunter*

Introduction

Herne the Hunter

This chapter is a follow-up with updates and new material to my book In Search of Herne The Hunter, published by Capall Bann (1994), to which I refer anyone who does not know the legend of Herne, the antlered spectre who haunts Windsor Great Park. However, for those unfamiliar with the subject, I shall relate a brief account of his legendary story first:

Back in the reign of Richard II there was in Windsor Forest a young keeper by the name of Herne, who worked on the King's estate and who was the King's favourite, which made the other keepers envious. At a hunt one day, Herne was injured whilst protecting the King from being gored by a fatally wounded stag. The King was at his wits end, as Herne lay dying but no-one seemed to able to help him. At this, a wizard named Philip Urswick appeared and said he could cure Herne, to the King's delight. Urswick then cut off the dead stag's antlers, tied them to Herne's head and, saying that he would recover in one month's time, rode off with Herne.

When the month was up, the keepers reluctantly went to Urswick's hut in the forest to collect Herne, but he heard them muttering against him

(Herne) and Urswick asked them what they would give him if he aided them in their revenge, to which they agreed to carry out the first request he made of them. In return, he promised that Herne would lose all his woodcraft skills. This turned out to be true and the King had to dismiss Herne, who proceeded to ride off with the antlers on his head, only to be found later hanging from an oak tree, later to be called Herne's Oak.

However, the keepers also began to lose their skills and they went back to Urswick to consult him, only to be told that to lift the curse they had to visit the oak at midnight, which they did. Herne's ghost appeared to them and told them to join him on a hunt the following night. This continued for some weeks, gradually depleting the deer herds and committing unspeakable outrages, until the King came to hear of it. He then ordered the keepers to meet him at midnight at Herne's Oak, where they encountered Herne's ghost, who told the King that the only way he would stop haunting the Park as he did was to hang the keepers. The next day the King did as he was bid and he was no longer troubled during his reign, although after his death Herne resumed his nocturnal hunts, which have been sighted over the centuries, including an appearance before Henry VIII.

The earliest reference we have of Herne is in Shakespeare's *The Merry Wives of Windsor*, but *Windsor Castle*, a novel from 1843 by W Harrison Ainsworth, contains a lengthy account of Herne's story, which the author has obviously elaborated.

Reported sightings of Herne's ghost seem to have mainly occurred just before a crisis in Britain. He is said to have appeared just before the Depression in 1931, before the abdication of Edward VIII in 1936, before the outbreak of World War II in 1939 and before the death of George VI in 1952. His last sighting was by a Castle guardsman in 1976.

Cernunnos and the Wild Hunt

It has been suggested that the figure of Herne may have been a folk memory of the Celtic horned god Cernunnos, who could have been revered by the inhabitants of the Berkshire area in Celtic and Romano-British times. Classical scholar Georg Luck in his study *Arcana Mundi: Magic and the Occult in the Greek and Roman Worlds* (1985) argues that Cernunnos was merged with the Greco-Roman god Pan/Faunus, another deity bearing horns. His findings indicate that this merged god could have been popular with those pagans who were reluctant to accept the new religion of Christianity, with his imagery eventually becoming the base of the idea of the Christian Devil.

However, Miranda Green, in her book *Animals in Celtic Life & Myth*, considers that "the protective character of the Celtic horned and antlered gods bears a far greater resemblance to the beneficence of Christ than to the image of the Devil". There is some evidence that pagan Celtic beliefs may well have lingered on into the Anglo-Saxon period, and the figure of the god could well have been kept alive in local Windsor folklore, who then morphed into Herne the Hunter, the leader of the Wild Hunt, which is a common theme in the folklore of northern Europe.

Wild Hunt stories tell of a spectral hunt which courses across country, through forest or across the sky, usually led by some form of demonic personage, with an entourage of ghostly horses, devils, murderers, blasphemers, unbaptised infants, other worldly beings and sometimes Freemasons (!). It was believed that anyone who was unfortunate enough to see the Wild Hunt was likely to be carried off with them, and to speak to the Wild Huntsman meant certain death. It was thought to be unlucky if one happened to see the Wild Hunt, but to ward it off, it was recommended to fix a pair of antlers to the gables of one's house.

Other Wild Hunt leaders are Gwynn ap Nudd, Lord of the Dead in Welsh mythology, the Saxon god Woden, Wild Edric in the Welsh Marches, King Arthur, Frederick the Great or Charlemagne in France and Germany, and also the Devil himself. The leader is normally accompanied by a pack of dogs called the Hounds of Hell and an owl, and in this guise Herne was presented as a bogeyman and used as a threat by parents in the Windsor area to keep their children in order.

Here are the last six verses of a translation in 1796 by Sir Walter Scott of a long poem by *Die wilde Jager* (*The Wild Huntsman*) by Gottfried Burger:

What ghastly huntsman next arose,
Well may I guess, but dare not tell;
His eye like midnight lightning glows,
His steed the swarthy hue of hell.

The wildgrave flies o'er bush and thorn,
With many a shriek of helpless woe;
Behind him hound and horse and horn,
And, "Hark away! and holla, ho!"

With wild despair's reverted eye,
Close, close behind, he marks the throng,
With bloody fangs, and eager cry,
In frantic fear he scours along.

Still, still shall last the dreadful chase,
Till time itself shall have an end.
By day, they scour earth's caverned space,
At midnight's witching hour, ascend.

This is the horn and hound and horse
That oft the 'lated peasant hears;
Appalled he signs the frequent cross,
When the wild din invades his ears.

The wakeful priest oft drops a tear
For human pride, for human woe,
When, at his midnight mass, he hears
The infernal cry of "Holla, ho!"

A vivid portrayal of the Wild Hunt indeed. However I shall continue with the topic of the tree upon which Herne was said to have hanged himself.

Herne's Oak

'Why, yet there want not many, that do fear
In deep of night to walk by this Herne's oak.'

The Merry Wives of Windsor

Oak trees have acquired a special reverence in British history and folklore. The tree was sacred to the Anglo-Saxons, who held it so because of it was rarely struck by lightning. Their runic symbol for the letter 'A', ᛣ, meaning *ac* or 'oak', runes being considered to have divine or magical properties. Indeed the Germanic peoples often looked upon the oak as being at the centre of their religious and social life. A charter dating to 955 concerning land in Abingdon mentions a "foul oak", and there is a record of a "Woden's Oak" close to Chieveley, both historically in Berkshire, which could point to the possibility of their having once been an oak-cult in the county. Many English surnames such as Oak and Nokes can be traced back to tree, notably one man named Thomas del Oke recorded to be living in Berkshire in 1275.

Many villages had what was called a Gospel Oak, so called as the Gospels were read out under the tree during the annual beating of the bounds tradition on Ascension Day. At the foot of Glastonbury Tor stand two ancient oaks named Gog and Magog, referring to the male and female giants who were said to have once walked the tracks of Britain. The most famous oak is Major Oak of Robin Hood fame in Sherwood Forest, and

May 29th is Royal Oak Day, which commemorates the return of the monarchy in 1660. Oaks represent strength and durability, the Druids especially revering the tree in their rituals. Oak leaves were depicted on the old sixpence and shilling coins, thus acknowledging the oak's almost magical properties. But now we turn to the oak upon which Herne the Hunter hanged himself.

The erroneous Herne's Oak just before its demise in 1863

Herne's Oak was cut down in 1796 on the orders of George III who wanted some of the old trees in Windsor Great Park felled and replaced with new ones, Herne's Oak being inadvertently included in the felling programme. There were various opposing views on the reason for the felling. One claimed that the King instructed that it be felled due to one of his fits of madness, which he was renowned for. An alternative had it that he was fed up with people talking about the fact that indeed it was Herne's Oak. On the other hand, the King refused a gift of some chairs which were alleged to have been carved from the Oak, because he was adamant that the tree itself was still standing. However, he seems to have accepted that the tree had been cut down, as one story goes. Despite denying on several occasions that it had happened, he eventually admitted the error and said that he was very sorry for the oversight.

The original Oak was not forgotten for many a year, and a recollection comes from a correspondent to the *Gentleman's Magazine* in March 1841 who said that as a singing-boy in 1786, he used he used to play in the Park and often climbed into the tree's hollow trunk. And there was also a delightful account about an old lady who was interviewed sometime in the 19th century about Herne's Oak. Apparently she distinctly remembered the original tree and dancing round it when she was a young girl. A charming little reminiscence, I think you will agree.

Around the mid-19th century there was much debate about which tree was Herne's Oak, which I covered in my *Herne* book, and further interesting comments on the subject from the 1841 *Gentleman's Magazine* include the following:

a) A bailiff at the Castle mentioned that on an occasion when George III once entered the Queen's Lodge he discovered that two chairs had been presented to him, which had been made from the wood of the deceased Herne's Oak. The King immediately threw them out, insisting that the tree was still in existence, which just shows how muddled his mind was becoming.

b) A "worthy" 84 year old shopkeeper in Peascod Street described that when he was a boy the hollow tree had been cut down about 45 years previously, which takes us back to 1796, the very year that it actually occurred.

c) Another correspondent stated that when he was a boy the tree was dead, and that it was so decayed that it was almost " a blotch" on the landscape. Again this would take us close to the end of the 18th century.

d) The father of the aforementioned singing-boy, a native of the nearby village of Datchet, was a Park foreman who assisted in the chopping down and grubbing up the tree. In addition, he stated that in 1783 his father collected an acorn from the tree which he hoped that would have been planted "with due ceremony" on the site of the original tree.

e) Another native of Windsor asserted that as a boy a portion of Herne's Oak's root, "big enough for a gun-stock", was given to him by the forester who actually cut the tree down.

A further correspondent added that there were two people in whom he highly regarded on this topic, namely the late Bishop of Salisbury, then

Canon of Windsor, and the President of   the Royal Academy, Mr. West, then a Windsor resident. Both were of the opinion that they recognised the true Oak when it was felled. Indeed West was so concerned that "so great a curiosity should be removed", that he made a request to have a fragment of the wood as a relic.

Another contributor to this *Gentleman's Magazine*, however, was of the opinion that on the subject of the real Herne's Oak "assertions of park-keepers and labourers should be cautiously received". So I shall leave it at that.

And now three more Herne's Oak reminiscences. A Royal Huntsman, Charles Davis, recalled that in the early 19th century when he was a young man, he used to perambulate around the fairy dell reading Shakespeare, whilst imagining to himself the fairies, which appeared in the play. Another sighting of Herne is recorded in *A Dictionary of Fairies* by the folklorist Katharine Briggs. Here she recalls that in 1915, whilst she attended a school in Edinburgh, one of her teachers related that her father, who was a retired colonel living in apartments at Windsor Castle, often saw Herne on moonlit nights under the branches of Herne's Oak, however which actual tree he was talking about is not known.

And finally, a 1940s sighting made by a schoolboy on his way from his Englefield Green to his school in Windsor. His route by bicycle took him down the Long Walk towards the Castle, and it was on a misty autumn morning when he suddenly caught sight of a person wearing a set of antlers sitting on a horse, silhouetted against the murky mist. His view was only a momentary glimpse, but it was enough to have turned his knees to jelly!

In my *Herne* book I related the tale of a guardsman at the Castle who was found unconscious on the East Terrace who swore he saw a statue sprouting horns and coming to life. Buckingham Palace stated that they had never heard of a ghost of any kind at the Castle and dismissed the report. However, the story was reported in the Windsor Express on 1st October 1976, and a lady reader contacted the newspaper saying that it was amazing that they had never heard of Herne the Hunter. She added that her grandmother told her 60 years previously of Herne sightings. The story she related was that Herne himself had a daughter who was seduced by Henry VIII, which drove her father mad.

There are a number of reputed secret passages, which run from the Castle used by Herne, not to be confused with sally port passages, which are controlled entrances into fortifications. One runs directly to Herne's Oak, with others leading to Datchet Mead, St Lawrence's church in Upton, Slough where the astronomer Sir William Herschel is buried, and Burnham Abbey and Bulstrode Camp in Gerrards Cross, both Buckinghamshire sites. Local legend has it that such passages were large enough to drive a coach and horses down, but traceable on the surface as ancient paths. Whether these tunnels actually exist, however, is problematic.

Such was the affection the locals had for Herne's Oak, that even after its demise it was said that the shadowy form of the fated tree was sometimes seen where it once stood, and the ghostly image of Herne's body was also witnessed swinging from its spectral branches. The current 2nd Earl of Gowrie, and former Conservative Party politician, also adds his opinion on Herne's origins. He spent a number of his childhood years at the Castle and viewed Herne as a folkloric legend featuring the survival of a fertility god, and Angus MacNaghten, author of *Haunted Berkshire*, goes along with this interpretation, surmising the existence of forest shrines, looked over by ancient priests. He considers that their rituals involved the wearing of headdresses adorned with antlers, and that Herne is a folk memory from pagan times, which ties up with Cernunnos discussed above. This sums up my researches into Herne sightings, but if anyone has any more please contact me through the publisher, I should be very grateful to hear about them.

The original Herne's Oak in 1783 (The Royal Windsor Forum)

To clarify the original Oak's position, it was situated in what was called the Little Park just east of the Castle, and it was also referred to as Sir John Falstaff's Oak, alluding to *The Merry Wives of Windsor*, and it was well liked by the locals. However, in 1838 Edward Jesse (1780-1868) suggested that an oak which stood in the avenue of trees in the Little Park was in fact the real Herne's Oak. A writer on natural history, including *A Summer's Day at Windsor, and a Visit to Eton* (1841), he became Deputy Surveyor-

General of the Royal Parks and Palaces. His views on the oak attracted many supporters, including Queen Victoria herself. However, this tree was blown down on 31st August 1863 and the Queen ordered a replacement to be planted in its place. It is said that after this tree blew down logs were collected and were burned at the Castle "to burn away the ghost of Herne the Hunter". However, one log was saved and a woodcarver got to work on the log, creating a bust of Shakespeare himself. This can be viewed at the Guildhall Museum in Windsor High Street (see below).

Bust of Shakespeare carved from the erroneous Herne's Oak

In the ensuing years much research was carried out and eventually King Edward VII had the matter looked into thoroughly, the original site being settled once and for all. The remains of the tree which fell down in 1863 were dug up and the Little Park's avenue was replanted. On 29th January 1906, Herne's Oak 2 was planted exactly on the site of the original Oak, which is still standing, but this is in the private section of the Home Park. It is interesting in passing though, that Edward VII, who passed away in 1910, dressed in full uniform, was buried in a huge oak coffin in St. George's Chapel.

Thus the history of the "Herne's Oaks" and their timelines can be summarised as follows:

1796 The inadvertent felling of the original Herne's Oak by George III

1838 Edward Jesse concluded that an oak tree growing just south of the original was Herne's Oak

1863 This erroneously named tree, accepted as the true one by Queen Victoria, blew down on 31st August

1863 Queen Victoria planted a replacement on the site of the erroneous tree on 12th September

1906 The replacement was cut down when the Home Park Avenue was replanted

1906 Edward VII planted another oak on the site of the original Herne's Oak on 29th January

All the illustrations of Herne's Oak between 1780 and 1796 reveal it to have been a pollard, a practice that took place in the winter when there was snow on the ground, in order that the royal deer were able to feed on the bark. I am grateful to the Crown Estate (in 2018) for confirming that Herne's Oak 2 is still standing, for providing the photo below, and pleased to report that it is also thriving. However, it is situated in the private section of the Home Park, which is not accessible to the public.

It is widely accepted that Shakespeare used local folklore when writing the story of Herne the Hunter, which he included in *The Merry Wives of Windsor*, and it is recorded that he spent some time in Windsor gathering material for the play. He stayed at a local hostelry, but there are three contenders for which inn it actually was. One was called the Bottle on the Moore and was situated at Frogmore, which changed its name to The Hope Inn, which does not now exist. Another vanished inn was The Old Kings Head in Church Street, and another was The Harte & Garter Hotel, previously two inns, The White Hart one and The Garter the other, in Thames Street opposite the Castle. This now possesses a commemorative stained glass window. The play was first performed in Vicars' Hall behind St George's Chapel, and was commissioned by Queen Elizabeth I to coincide with the making of her cousin, Lord Hundson, as a Knight of the Garter.

Herne's Oak was featured in what became known as the Windsor Tapestries, a series created in Victorian times by a firm called the Old Windsor Tapestry Manufactory, established in 1876. This was based in a now long demolished building named Manor Lodge in Old Windsor, and its founders were two Frenchmen, Marcel Brignolas (Manager) and Henri C.J. Henry (Director). The firm was part of the Arts & Crafts movement which was coming into popularity at that time. The only other such establishment turning out tapestries contemporaneously though was that of William Morris, which was founded at Merton Abbey in 1881.

Herne's Oak 2 (Crown Estate)

One of the early works was a commission depicting scenes from Shakespeare's *Merry Wives of Windsor*, in which the story of Herne is told, which were designed by the artist T.W. Hay, displayed at the Paris Exhibition in 1878 and exhibited at Windsor Guildhall in the December of that year. One of the eight scenes was that of Herne's Oak, the scene being that of Act V, Scene V, where Falstaff is depicted in the dell hard by the Oak. He is surrounded by Anne Page as Queen of the Fairies, her troop of masked fairies and eleven other figures making up quite a complex picture. Falstaff is disguised by having a stag's antlers on his head and is depicted as crouching down and having his face lit up by one of the fairies' torches.

Herne's Oak is shown in the background, with Windsor Castle on the skyline. The scene is portrayed as a summer night's revel lit by the fairies' lights, with the Oak's green leaves behind Anne Page, framing her bower. The size of the tapestry is eight feet eight inches by six feet. Illustrations proved not suitable for reproduction here, so for those wishing to view the tapestry, an image can be found on the Royal Windsor Forum website.

The erroneous Herne's Oak which blew down in a storm in 1863, was cut up and many objects carved into souvenirs, one special item being a compartmented casket made in an Elizabethan style. This was carved by a William Perry, Wood Carver to the Queen, who wrote "*A treatise on the identity of Herne's Oak, showing the maiden tree to have been the real one*", and described the casket as a receptacle to house "relics, or interesting memoranda relating to the immortal Bard". At the corners are niches, each displaying an oak tree in bas relief in the background, together with ivy creeping around the trunks. The niches contain in full relief figures from *The Merry Wives of Windsor*, Falstaff, Ann Page and two other minor characters. The centre of the top features a portrait of the Bard with the inscription "Shakespeare", together with his dates. On the inside of the drop front is a silver plaque containing an inscription detailing the casket's provenance and the name of William Perry, carver, and the date 1866. Queen Victoria also had a cabinet made from the timber, and as you will expect, Herne's Oak carvings are highly collectable. There is also in existence a 19th century oil painting of the erroneous Oak by a Windsor local Mr. Dennis Lightfoot, although where it is now housed, I have not been able to ascertain.

The full story of the 1863 demise of the wrong Oak is as follows. A newspaper report from Saturday September 5th 1863 described how "the shattered trunk of Herne's Oak" was blown down on Monday morning. Consequently, it was important to report this to Queen Victoria, who at the time was in Germany. She immediately ordered that the trunk should not be removed until she returned to the Castle. Whilst she travelled back to England a day and night watch over the trunk was arranged to deter souvenir hunters. On the morning after her return, she, along with lesser members of the royal family, visited the site, and the Queen was adamant that the tree be treated as Herne's Oak. The accepted view of Herne at this time was that he had been a forest keeper in the early part of Queen Elizabeth's reign, when he committed some offence. Angered by this, Elizabeth dismissed him immediately and he "formed the desperate resolution to hang himself upon this tree".

The year before the tree's demise, an historic event had occurred. Royalty, including Frederick William IV of Prussia together with a party of German notables, arrived for the baptism of the Prince of Wales, the future Edward VII. Whilst they were in Windsor they expressed a desire to see Herne's Oak, where they stood for a while in silence, such was the fame of the tree through the Shakespeare connection. Before the Prussians departed, they plucked ivy leaves from the tree's trunk as mementoes.

This is just one instance of visits to the Oak by "pilgrims" from all over the world. It is notable that Herne's Oak must have been famous before *The Merry Wives of Windsor* was first performed, since a map published by John Norden, compiled about 1597, shows a copse labelled as Herne's Wood five years before the play was registered for publication in 1602.

To bring things a bit more up to date, in 2017 Windsor & Royal Borough Museum held an exhibition entitled *Tree Tales from the Great Park*, which included an event for children to mould a model of a tree and to explore the legend of Herne the Hunter and Herne's Oak. It is good to see to see local folklore and folktales being promoted in this way.

There is also a Herne's Oak in Carthamartha Woods in Cornwall, but this has no connection with the Windsor one, probably just being a haunt for hunters!

Herne's Oak Public House

For many a year there was a public house named Herne's Oak in the nearby village of Winkfield, but unfortunately the pub is no longer there, as the building has been converted into offices, however the building has an interesting history. The structure appears to have been built in the late 16th century or sometime in the 17th century, the earliest extant deed dating from 1752, which refers to a messuage (a dwelling with out-houses), a barn, a garden, an orchard, as well as six acres of pasture, six acres of meadows and one acre of woodland.

In 1764, the property changed hands for a sum of £60, but the deeds make no mention of a beer-house or the name The Herne's Oak. After several changes of hands, the property was acquired in 1820 by a John Tull, a Windsor baker, still without mention of the name. In 1826 a John Jennings bought the property and it is assumed, as his occupation was that of a brewer, that it was he who turned it into a public house and named it The Herne's Oak.

The Jennings family auctioned the estate in 1862 at The Star & Garter in Windsor, which went under the hammer to the brewer Lawrence Wethered, when the property was first officially referred to as The Herne's Oak. The pub was taken over by Whitbread, which owned the premises until it was sold off in 2009. "Harry" Harrison, the landlord in the latter years, used to have a brief summary of Herne The Hunter's story pinned up inside the pub. There is also a local Winkfield legend that the ghost of Herne has been encountered outside the premises, but other than that, I have not been able to discover why the name was chosen, as it was some three miles from the tree itself.

Just before its demise I managed to take a photograph of the last inn-sign, which was quite different from the one that I photographed for my

Herne book, and I reproduce it here (it is not known why the figure of Herne has not been portrayed with his antlers though). It is sad that an old pub with its Windsor Forest and Herne associations has had to go, but I suppose it is a sign of the times. I have also discovered that there was once a pub named The Herne's Oak in Windsor itself, which was situated in Rectory Terrace, Parsonage Lane. It doubled as a general store and has now been converted into a local shop, but unfortunately, I have not been able to find any more of its history.

I should add that the public house *The Merry Wives of Windsor* in St Leonard's Road, Windsor, is now *The Windsor Grill* restaurant, another drinking establishment and a traditional name gone. It was once one of the oldest Windsor pub names, but its character has been maintained, even though there are obviously alterations. The 17th century timber framed building is Grade II listed, and the public house frontage was constructed around 1900.

The last inn sign - but why no antlers?(Valerie Fitch)

Adjacent to the Winkfield pub there was also a Herne's Cottage, now Herne's House, reputed to have been a Royal Park keeper's cottage in Henry VIII's time, local legend having that it was inhabited by Herne himself. It is conjectured that Nell Gwyn may have once owned it, as it was rumoured that she owned a nearby farm; she certainly had other property such as 61-63 King's Cross Road in London, which later became the popular Bagnigge Wells Spa. From 1680 to her death in 1687 she was given by Charles II the freehold of Burford House near the Home Park, 250 yards from the Castle, so it is possible that Herne's Cottage was once her property. At the auction of 1862, the title to the house was the same as that of The Herne's Oak, when the estate was split into lots. It could well be, therefore, that the legends surrounding Herne's House may well relate to the pub. It must be pointed out that Herne's House is in private ownership and thus the owners' privacy must be observed.

The inn after closing (Valerie Fitch

And to end this section, I should like to quote a notice that was displayed in the Herne's Oak inn, as told by the landlord "Harry" Harrison in 1999:

The ghost of Herne the Hunter roams the trees of the

ancient forest of Windsor. Once a royal huntsman he

became a favourite of the King when he saved the
life

of the monarch from a charging stag. Fatally wounded

in his act of bravery Herne lay dying from his wounds

when an old wizard appeared from within the trees.

Pointing to Herne he spoke, "if that life you wish to

save then those there antlers to his head you must tie."

The King gave the order for the dead stag antlers to be

cut and placed on the head of Herne. As the life

returned to this once limp body the old wizard

disappeared. The favours shown by the King made the

huntsmen envious and tales of untruth and hatred left

their tongues. Herne was soon dismissed from service.

Sad and dishonoured he went out into the forest and

took his own life. Hanging from an old oak tree was

found the lifeless body. From that day this tree was to

be known as the HERNE'S OAK.

Thus this concludes the story of a traditional English pub with its own legendary history, gone the way of so many others.

Antlers and Deer

Deer and their antlers feature in the folklore of many countries, but I shall keep to Britain and the relevance to Herne. There are several tales from Irish and Scottish sources which include deer which they call "fairy cattle" and in which they are milked and herded by a supernatural woman who is able to shape shift into a white or red deer. The Celts revered the stag, as it acted as a symbol of wild nature, its antlers imitating branches of trees. This may be connected to a figure on the Celtic Gundestrup Cauldron discovered in Denmark, which shows, amongst other strange images, a seated man with antlers on his head accompanied by an antlered deer and other animals. This obviously brings to mind Herne himself, the Lord of the Animals.

It is apparent that the Anglo-Saxons regarded the stag as an important symbol of regal and political power. Indeed Woden himself was described as being led to the abode of the goddess Holda by a stag, and it is recorded that he was also known as the stag himself. In Norse mythology the fertility god Freyr is killed by a deer's antlers, and the stag Eikthyrnir that stood in Valhalla, and was known to cause cows to yield not milk but blood, just as Herne himself was said to have done.

In the Anglo-Saxon poem *Beowulf* there is a great feasting hall called Heorot, which translates as "Hall of the Hart", and in the great Anglo-Saxon ship burial of Sutton Hoo, archaeologists discovered a stone sceptre/whetstone mounted with the figure of a bronze stag complete with antlers. It is thought that the piece represented the power and authority of the king, who is thought to have been Raedwald of East Anglia who hedged his bets by worshipping as a Christian as well as a pagan. St. Patrick and his followers turned themselves into deer to avoid a trap laid by a pagan king, and in Welsh mythology the stag was one of the oldest animals in the world. The importance of deer in British folklore cannot be overemphasised, with Sir Francis Drake's ship named the Golden Hind.

Stag-headed trees are those that have dead branches at their top, which stick up above the green-leaved branches, looking rather like the antlers of a stag. It is said that oak trees, which sometimes show this feature, live a life of three stages: 300 years of growth, 300 years of rest, and finally 300 years of decline. The original Herne's Oak when illustrated in the 18th century, was obviously in the latter stage and stag-headed and, if it had not been inadvertently cut down, it probably would not have lived that much longer.

The antlered deer is intimately linked with the idea of the hunt or chase, especially involving red deer, which are the species which inhabit Windsor Great Park, numbering now around 500. They are all descendants of 40 hinds and two stags, which were reintroduced in 1979 from Balmoral by the Duke of Edinburgh, the original herd having been removed during the

Second World War. Thus antlered deer have a long history in the minds of humans, stretching back to prehistoric times. The chase was immortalised by a poem by Sir Walter Scott:

Hunter's Song

> *The toils are pitched, and the stakes are set,*
> *Ever sing merrily, merrily;*
> *The bows they bend, and the knives they whet,*
> *Hunters live so cheerily.*
> *It was a stag, a stag of ten,*
> *Bearing its branches sturdily;*
> *He came silently down the glen,*
> *Ever sing hardily, hardily.*
> *It was there he met with a wounded doe,*
> *She was bleeding deathfully;*
> *She warned him of the toils below,*
> *O so faithfully, faithfully!*
> *He had an eye, and he could heed,*
> *Ever sing so warily, warily;*
> *He had a foot, and he could speed —*
> *Hunters watch so narrowly.*

In 2016 a red deer skull and antlers were found on a beach at Borth in Wales, dating back 4,000 years. The antlers were four feet wide, and they belonged to a huge stag, which once roamed the land in the Bronze Age. In addition, stumps of yew and oak trees were uncovered on the same beach, leading to the fact that there was once a forest in the region, thus connecting once again to the theme of sacred trees, Windsor Forest and Herne's Oak.

The Merry Wives of Windsor

Now to Shakespeare, and the appearance of a pirate edition of *The Merry Wives of Windsor* dated 1602 where the following alternative version of the Herne legend appears:

> *Oft have you heard since Horne the hunter dyed,*
>
> *That women to affright their little children,*
>
> *Ses that he walkes in shape of a great stagge.*

Now for that Falstaffe hath bene so deceived,

As that he dares not venture to the house,

Weele send him word to meet us in the field,

Disguised like Horne, with huge horns on his head,

The houre shalbe just betweene twelve and one,

And at that time we will meet him both:

Then would I have you present there at hand,

With litle boyes disguised and dressed like Fayries,

For to affright fat Falstaffe in the woods.

We have come across Falstaff in connection with the Windsor Tapestries, and it is apposite here to mention the thrust of the play, which is a comical work full of intrigues. Sir John Falstaff is an impoverished knight who tries to seduce two married women, Mistress Page and Mistress Ford, in order to obtain money from their well-off husbands. However, he does not succeed and the two women plan to dupe Falstaff. Mistress Ford invites Falstaff to meet her one night at Herne's Oak disguised as Herne the Hunter with a set of antlers on his head. Mistress Page is dressed as the Queen of the Fairies, along with some children dressed as fairy folk, who taunt and pinch Falstaff. Mistress Quickly also prepares the fairies with this instruction:

But till 'tis one o clock

Our dance of custom round about the oak

Of Herne the Hunter, let us not forget.

Mistress Page encourages everyone as follows:

Let them from forth a sawpit rush at once

With some diffused song; upon their sight

We two in great amazedness will fly:

Then let them all encircle him about

And, fairy-like, to pinch the unclean knight,

And ask him why, that hour of fairy revel,

In their so sacred paths he dares to tread

In shape profane.

To which Mistress Ford adds:

And till he tell the truth,

Let the supposed fairies pinch him sound

And burn him with their tapers.

And Falstaff appears to be quite willing to
impersonate Herne, as he states in Act 5:

Divide me like a bribe-buck, each a haunch;

I will keep my sides to myself, my shoulders for the

fellow of this walk,

and my horns I bequeath your husbands.

Am I a woodman? ha! speak I like Herne the
hunter?

Falstaff, The Merry Wives of Windsor

The play ends with everybody laughing at the antics they had all got up to and at Falstaff's humiliation, with the two women turning out to have the upper hand.

Shakespeare used local folklore as well as references to real Windsor people and events in the play; Anne Page for instance is recorded to have been buried at Windsor Parish Church in 1617 at a cost of two shillings, paid for by the parish council. Queen Elizabeth I was so taken with the character of Sir John Falstaff in Shakespeare's plays Henry IV parts I & II that she wanted him to write a sequel, which he duly did. It is highly unlikely, therefore, that the playwright would have invented the legend of Herne the Hunter any more than he would have done for the inhabitants and goings-on at Windsor.

The Fairies' Dell near Herne's Oak gradually became filled in over time and Prince Albert, wishing to preserve the area associated with Shakespeare, decided to dig out the accumulated earth with a view to recreate the Fairies' Dell itself. As to the supposed Herne's Oak, which blew down in 1863, it was hoped that the memory of the tree could be maintained, thus leading to the carvings mentioned above. A branch from this tree broke off in 1843 and was preserved in the royal stores at the Castle.

*Note :*There is an opera based on the play by Otto Nicolai published in 1849, which includes an overture for non-opera lovers.

The Legend of Herne the Hunter

Another depiction of Herne

To expand on Harrison Ainsworth's account of Herne in his novel *Windsor Castle*, he tells of the Earl of Surrey's unaccompanied walk in Windsor Forest where he came upon 'a blue, phosphorescent light' shining through some bushes. He then espied an enormous oak tree, at the foot of which he saw "a wild, spectral-looking object, possessing some slight resemblance to humanity", the ghost being Herne the Hunter himself. Herne then let out "a horrible burst of laughter, then a fearful wail", which frightened Surrey enough to quickly to return to the Castle.

As the novel progresses, Herne appears on several more occasions, sometimes accompanied by a pack of hounds. Surrey persuades the Duke of Richmond to go with him into the Forest in order to gain another witness, whereupon they caught sight of him, but Herne just blew flames out of his horn and promptly disappeared. These events, of course, are just the work of Ainsworth's imagination, but are vivid nonetheless.

In *The Merry Wives of Windsor* one of Herne's attributes is that Herne "makes milch-kine yield blood", or in modern terms "causes cattle to produce blood instead of milk". It was considered that as cows have their offspring about April/May time this could be connected with the traditional custom of placing honeysuckle and rowan sprigs in cow sheds on 2nd May in order to protect the cattle from coming to any harm from witches, and to make sure that the milk produced is up to standard and a good yield. Rowan is well known to have been used to prevent the evil deeds of witches, and honeysuckle was also seen as a powerful protective agent. However, either these remedies were not used in Windsor or Herne was impervious to them.

Going on to the 18th century, author Samuel Ireland (1744-1800), in his two-volume work entitled *Picturesque Views on the River Thames* (1792), related another version of the story of Herne, this time placed in the reign of Elizabeth I:

> *"That having committed some great offence, for*
> *which he feared to lose his situation and fall into*
> *disgrace, he was induced to hang himself on this*
> *tree [Herne's Oak]. The credulity of the times easily*
> *worked on the minds of the ignorant to suppose that*
> *his ghost should haunt the spot. This rendered it a fit*
> *scene of action for the purpose of our bard*
> *[Shakespeare] to terrify and expose the cowardice*
> *of the fat knight [Falstaff], who confirms the idea of*
> *Herne's ghost being supposed to walk near this*
> *place, and is even desirous of imitating the keeper's*
> *voice, as described above."*

Moving on in time, the folklorist and mythologist Lewis Spence also wrote on Herne. Spence saw Herne and his healer Philip Urswick (see below) to represent a rivalry between the spirit of a beech tree and that of an oak. In Ainsworth, Urswick resides in a beech tree, from which he appears in flames, which Spence saw as the "lightning spirit who animates the tree". He surmised that the name Urswick could be a corruption of Okuthor, another name for Thor, "the god who drives the thunder-chariot", but this author feels that this is probably a step too far in conjectural supposition. However, Urswick certainly cuts a strange almost shamanic figure, especially with his healing skills.

And now a possible alternative answer not covered in my book. Where did this name come from? My research has led me to a former Dean of Windsor, Christopher Urswick (1448-1522), who took up his post of Canon of Windsor in 1490, becoming Dean in 1495. During this period he oversaw the rebuilding of the Windsor Deanery and the redevelopment of St. George's Chapel, and there is still an Urswick Chapel situated in the north west of that building. A stone screen with an inscription requesting prayers for Urswick is still extant, but now in the south aisle. The Albert Chapel contains a window depicting eminent figures connected with St. George's

Chapel, in which Urswick is included, and on the roof, his coat of arms is featured several times.

Now, could Christopher Urswick have been the inspiration for the figure of Philip Urswick? Of course, the latter does not appear in print until W Harrison Ainsworth's novel *Windsor Castle* in 1843, but could his name have easily been recorded in local folklore, as did Herne's? The historical Urswick died in 1522, *The Merry Wives of Windsor* was published in 1597 (see below), and Shakespeare's play *Richard III* from 1592 included Urswick as a minor character in one small scene where he acts as envoy between the Earl of Derby and the exiled Earl of Richmond, the future King Henry VII.

Urswick was obviously known to Shakespeare and the playwright incorporated local folklore into *The Merry Wives of Windsor*. Ainsworth also was well versed in folklore, and it may well be that he picked up the name of Urswick from the locality of Windsor, as did Shakespeare before him. Perhaps Urswick had some kind of reputation, which became part of Windsor lore. As to the forename Philip, my researches have not found anything further on this, so here we must leave the matter as an unresolved enigma.

The origins of Herne have already been described in my earlier book, but there is one further suggestion not covered there. This version tells that Herne was a drunkard, with his drinking horn giving rise to his name being spelt sometimes as the alternative Horne. The surnames Herne and Hurne date back to Saxon times. For instance in the Berkshire hundred rolls of 1279 there is a record of one Henry en le Hurne, the name deriving from the Anglo-Saxon word *hyrne*, which indicated that a person lived on a corner of a plot of land or on a bend of a river.

The place-name Windsor itself derives from the Anglo-Saxon words meaning a "river bank with a windlass", which appeared in the 17th century as Windlesor. Also in Windsor there used to be a Horne Weir on three islands in the Thames, which may, or may not, have any connection with Herne. Continuing with place-names, Berkshire is said to have been derived from "bare oak shire", a 15th century reference referring to a bare oak in Windsor Forest around which the local populace would gather round, but this is rather speculative.

However, in his poem *The Battle of Agincourt* (1627) Michael Drayton writes about Berkshire's traditional emblems which were borne by Berkshire men at the Battle of Agincourt:

Barkshire a Stag, under an Oake that stood,

Oxford a White Bull wading in a Flood.

In 1889 the emblems of the Oak and Stag were adopted by the new Berkshire County Council, and when the county was granted its own coat of arms in 1947 it incorporated them into its design as well. It has been thought by many over the centuries that the oak referred to Herne's Oak and that the stag related to Herne himself, but whatever their origins, they go back into the mists of time, perhaps deriving from a pagan stag cult and tree worship.

Apparently, Herne was also said to have haunted Feckenham Forest near Redditch in Worcester. Here he was said to have killed a sacred stag which belonged to the Abbess of Bordesley Abbey, the ruins of which are still visible. The story continues in a similar vein to that at Windsor, in that as a punishment for this deed, Herne was destined to lead the Wild Hunt forever. How Herne has travelled as far as Worcestershire is a mystery, especially since factually an Abbess of Bordesley never existed.

Now moving further afield mention must be made of American author William Perry Brown (1847-1923). I have come across a short story he wrote, now very dated, in which he writes about a misogynist character called Herne the Hunter who lives in a cave in a "weird, wild region of brake and laurel, walled in by lonely mountains". The story describes him in this way: "Some town-bred Nimrod, with a misty Shakespearean memory, had added to his former patronymic of 'Old Herne' that of Windsor's ghostly visitor. The mountaineers saw the fitness of the title, and 'Herne the Hunter' became widely current". The figure of Nimrod was described in the Bible as "a mighty hunter before the Lord", thus once again we have the link with Herne.

The legend of Herne was kept in the popular imagination by a number of printed accounts, which included a penny dreadful entitled *Herne the Hunter: A Legend of Windsor Forest* from the 1850s. As mentioned in my 1994 *Herne* book, there was a nineteenth century opera based on his legend, and in 1879 a playwright named Thomas Plowman penned a play entitled *Herne the Hunter: Or the Days of the Bluff King Hal, an Historical Improbability*.

Finally, returning to my original book, I have an addition concerning the Mask of Herne, a stone carving of a head unearthed in Park Street in Windsor in the late 1920s. In an article submitted to The Times by the Rev. Leslie Badham, Vicar of Windsor, he referred to the mask as: the "curious head with deep-set eyes under the fierce brow and antlered horns". The mask was made of coad stone (not load stone, as I incorrectly stated in my book) and it could simply have been a Victorian wall ornament. Apparently, it has medieval counterparts and bears some resemblance to the grotesque heads on the parish church at Hitchen in Hertfordshire. It was stolen from Windsor Parish Church in 1963 and has never been recovered.

An illustrated article in the Windsor, Slough & Eton Express on 1st February 1963 tells its story, written by the late local historian Michael Bayley of Maidenhead.

Herne & Burnham Beeches

As everyone knows, the Wild Hunt is associated with Herne, and I should like to draw readers' attention to another connection with a woodland near where I used to live in Burnham in Buckinghamshire, and that is Burnham Beeches. This vestige of ancient woodland contains the largest collection of old beech trees in the world, renowned for its weird, gnarled beeches, and it is often used as background for films and television. Films include *Goldfinger*, *Robin Hood Prince of Thieves* and *Harry Potter*, and TV productions include *Midsomer Murders*, *New Tricks* and *Doctor Who*. In the past it attracted people like the poet Thomas Gray and composer Felix Mendelssohn.

The woodland contains an old enclosure named variously as Hartley Court Moat, Harlequin's Moat or Hardicanute's Moat. The latter name has led to local folklore connecting the enclosure with King Canute's son King Hardicanut, but the dating shows this to be false. Enclosing one and a half acres, it consists of an irregular moat surrounding an area with a continuous bank on the outside and dividing banks within, and the whole is further enclosed by a bank and ditch covering over nine acres. The date of the site is uncertain, but such moated homesteads are considered to date from the 12th to the 14th centuries, although its origins may well lie in the Anglo-Saxon period or perhaps even earlier. Elsewhere in the woodland there are earthworks dating from the Iron Age Celtic period, so it is obvious that people were here from at least around 300 BCE. One old oak tree in the Beeches is known as Druid's Oak, but obviously, it does not date back to the Celtic period, being approximately 500 years old.

The site's name in its Harlequin form is of interest in that it is a variant of Herian, which was an alternative name for the Saxon god Woden, another leader of the Wild Hunt. Harlequin's Moat could possibly be named after a folk memory of when Woden and his entourage raced through the Beeches way back in Saxon times. Burnham Beeches is not far north from Windsor over the River Thames, so can we speculate that it may have been rumoured that Herne himself sometimes led the Hunt through the Beeches?

Herne and Paganism

The modern Pagan movement, largely influenced by the writings of Gerald Gardner and Margaret Murray, has flourished since the 1950s and is now the fastest growing religion in Britain. Herne is a major figure/god in many of the branches of Paganism, and is held by some to be a folk memory of the Celtic horned god Cernunnos. There is a suggestion that the haunt of Herne, Windsor Forest, remained a Celtic stronghold for longer than the most of southern England, with the worship of Cernunnos lingering on into the later Saxon period and then merging with the Wild Hunt.

The horned god is often equated with Herne and was first used in British Pagan rituals in the 1950s. In his influential book *The Meaning of Witchcraft* (1959), Gerald Gardner described him as "British example *par excellence* of a surviving tradition of the Old God of the Witches." This theme of witchcraft being a survival of an ancient pagan religion, originally put forward by Margaret Murray in the 1930s, has long been discredited, but the idea of Herne/Cernunnos has been incorporated into Pagan beliefs and rituals, and is as valid a god as any other. Artist and authoress Chesca Potter, in her pamphlet *Mysterious King's Cross* (1990) describes the stag-headed god as "The male fertilic power of nature, physically and spiritually. In prehistoric times, the Shaman would have dressed in deerskins and a mask with stag-horns becoming as the God . . ."

Within the religion of Wicca the horned god/Herne is seen as the consort of the triple goddess, a theme that is virtually absent from the main religions. He is seen as an ancient fertility god, presiding over fields and forests and, of course, the hunt. He is the lord of life, death and resurrection, the hunter and the hunted, and also the protector of the goddess. Herne is now a powerful figure and image in Pagan circles, and his importance is illustrated by the following news item. In 2016 a Scottish Pagan wished express his beliefs by building a sacred shrine to Herne the Hunter on his land, only to be refused planning permission from his local council. Such is the suspicion still held by ignorant people against "pagan" practices.

There are many strands of modern Paganism, from Wiccans to Odinists, and most of them accept the notion of a god and a goddess, a belief in the balance of male and female in the world, an idea largely lost, especially in the Western world, with the influence of the Abrahamic religions. It is a positive theme, which is gaining ground more and more, with Herne up there in the hierarchy of deities honoured by the modern Pagan community.

Books, Films and Music

There have been quite a few Herne appearances in books and films, such as Herne the Hunted in the late Terry Pratchett's *Discworld* series. However, there is one I should like to bring to the reader's attention, and that is the book entitled *The Dark is Rising* by Susan Cooper, published in 1973, the second of a series of five linked children's novels of the supernatural, which are also good reading for adults as well. *The Dark is Rising* is set in south Buckinghamshire, where Cooper was brought up. It tells the story of Will, an eleven-year-old boy living with his family in the village of Huntercombe, last of the Old Ones, who had to find and join together the five remaining Signs of the Light to prevent the Dark from rising.

The book interweaves ancient Celtic and English traditions with local legends and folklore of Buckinghamshire, which add to the atmosphere of the tale. Being set in the Thames Valley, it is not surprising that Herne the Hunter makes an appearance, as does Herne's Oak. As one reviewer put it: "It is almost as if the magic forces within the story were themselves reaching out to spellbind the reader". Cooper also brings in Herne in the last of the series *Silver on the Tree*, and this author cannot recommend these books too highly, and I mean books, for there is a film.

The Seeker: The Dark is Rising is an American film released in 2007. An American family, including Will, move to a small English village whence Will's ancestors originated. In fact, the film was made in Romania, which about sums up the scenario. The legends and folklore of the book have all been deleted and, worst of all, Herne the Hunter does not even make an appearance! The film was obviously influenced by those of Harry Potter, and Susan Cooper herself was not impressed by the result, to say the least. In my estimation, I would rate it at 2 out of 5. If you like fantasy, have any interest in British legends and folklore and like a real, engaging read, then get hold of the books - you will not regret it!

Listed here are other main places where Herne appears:

Robin of Sherwood TV series (a 1980s production in which Herne prominently appears)

Windsor Castle, by William Harrison Ainsworth (an 1843 novel with the Herne legend)

The Box of Delights, by John Masefield (novel & 1984 TV series)

Call of the Hunter (2009 film)

Herne, music by Clannad (*Legend* album 1984, soundtrack to TV series *Robin of Sherwood*)

Face of the Hunter, music by the pagan metal band Herne (2011 album).

There are quite a number of other Herne appearances, which can be found on the internet.

Conclusion

And finally, a more recent experience of Herne. In a series on BBC Radio 4 in 2015 dealing with the folklore of Britain, one episode was devoted to Herne the Hunter. During the programme, there was a brief interview with a warden of Windsor Great Park, who told of his encounter with Herne. He and a couple of friends were doing some late night fishing at Russells Pond in the Park when they heard the sound of a galloping horse emanating from a nearby copse. They immediately formed an opinion that it was the sound of a hunt, but who would be hunting in the middle of the night? - it must be Herne the Hunter.

Thus this chapter has now closed the chance of this author writing any further on the subject of Herne the Hunter. It has been a long journey, but I have enjoyed the search for Herne, and I hope this chapter is of some interest to those new to Herne, or to those who have read *In Search of Herne the Hunter* and wish for an update.

Looking back, if I had written the book now 25 years on, apart from the new material in this chapter, there are a few minor amendments I would make, but 95% of the text I would not touch. These are my final words on this exhilarating and spellbinding subject.

Works Consulted:

In Search of Herne the Hunter, by Eric L. Fitch (Capall Bann 1994)
Herne the Hunter: A Berkshire Legend, by Michael John Petry (1972)
The Winkfield Chronicles, by Ruth Timbrell and the Revd. Simon Baynes, M.A. (2000)
A Dictionary of Fairies, by Katharine Briggs (1976)
The Romance of Windsor Castle, by Hector Bolitho (1946)
Animals in Celtic Life & Myth, by Miranda Green (1992)
The Minor Traditions of British Mythology, by Lewis Spence (1948)
Herne, the Windsor Bogey, by Simon Young (in Gramarye journal, Winter 2017, issue 12)
Round & About 109 (December 1997/January 1998)
The Lore of the Land, programme 3 (Radio 4, 2015)
ancient-tree-hunt.org.uk/discoveries/newdiscoveries/2007/23+jan+2007

I should also like to acknowledge the invaluable assistance I received in relation to this chapter and my book In Search of Herne the Hunter *from the late Maidenhead historian Michael Bayley.*

Susan Cooper's The Dark is Rising interlinked sequence comprises:
Over Sea, Under Stone (1965)

155

The Dark is Rising (1973) - features Herne
Greenwitch (1974)
The Grey King (1975)
Silver on the Tree (1977) - features Herne

There is now a premium bitter beer named Herne the Hunter, brewed for the Herne Brewing Company by Wanaka Beerworks in New Zealand. Their recommendation: The inaugural brew, this is an Extra Special Bitter, with gentle hop bitterness from the Challenger hops, and deliciously aromatic fruitiness from the Styrian Golding. Made from UK malts. Also, there is The Herne Tavern in Honor Oak, London, SE22 0RR

WITCHES

16 - The Witch Of Endor: The Summoning Of The Spirit Of Samuel By Saul

One of the strangest and most incongruous narratives in the Bible must surely be that of the calling up of the ghost of Samuel by a necromancer who has come to be known in popular lore as the Witch of Endor. Such a practice was at variance with the beliefs of both the ancient Hebrews and later to Christians, both of whom denounced supernatural pursuits such as witchcraft, divination and speaking to the dead, believing them to be evil and against the will of God. For instance Deuteronomy 18.10-12 warns against necromancy, augury and sorcery, "For whoso doeth these things is an abomination unto Yahweh" (this term being the tribal Hebrew name for God). Consulting departed spirits was something that was obviously taking place at that time and, amongst many different societies, it still is. So, why did this account find its way into holy writ?

The story occurs in 1 Samuel 28, the background of which concerns the banishing of "those who had familiar spirits and the wizards" out of the land by Saul, King of Israel from about 1025 BCE to 1010 BCE following the death of Samuel, last of the Judges. It was during Saul's reign that a host of Philistines arrived at the border of Israel, ready to do battle again now that Samuel was dead, at which Saul "was afraid, and his heart greatly trembled". He was obviously at his wits' end as to what approach to take against this threatening throng and, even though he prayed to Yahweh, "the Lord answered him not, neither by dreams, nor by prophets". So it is at this point that Saul decided that drastic action had to be taken.

Aware of the teachings against such practices, he decided to risk his soul and instructed his servants to "seek me a woman that hath a familiar spirit, that I may go to her, and inquire of her" in order that she would be able to obtain advice for him by supernatural means. His servants, apparently without much trouble, found such a woman living at Endor, four miles south of Mount Tabor, which rose from the Plain of Jezreel. This town was never fully assimilated by the Israelites and remained largely Canaanite, a people who worshipped their own gods and goddesses and practised the magical arts. This woman was likely to be of Canaanite stock and, because of her "pagan" beliefs, became known as the Witch of Endor. She was reputed to be able see the future with the aid of a spirit.

So Saul, to ensure that he was not recognised, disguised himself before his visit to the necromancer, because he did not want the witch or the spirit she was about to call up to recognise him, especially the latter, as in the ancient world spirits of the departed were generally considered harmful. Accordingly, accompanied by two servants, Saul was taken incognito to a secret spot to meet the witch at the dead of night, as spirits of the departed do not like the light. He requested of her that she raise a spirit, whose name he would divulge in due course, who would be able to predict the future and thus advise him on a course of action.

At this, the witch exclaimed that she could not carry out such a task, because of the laws against occult practices, which had been passed by Samuel, and she accused Saul of trying to trap her and have her executed. But Saul, swearing by God, assured her that she would suffer no punishment, to which she asked the name of the ghost whom he wished to raise. Saul then revealed that it was the spirit of Samuel himself he wanted to be summoned.

Upon hearing this name, the witch performed her magical signs and incantations and called up Samuel's ghost. It was then that she realised that it was Saul himself who had come to her and she cried out to him asking him why he had deceived her. He told her not to be afraid, but asked her what she saw, to which she replied "an old man cometh up; and he is covered with a mantle". This description confirmed to Saul that it was Samuel's ghost, since earlier Samuel had been described as being old and grey and clothed in a mantle or robe. Recognising his predecessor, Saul "stooped with his face to the ground, and bowed himself".

Struck with awe, Saul then heard the voice of Samuel's spirit say "Why hast thou disquieted me, to bring me up?" to which Saul replied that he was sorely distressed about the Philistines' threat to wage war against his people. He added that, even though he had sought advice from prophets, dreams and God himself, no guidance was forthcoming. Thus, despite reservations, he felt his only avenue was to consult Samuel by way of summoning his ghost in order to obtain his counsel as, in life, he had been viewed as the greatest figure since Moses.

However, Samuel's spirit pointed out to Saul that the reason for Yahweh's silence was that Saul had twice displeased Him. Firstly, he had taken upon himself to adopt the role of priest, which was considered to be sacrilege, and secondly he encouraged his people to sacrifice sheep and oxen to the Lord, who was not pleased. Samuel was still alive on this occasion and had reported to Saul Yahweh's words "to obey is better than sacrifice, and to hearken than the fat of rams". Thus, Samuel's ghost was now rebuking Saul for the third time for disobeying Yahweh's wishes and, this being the last straw, Yahweh had decided that Saul would lose the battle with the Philistines, the kingship of Israel would be handed to David, and Saul would die.

The Witch of Endor summoning the Spirit of Samuel

Hearing these words from the spectral Samuel, Saul fell stretched out to the ground, terrified. He had not eaten for a day and a night and all his strength had left him weak and exhausted. The witch then approached him and, seeing he was greatly disturbed, exclaimed to him that she had risked her life to obey him and it was time for him to listen to what she had to say. However at first she offered him some food to keep his strength up for his return journey, but he refused any sustenance. Nevertheless, after she and his servants urged him to eat, he gave in and ate of the fatted calf the witch had slaughtered. She then prepared some unleavened bread, which Saul and his servants ate and they departed on their return journey.

So, how can we view this strange Biblical episode? Firstly, even though the Endor woman has been popularly known as a witch, her craft seems rather to describe her as a medium, an ancient practice that has continued up until today. As we know, mediums have a bad press, but there are well-meaning practitioners as well as charlatans. The Witch of Endor seems to have been successful in calling up Samuel's ghost, but the interpretation of this event varies, with some Christians believing that it was not Samuel who was raised, but a demon, because such sorcery could not be associated with God. An alternative view is that the witch was a fraud and used ventriloquism and foggy smoke from a fire to disguise her ruse.

It is considered by historians that the early Israelites believed that spirits of the departed continued to live and that they could foresee the future and could return to the world under certain circumstances, as we have seen in this account. The Israelites placed plates of food, drinking vessels and lamps in graves, as gifts to the deceased, which shows that they thought that what men had required on earth, they would also require in the spirit world. This world, called Sheol, was considered, according to Job 10.21, to be "the land of darkness and the shadow of death" beneath the earth where the spirits lived a shadowy existence. Thus, they had no notion of a "heaven" or "hell", which future Christians would formulate, and their belief was not dissimilar to the ancient Greeks' idea of Hades, which was not a place of punishment or reward, but rather just a place of gloom. (Sheol has often been mistranslated as Hell by Christian clerics but, as we have seen, the Israelites had no such concept.)

Another way at looking at the story is as a satire on Saul. Having driven necromancers and magicians from the land, Saul proceeded to disobey God's wishes and then went ahead himself to dabble in the forbidden arts. After the witch had summoned the ghost of Samuel, the spirit did not give Saul any good advice, but preyed on Saul's fears and forecast his doom.

However one treats this story, it is certainly a strange one to find in the Bible, which otherwise teaches that anything occult or magical is decidedly against the will of God. Nevertheless, since time began, humankind has dabbled in arcane practices, sometimes for good, other times for bad, and despite the prevalence of science, I think they always will. But hopefully people will be wary of charlatans and possible psychic damage, which is always a danger if contacting the other side is approached with the wrong attitude and frame of mind.

This chapter first appeared in Merry Meet Magazine no. 51 Winter 2013/2014.

17- The Witches Of Windsor: The Unfortunate Fate Of These So-Called Witches

In the 16th and 17th centuries witchcraft trials were taking place around all of Europe, the practice being believed in by everyone from superstitious and illiterate peasants to monarchs, a prime example being James VI of Scotland and James 1 of England. The action in this chapter takes place in the reign of Elizabeth I, whose successor was James I. The latter had a great interest in witchcraft, which he considered as a branch of theology. He was present at the North Berwick Witch Trials and several "witches" were convicted of cursing the ship in which he was sailing by sending storms, whilst en route from Denmark to Scotland. In 1597 he wrote a book entitled *Daemonologie* and he personally supervised the torture of women accused of witchcraft, but in later years his views became more sceptical. This was the background to the story, which will now unfold.

It was in 1579 that Windsor became the focus of witchcraft activity after the Privy Council wrote a letter to the Dean of Windsor and Sir Henry Neville, Member of Parliament for New Windsor requesting that they investigate witchery in the town, especially with regard to image-making. Four suspect women were taken into custody accused of the practice and sent to Reading for trial. The key perpetrator seems to have one Elizabeth Stile or Rockingham, a widow aged around 65. She lived alone apart from a rat named Philip, described at the trial as a "wicked spirit". Apparently she fed it with blood from the wrist of her right hand, where the tell-tale marks were supposedly found, and she also "gave her right side to the Devil". She was apprehended in January 1579, after being indicted by her neighbours as being a lewd, malicious and hurtful woman to the local inhabitants in Windsor, which were also accusations held against the other women.

In fact, the four accused witches were said to have acted together on many occasions, but they also performed wicked deeds by themselves. For example, Elizabeth caused the death of a man named Saddock, who had promised her an old cloak but who had failed to keep his promise. She evidently clapped him on the shoulder, after which Saddock went home and promptly died. On another occasion, she confessed to having walked unsuccessfully to Old Windsor begging for milk, and when she returned home, she found that her rat had provided her with both milk and cream[9].

---

9 : New Windsor is where the Castle stands; Old Windsor is a couple of miles downstream on the Thames and is where the Anglo-Saxon kings held their court. Runnymede is adjacent, where Magna Carta was signed by King John in 1215

Elizabeth Stile and her Familiars

In addition to her confessions, others gave evidence at her trial, including that put forward by a Windsor ostler. On oath, he claimed that one Mother Stile was wont to visit his master's house in order to beg alms, which he often willingly gave her. However, on one occasion she arrived only to find that the ostler was short of money. He gave her what he could, but she was apparently not satisfied with what she had received and returned home very angry.

Soon after this incident, the ostler reported that he developed a severe aching in his limbs which hindered him not only working but also from resting until he was able to do neither. He tried all kinds of remedies, but all to no avail. It was as a last resort, therefore, that he paid a visit to a wise, or cunning, man named Father Rosimund, more of whom later. He informed the ostler that there were many evil women in Windsor and that it was apparent that one of them had bewitched him. Upon being asked whom he mistrusted, the ostler immediately referred to Mother Stile. Rosimund's solution was to advise the ostler to scratch her next time they met and, as long as blood was drawn, he would recover. An opportunity eventually arose and the ostler managed to scratch Mother Stile's face and drew blood, after which his aches disappeared and he had been better ever since.

One further incident involving Mother Stile concerned the son of another Windsor man who had come to fetch water from a well, which happened to be positioned near her door. Unfortunately, the boy took it into his head to throw a stone at her house and she, perhaps justifiably, did not take kindly to this. She took the boy's pitcher from him and added that she would be even with him. On his way home, the boy bumped into his father and told him that Mother Stile had taken the pitcher away from him. It seems that his father recognised that his son had caused the old woman some grief and so he said that he would speak with her.

However, on their way back to Mother Stile's house the boy suddenly exclaimed "Oh, my hand, my hand!" Upon turning to his son he saw that the boy's hand was bending backwards and, horrified, attempted to stop the process, but to no avail. It was then that one of their neighbours arrived on the scene and both he and the father tried to stop the boy's hand from bending, but even their combined strength could not stop it. Fortunately for the boy, his hand was bent back to its rightful position either by Father Rosimund or one of the other accused witches named Mother Devell, to whom we now turn.

Mother Devell lived near Windsor Pound and was very poor. Like Mother Stile she lived alone with a familiar, or spirit as it was called at the trial, in the form of a black cat named Gille which, it was alleged, helped her in her witchcraft activities. It was Mother Devell's habit to feed the cat daily with milk mingled with her own blood, it was said.

Mother Stile, in her confession, implicated the other three women, and in Mother Devell's case claimed that she had cursed a fisherman named William Foster and a baker, the wife of a man named Willis. It seems that her witchery did not cease after her apprehension for, having been brought to Reading Gaol after Mother Stile, she apparently bewitched the latter and others. She took away from Mother Stile all use of her limbs and in addition induced her to take leave of her senses. Furthermore, her toes rotted and she had to be borne on a barrow before the judges, "a most ugly creature to behold". So it seems that these women, even though they were said to work together as we shall see later, were not averse to attacking each other.

The third accused was Mother Dutten, whom Mother Stile claimed was involved in devilish deeds. This old woman lived somewhere in the parish of Clewer together with "a spirit or fiend in the likeness of a toad", which used to reside in her garden amongst a border of green herbs and which she fed from blood pricked from her side. She was also accused of being clairvoyant. Mother Stile's confession included incriminating evidence against all of the other three women, all of whom were involved in the murder of various people, as will be described below. On one occasion Mother Dutten was accused of making the image of a man or woman which, Mother Stile could not say, but she did state that this person subsequently died, but she did not know his/her name. Thus, we are introduced to accusations of a serious nature.

Finally we turn to Mother Margaret who resided in one of the Windsor alms houses and was obviously crippled in some way, as it was reported that she had to get around with the aid of two crutches. In her particular case, her fiend was a kitten named Hinnes, which she fed with breadcrumbs mixed with her own blood. Mother Stile's confession included a claim that when she was apprehended, Mother Margaret came up to her and gave her some money and urged her not to divulge their secrets, and she threatened that if she did so, then she would be harshly treated. There are no further accounts of Mother Margaret, except inasmuch as when she was implicated in joint ventures, as we shall now investigate.

Included amongst her confessions Mother Stile stated that she used to meet with the other three women, Father Rosimund and his daughter. The place they met at was in "the pits" behind Master Dodge's abode, which could be the sawpit in Windsor Forest, which was mentioned in Shakespeare's *Merry Wives of Windsor* (see also chapter 15). It was there that they carried out their "heinous and villainous practices" according to whatever they individually or as a group had devised. They were also wont to meet at the pond at about 11 o'clock at night. It was here, Mothers Stile said, that Mothers Dutten and Devell persuaded her to forsake God and his works and to giver herself to the Devil.

It is perhaps most convenient to list the evil doings they were supposed to have had a hand in using their devilish spells:

1. The murder of a farmer named Lanckforde who lived by the Thames in Windsor. This was carried out by Mother Dutten making an image of the man in red wax, about the width of a hand long and three or four fingers broad and, with the agreement of all four women, sticking a hawthorn prick into the left side of the image's breast. This had the affect of producing a sudden death within a short space of time.

2. One of Lanckforde's maids was dispatched in a similar manner.

3. Another victim was a previous Mayor of Windsor by the name of Richard Gallis, landlord of the Garter Inn, again using the wax image. It is interesting to note however, that he found time to write a book, *Discovery of Witchcraft*, about the witches before he expired. Initially Gallis started persecuting the women and in one instance he tied a rope round Mother Stile's waist and dragged her to Sir Henry Neville, who immediately said that Gallis had no right to do what he had just done, ordered him to release her and told him never to do anything like that again. Ultimately though, as we shall see, this did not change Mother's Stile's fortune.

4.   A butcher named Switcher was likewise dispensed with. This could have been a person originating from Switzerland; apparently Windsor housed a fair sized foreign contingent.

5.   Another butcher, named Mastlin, was also bewitched, but Mother Stile claimed she did not know whether he died or not, although elsewhere it was reported that he consumed away.

6.   There were four instances where people were allegedly bewitched, but did not die. In the case of Humphrey Hosey and his wife, Richard Mills and John Mathinglise, they all caught a   strange sickness which lasted for a long time, but they recovered eventually.

7.   One image was made by Mother Dutten at her house in the presence of Mothers Devell and Stile. This was used against a man named Foster. After finishing making the image, Mother Devell said to her black cat "plague him and spare him not!", and she thrust a prick into the   image's heart. The result was that Foster remained at death's door for a long time, but it seems that Mother Dutten allowed him to recover. However, they went on to kill one of his cows instead.

8.   Mother Stile also confessed that they all dealt viciously with anyone who angered them. They would summon their spirits and say "such-a-one hath angered me, go do them this mischief", and as payment would give the spirits a drop of their own blood. These actions would then result in the unfortunate victim receiving some dire misfortune. The death of Saddock (see above) by Stile was effected by working upon an image of the man.

As can be seen from the above, which are only some of the accusations, this is quite a catalogue of supposed evil spells meted out by Elizabeth Stile and her companions. But there is one more figure we have not considered yet and that is Father Rosimund who, along with his daughter, were both accused by Mother Stile of being witches. As previously mentioned these two also joined the meetings in the pits behind Master Dodges.

Rosimund was apparently a widower who lived in a hut at Farnham Royal, and he seems to have been a popular figure in the community, as he was known to be a cunning man. But Mother Stile accused him of being able to change himself into any animal he wished. Indeed, she reported that, not only could he bewitch or even reverse the effects of anyone bewitched, she once found him in a wood nor far from his house sitting under a tree and transforming himself into an ape or a horse.

Whatever the truth behind these fantastic accusations, it seems that Father Rosimund and his daughter were not brought to trial and they both apparently got off scot-free. Perhaps even the credulous people of the 16th century would not accept such wild stories as shape shifting. However, the same could not be said of the four unfortunate women, who were all found guilty.

Upon being thrown into gaol, Mother Stile was urged by her gaoler to confess all her deeds of witchery, promising that this would look good in the eyes of God and ensure her a lenient sentence. She believed this, then made her confession in Reading Gaol on 28th January 1579 in the presence of a knight, the right worshipful Sir Henry Neville, a constable John Knight, the gaoler Thomas Rowe and an innkeeper John Griffith. She is reported to have had some remorse for her evil deeds and wished to confess her misdemeanours, which led to the sentencing of herself and the other three women to capital punishment. It seems that Mother Stile's confession was responsible for the other three witches to be condemned as well.

And so it was that on 26th February, almost a month after Elizabeth's Stile's confession, the four women were taken to Abingdon and there hanged. This was the first recorded instance of a group of witches working together, English trials usually consisting of a witch acting alone.

Works Consulted:

Stories of Great Witch Trials, by Ronald Seth (1967)
Witchcraft in the Thames Valley, by Tony Barham (1973)

18 - Witchcraft In Buckinghamshire: Four Quite Different Cases In The County

Typical witch woodcut

Introduction

"Thou Shalt Not Suffer a Witch to Live" (Exodus 22:18) is part of a list of transgressions together with their respective punishments, such types of commandment being common in the Old Testament. However, witchcraft has been understood and treated in many different ways, notably in the witchcraft trials which took place in the Early Modern period. The interpretation of witchcraft in the Old Testament at that time became the source of dreadful tortures and executions enacted upon so many innocent women and men, especially on the Continent. In England, it was carried out on a smaller scale, and it should be pointed out that no "witch" was burned alive in this country, the preferred method of execution being that of hanging. Records of witch trials reveal that there were 228 executions in England and 599 in Scotland, the latter country being more obsessed with witchcraft, especially during the reign of James VI. Scotland also practised burning at the stake, but usually the victim was strangled first.

In the phase of the witchcraft trials, much was made of witches' Sabbaths, the Devil, and the goddess witches were supposed to worship, i.e. Hecate, the Greek goddess of magic and the underworld. She was also associated with the Moon, as was Artemis, the two goddesses eventually becoming entwined into one. In this form, she was a goddess of the night, calling up ghosts and demons from the lower world, with the Romans revering her, using the name of their own moon goddess, Diana. In late Medieval times, Hecate herself became prominent as the witches' deity, along with the horned god, and for Christians she was seen as a devil, her patronage of the magical arts and her nocturnal activities neatly fitting in with the expectations of what witches got up to. The Egyptologist Margaret Murray made much of Hecate and witches in her books, seeing witchcraft as a survival of a secret pagan religion from ancient times, but nowadays her ideas have been discredited.

The last person to be convicted under the Witchcraft Act of 1735 was Jane Rebecca Yorke, a 72 year old medium of Forest Gate, London. On September 26th 1944, she was found guilty of seven counts of exploiting people's wartime vulnerabilities and expectations. She claimed to have a Zulu spirit guide and on many an occasion she would call up the spirit of Queen Victoria. Unlike earlier times, she was simply fined £5 and was placed on good behaviour for the following three years, and promised not to hold any more séances. The 1735 Act was repealed and replaced by the Fraudulent Mediums Act of 1951, which aimed not at "true" witches, but fake mediums. This came about due to the notorious case of the medium Helen Duncan, also convicted in 1944, but that is another, though fascinating, story.

Since World War 2, however, with the repeal of the 1735 Act, the practice of Wicca has flourished and is now recognised officially as a genuine religion in this country. It respects the feminine as well as the masculine, worshipping both a goddess and a god, and its emphasis is on good magic, healing and the environment. Even within Wicca, though, there are different persuasions including pantheism, polytheism and goddess monotheism to name three, but all are quite distinct from what is popularly called "black magic". Wicca has no repellent aspects any more than most religions, despite what fundamentalist Christians may say.

There appears to have been little "witchcraft" activity in the county of Buckinghamshire during the period of the witchcraft trials, but having been born in the county and lived there for over 30 years I have picked up some tales concerning the topic. This chapter thus deals first with two cunning women and some "traditional" witches from the South Buckinghamshire area where the author used to live, and finally an account from further north in the county.

The White Witch of Burnham

The traditional witch figure is the toothless crone who lives on her own with here familiars such as a black cat, a toad or an imp, and who rides through the air on a broomstick. More often than not these attributes were attached to old women who lived alone, but who had powers of natural healing and were well versed in herbal lore. The witch we are concerned with here is of the latter persuasion, the harmless village "wise, or cunning woman", the inheritor of hundreds, if not thousands of years of ancient wisdom. (That is not to forget "cunning men" as well). Such folk were normally Christian, along with their neighbours, and were mostly concerned with curing sickness, locating missing persons, finding true love, counteracting "witchcraft", fortune telling and the like. However, even though they were often accused and hanged for practising witchcraft during the persecutions, they were largely innocent of such "crimes". In Britain cunning practices had largely died out by the end of the 20th century, although they may linger on in other European countries.

One such woman resided near Burnham Beeches during the years leading up to the Great War, who claimed to be what is known as a white witch, practising only "good magic". She had an intimate knowledge of herbal medicines, a discipline that has had something of a revival in recent times, along with other forms of alternative medicine, many of which are very old and largely forgotten in the Western world. Her familiarity with such substances led her far and wide outside of her immediate locality in order to obtain her efficacious plants.

She would often walk to the Slough arm of the Grand Union Canal, a distance of three or four miles, so that she could procure the herbs she required that were not available in the near vicinity of her home. Her reason for exploring so far was that in years gone by market sweepings from London used to be dumped on the banks of the canal by the barges, which used to arrive from the metropolis. Amongst these sweepings were exotic plants that subsequently took root and grew alongside the canal. Making use of this serendipitous opportunity to harvest such foreign and fruitful growths, she considered it worthwhile to make the journey now and then to glean ingredients necessary for her herbal cures.

Here we see the use of natural magic for beneficial purposes, and it is pertinent to note that this old lady was never known to curse of throw a bad spell over anyone. An interesting footnote to this account is that the character of "The White Witch of Burnham" was used by Walter de la Mare in one of his stories. The author once lived at Hill House, a Georgian property in Taplow, a parish adjacent to Burnham, where he and his family resided for from 1924 to 1939. I have tried to identify the story in which she appeared, but have not been successful.

The Wise-Woman of Rotten Row

Rotten Row is a hamlet situated three miles or so west of Marlow in Buckinghamshire, where another cunning woman once lived in the 19th century, as far as I can tell. She was known for her insistence that she had no otherworldly powers, saying that her abilities were entirely natural and that she used them in a manner that did not involve the occult in any way. For instance, she recommended that the local young girls wash their faces using a distillation of elder leaves, which had been collected in the month of May. Elder trees were traditionally believed to be transformed witches, and the local witch who lived near the Rollright Stones is said to have turned a company of knights into the stones we see today, after which she transformed herself into an elder tree. To have elder wood inside a house or to burn it on a fire was thought to attract bad luck. I am sure, though, that this wise woman would have no such evil-minded dealings.

She no doubt had a stock of various ointments and medicines, but one requires a special mention. It was an ancient remedy that she took over from her mother, who used to sell it walking from house to house. Interestingly the bottle in which the remedy was stored had an old label upon which was written:

> *The Golden Pills of Life and Beauty also known as the Trowbridge Pills. For the complaints incident to the female constitution. Prepared by Mrs. Jane Ludlow of Warminster.*

Whether this indicated long-range communication between cunning folk from all parts of Britain is not known, but it is a worthy topic for future folkloric research.

One of her tasks involved a kind of exorcism, for the people of Marlow came to her to rid them of a ghost, which had been haunting the neighbourhood. The spectre appeared at a particular place in the town and was known locally as "the Whistling Milkman", a young man who was hanged years ago for a murder committed in the town. It is not known by what means she used to expel the ghost from the neighbourhood, but she was successful, the ghost disappearing from then on.

The wise-woman lived to a ripe old age, continuing to advise and assist people with their problems. Such advice included warning folk not to pick up a pin found in the road, as she said that a witch may have placed it there when she was aware that someone was approaching. She warned that if they picked the pin up and kept it, they would then be under the witch's power.

Here we see a "white witch" referring to a "black" witch, the latter still being believed in up to the 19th century.

The Grenfell Curse

This section deals with what are considered in folklore as "traditional" witches, who were thought to practise the shadowy arts of cursing, blighting people, livestock and crops, amongst other ungodly actions. Enough has been written about such figures, the most famous being the three witches in Shakespeare's play *Macbeth*. In popular culture, they are the embodiment of wickedness from fairy tales to Disney. The following account deals with such a company of 19th century witches who were said to live in the village of Taplow.

In 1852 the stately home of Taplow Court was in the hands of the Grenfells, the family whom the comedienne Joyce Grenfell married into. There has been a house on the site since the Norman Conquest, but the present building was purchased by Charles Pascoe Grenfell in 1852 from the Earl of Orkney, and Grenfell rebuilt the house in 1855 in mock Tudor style. After the Second World War, it was owned by British Telecommunications Research, but from 1988 it became the home of the Soka Gakkai International, a Buddhist movement based on the teachings of Nichiren Daishonin. The Taplow Court estate lies adjacent to that of the Natural Trust house of Cliveden (see chapter 24 for more on this property).

After their acquisition of the house and its surrounding estate, the Grenfells decided to enlarge the grounds to take in the old adjacent churchyard. This area is owned by the Church of England as it contained the ruins of the old village church, as well as the great Saxon burial mound, whose contents excavated in 1883 were the finest of their kind until the finds at Sutton Hoo in East Anglia. They had the church ruins demolished, and a spring which flowed into Bapsey Pond was culverted and the pond itself lined with brick (see also chapter 23).

It appears via local lore that the witches were angered with this desecration of what they regarded was a sacred pool. They gathered together to decide how they could punish the Grenfells, coming to the conclusion that the family should be cursed, and decreed that the ownership of Taplow Court would never descend from father to son. Indeed, not only was the family generally considered by the locals to be ill-omened, but history has borne this out in that the three sons of William Henry Grenfell, Lord Desborough, were all killed before their time. Julian and Billy, both scholars, poets and sportsmen, who would doubtless have risen to eminent positions had they lived, died during the Great War at Ypres. The third son, George, was killed in a car accident in 1926.

It is quite probable that the spring was considered by the same "witches" to be sacred, and it would have been seen a desecration to culvert the spring. Such an act would have to be paid for by the family who perpetrated the deed. So the curse came to be. Truth or fantasy? Who knows.

The Wingrave Witch (or not)

In the Buckinghamshire village of Wingrave, four miles northeast of the county town of Aylesbury, a witchcraft trial ended happily. The origin of the village's name comes from an Anglo-Saxon man called Withun, appearing in the Domesday Book as Withungraue, which seems to mean Withun's Grove. This would indicate that there may once have been a heathen grove in the vicinity, but whether pre-Christian paganism continued there down the centuries is unlikely, especially as an 18th century trial cleared an old lady of practising witchcraft. But the way in which she was found innocent is unusual.

In 1759 Susanna Hannokes was accused of bewitching the spinning wheel belonging to a neighbour, putting it out of action. The normal procedures of testing if someone was a witch or not, often including torture or finding a so-called witch's mark on her body, was not pursued in this instance. The method adopted here was to weigh the old woman against a church Bible, in the presence of the accusing neighbour. Upon being taken to the parish church, she was stripped to her underwear and the weighing then commenced. Fortunately, it turned out that she was heavier than the Bible and so she was deemed innocent, much to the displeasure of her accuser. What an enlightened, if dubious, method of making a verdict!

Accounts of the witchcraft trials and executions do not make pleasant reading, but one wonders how many trials, like Susanna's, did not result in punishment or execution. Perhaps one day a historian could write a book on such a topic, relating the accusations, trials and acquittals of those more fortunate than many unfortunates.

Works Consulted:

Witchcraft in the Thames Valley, by Tony Barham (1973)
A Mirror of Witchcraft, by Christina Hole (1957)
Victoria County History of Buckinghamshire Vol 3, at the website of British History Online
Wikipedia - Witchcraft Act 1735, Jane Rebecca Yorke

I am also grateful to Michael Bayley, late local historian of Maidenhead, for allowing me to use of some of his material in this chapter, elements of which were first published in my book Unknown Taplow & Environs, published by Windsor Publications in 1988.

19 - Witches & Cats: Perhaps The Favourite Witches Familiar

Section of a woodcut depicting a witch and familiars

The cat has been a companion of humankind since the Near Eastern wildcat was domesticated somewhere around 10,000 years ago. Its scientific name is *Felis Catus*, named as such by the Swedish biologist Carl Linnaeus in the 18th century. Various kinds of wildcat are to be found all over the world, although Britain's native species, *Felis Silvestris Grampia*, is now to be found only in Scotland. Once living throughout Britain, it is in danger of extinction, its numbers being estimated to under 100 pure individuals. It is probably the most endangered mammal in the world, with the female producing one litter a year in May. Measures are now being taken to save the species, its main problem being hybridisation with feral domestic cats.

Over the millennia, cats have been regarded as either good or bad, being revered as a god or condemned as a demon. It seems that the purring gentle animal, which can also be a predatory killer, affects people so much that they either love them or hate them. As we shall see, they have often been at the sharp end of their relationship with humans.

Perhaps the most well known society, which seemed to have held cats in high esteem was that of the ancient Egyptians, who worshipped the cat goddess Bastet. Cats themselves served in temples and were seen as representatives of the goddess, and after their death they were mummified, thousands of cat mummies having been excavated in Egypt over the years. In 1890, about 180,000 mummified cats were delivered to Liverpool Museum, which were auctioned off and ground down as fertiliser, showing how little importance they were given, although storage may have been a bit of a problem!

Embalmed cats used to be sent to the city of Bubastis, where they were arranged on shelves in a cemetery dedicated to them. Bubastis was the centre of the cat cult, its temple being a glorious building made from red granite, with a statue of Bastet placed at the centre of the shrine. The cats' mummified bodies, as well as those of other animals such as falcons and crocodiles, were used as votive offerings, and their mummies have been found literally in their millions. X-ray examinations have revealed they were purposely sacrificed as votive offerings, which was in contrast to the death penalty for killing cats. Paintings in Egyptian tombs also depict cats receiving privileged treatment, revealing their presence living amongst humans dating from early times, a fact that has now been discovered amongst other civilisations such as Mesopotamia and China.

It is an interesting, if not curious, fact that domesticated cats are not mentioned in the Bible, even though other creatures as diverse as dogs, lions, sheep, donkeys, camels, all kinds of bird, and unicorns appear. This is surprising given the historical links between the Jews and Egyptians. There were small cats such as wild lynxes and caracals in the Middle East, but these did not have a mention, and it may be that domestic cats were not known in the Holy Land until the Roman occupation. Cats generally are seen to have very good memories, but in Jewish folklore they are connected with forgetfulness. For instance, Jewish boys in Russia were forbidden to stroke a cat, for to do so would cause them to lose their memories. In the Christian world, the cat symbolises apathy.

Entering the world of Celtic myth we come across the powerful *Cath Palug*, or Palug's Cat, which was slain by Cei Wynn (Sir Kay in the Arthurian legends) or by Arthur himself. North of the border in Scotland there is the figure of the *Cailleach*, or blue hag of winter, who takes the form of a cat. She was a shape-shifter, similar to the Welsh *Cerridwen*. And in Norse mythology the goddess Freyja, who ruled over death and the afterlife, had a chariot drawn by two magical cats, and was associated with witchcraft. The Isle of Man has its own, tailless, cat, which Manx folklore has it that Noah closed the door to the Ark because it began to rain, and caught the Manx cat which had almost been left behind, its tail being was cut off by the closing door.

Which brings us to the Christian Middle Ages, when the reverence for cats disappeared, especially in Britain and Europe where they were associated with witches. At this period, those suspected of witchcraft were intimately examined, tortured and sentenced to death, sometimes being weighed against the large Bibles kept in the local church, as described in chapter 18. There is much folklore surrounding cats, some of which led to the animals being deemed to be evil, and it appears that in Medieval times they were even burnt alive. *Taigheirm* was a practice that took place in Scotland, and lasted on the Isle of Mull until the 17th century, which involved black cats being slowly roasted on a spit as a kind of spiritual ritual to rid them of their supernatural powers. The perpetrators wore black clothes and the event lasted for four days and nights.

Cats were generally seen to be evil, and at the coronation of Elizabeth I, live cats were thrown into a wickerwork figure depicting the Pope, which was carried through the streets and hurled onto a great bonfire. Protestant participators then shouted out that the cries of the poor animals were "the language of the devils within the body of the Holy Father". One cannot imagine nowadays how these tortures could ever have taken place, and shows how ideas about animals were so different from today's. Indeed these notions were so ingrained that in 1233 Pope Gregory IX issued a Papal Bull giving people the freedom to exterminate cats altogether, especially black ones. Not much changed after this, as the Swiss scholar Conrad Gessner (1516-1565) referred to cats thus: "The beast is dangerous to soul and body" and has a "cunning character" in his magnum opus *Historiae Animalium*, a 4,500 page work on zoology.

It was against this background that cats, especially black ones, became associated with witchcraft. In Britain and Europe, black cats in general were seen as harbingers of bad luck, although in Britain today a black cat crossing one's path is seen to be a sign of good luck. But in the past black cats were believed to be able to assume human form in order to assist witches carrying out their demonic deeds. At one Scottish witch trial in 1662, Isobel Gowdrie declared that she could transform into a cat by the chanting three times the following magical verse:

I shall goe intill ane catt,

With sorrow, and sych, and a blak shott;

And I sall goe in the Divellis nam,

Ay quhill I com hom againe.

"Hom againe" means returning to human form. She confessed also that members of her coven could turn each other into cats, which involved one witch already transformed saying "The Devil speed thee, go thou with me".

Another Isobel, this time Isobel Grierson from Prestonpans in East Lothian, was an infamous witch accused of changing herself into a cat and breaking into a house along with other cats and the Devil himself. Her fate was to be strangled to death and her body burnt to ashes in 1607, having been found guilty of sorcery and making a living from ungodly and devilish practices.

A tragic account from Scotland tells of a boy who inadvertently came across three old women in the process of transforming themselves into black cats. Although he swore not to divulge this to anyone, his mother eventually got it out of him. Inevitably, the witch cats took their revenge and clawed the poor lad to death.

16th century ecclesiastical courts accepted that witches could turn themselves into cats and in the feline form could converse with human voices, although in a secret language. There are instances whereby a witch could be identified by injuries that had been inflicted on cats. A Scottish case tells of a laird who noticed that his stock of wine seemed to be diminishing. Suspecting that witchcraft was involved he descended to his wine cellar one night armed with a sword, only to be suddenly surrounded by innumerable black cats. Waving his sword, he managed to clear the cellar of the feline infestation, but in the process, he mutilated one of them. On the following day an old woman who was reputed to be a witch was discovered lying in bed with a leg missing.

A similar case dating from 1718 occurred in Caithness where a mason attested that he had been kept awake nightly by the awful crying of cats, which he considered were in fact witches. The cacophony got so bad that eventually he ran outside with a sword and a hatchet, slaying two of the cats and inflicting injuries on a number of others. On the following day, two women were discovered to have died overnight without any warning, and one other had a hatchet wound to a leg so severe that it finally broke off.

Staying in Scotland, one witch confessed that she and her associates transformed themselves into cats and attempted to gain access into farmers' houses by night, but they were unable to achieve their goal when the farm was protected by charms and the power of prayer. How witches actually changed into cats was revealed by another Scottish witch, who said that whilst about their evil works, her coven was joined by the Devil himself by turning them into cats by waving his hands over their heads. Travelling southwards to Morpeth in Northumberland we come across one Anne Baites accused of witchcraft who claimed that she turned herself into a hare, a bee, a greyhound and a cat so that the Devil could see the number of diverse animals into which she could change.

Shapeshifting is a concept that dates back millennia, with such figures as Zeus from Classical mythology and Odin from the Norse able to transform themselves into animals, the idea continuing into folklore with such shapeshifters as the selkie folk in Scotland and ultimately with witches. The animal most likely a witch would change into was the hare, with the cat as second, and lastly a magpie or raven (see also chapter 10). In folklore, cats were more benign, for instance, their actions were interpreted in weather forecasting and in curing sickness.

There were many "indications" that someone, usually a woman, was a witch, one of which was the fact that she had with her in her home an animal, or familiar. These were believed to be supernatural creatures who helped the witch in her magic-making, often having occult powers themselves. Of course the black cat one was one of these animals, others being toads, ferrets, rats and frogs, mice, dogs, birds and hares and even horses, butterflies and wasps. There was an early 19th century case in Monk Soham in Suffolk, where one old woman who had a pet cat, was accused of being a witch merely because she owned such an animal. As this was "obvious" evidence that she was a witch, she was taken away and hurled into a pit.

Witches' black cats were given names such as Pyewacket and Grimalkin. There is a story that a cat had entered a witch's cottage during the night while she was leaning over her fire, whilst dreaming up angry thoughts against a farmer's wife. The cat stayed on at the cottage for several months, creeping out at night to collect food for the witch, until nearly all the village women had suffered its from its marauding. It seems that many old women were hanged for sending out a cat to enact evil upon those who had offended them. Another cat caused the death of a young child by blowing on him, whilst another was instructed to prevent persons from reading the Bible. The witch cat was often associated with the Devil who turned himself into cat form so he could enjoy sexual congress and bind the two together, the Devil's ice-cold semen generating hatred instead of love.

"Witches" were said to have chosen black cats as their familiars because of their colour, associated with the night and dark deeds, and their otherworldly bloodcurdling cries. Depending on where and when one lived, black cats could be associated with good or bad luck, but within the UK, it has usually been the former, such as when a black cat crosses your path. Witches were also alleged to have suckled their cat-familiars, and even to have offered their blood to the cats by pricking a finger. In "witch-lore" the black cat was supposed to have been worshipped as the Devil incarnate at

Witches' Sabbaths. As the Devil was said to manifest himself as an animal, the cat was a favourite because of its lasciviousness and the fact that its glinting eyes in the dark led to its possessing demonic and psychic powers.

Not all cats owned by "witches" were black, one white spotted cat being spoken of at a witch trial in Chelmsford in 1566. Here Elisabeth Francis owned the animal, having acquired it from her grandmother, Mother Eve, who had initiated her into the practice of witchcraft from the age of 12. She was instructed to call the cat Sathan, the animal remaining and "serving" her for many years. She claimed that the cat conversed with her in a queer "hollow" voice, and that each time he performed a task for her, she rewarded him with a drop of her blood which she produced by pricking herself.

Having looked after the cat for fifteen years or so, Elisabeth eventually gave Sathan to her neighbour Agnes Waterhouse, who was also tried at Chelmsford. She was said to use him to destroy cattle and even to cause the death of a man who had insulted her by rendering him with a wasting disease. Agnes apparently kept Sathan for nine years or so, which meant that he must have lived to at least the age of 25. Another cat familiar was associated with an individual named locally as the Black Witch of Fraddam in Cornwall, who was believed to ride an enormous black cat up into the air. This activity was supposed to take place when she was out searching for magical herbs and poisonous plants, a common pursuit for witches, as we have seen.

Another woman, Dorothy Ellis of Cambridgeshire, confessed at her trial in 1647 that the Devil had appeared to her in cat-form, which demanded blood in the same way as Elisabeth Francis. The cat then did her bidding. Its doings included killing cattle, laming a man who had called her an old witch, and seeking revenge on one Thomas Salter for some unknown injury. With the latter, the cat was responsible for laming Slater's wife, and for causing their young baby daughter to have severe fits and ultimately dying at the age of 18 months.

The last trial of a witch, though now known not to be the last, was said to be that of poor widowed Jane Wenham, aged 70, which took place in Walkern, Hertfordshire in 1712, where she was known as a cunning woman. She was accused of bewitching livestock and also a farmhand, and owning cat familiars. Here the wretched sounds of cats were said to have been heard around her house, with several people claiming to have seen these cats, which prompted the animals to race to Jane's abode. She was also accused of having converse with the Devil himself who manifested himself in the form of a cat. The end result was that Jane was acquitted of being a witch by the Chief Justice, despite the jury having found her guilty, and he arranged that she be pardoned and cared for thereafter.

At a witchcraft trial at Lincoln in 1619, Margaret and Philippa Flower were accused of bewitching two children of the Earl of Rutland, and previously had caused the death of his eldest son. The two women worked at Belvoir Castle, but Margaret had been sacked for theft. She carried out her revenge with the assistance of a cat called Rutterkin, owned by her mother Joan Flower, who was locally deemed to be a witch. She pilfered one of the Earl's gloves and gave it to her mother who stroked Rutterkin with it, immersed it in boiling water, pricked it a number of times and then finally buried it. This resulted in illness and the death of the Earl's youngest son and heir.

But this proved to be insufficient revenge upon the earl's family, and the three women tried to prevent the Earl and his wife from having any further children by obtaining feathers and wool from their bed, boiling them in a mixture of blood and water and lastly rubbing them on Rutterkin's belly. These confessions led to the hanging of the two sisters, but their mother evaded the death penalty by denying everything. The involvement of the cat appeared to be essential for the bewitching to work, but in all these cases the poor animals were of course innocent of such malevolence and involvement in witchcraft.

Now we come to a 19th century white witch named Betty Swan from Kidderminster who was alerted by scratching at her front door, which did not stop until she opened it and in entered a large black cat. This animal stayed with Betty for a few days, where it was seen by the locals now and then, but one day Betty's door was seen to be shut all day and no smoke from her fire was emerging from the chimney. Eventually some alarmed locals broke in, and all that they could see were Betty's ashes lying on the floor. A strange tale indeed.

In the Middle Ages the only animals permitted to reside in monasteries and convents were cats, despite the beliefs of ordinary folk, but with the coming of the Enlightenment, cats began to be treated more humanely, but they still featured in popular folklore. In Britain black cats were said to be lucky, whilst white cats were seen to be unlucky, although cats' attributes and actions leading to prognostications varied in different areas of the country. Superstitions concerning cats extended to leaving them to die in roofs or other cavities of buildings, their mummified remains acting as guardians against any witch trying to gain access to the house. It was believed that witches could enter houses via windows, doors and chimneys, so it was felt that some kind of magic had to be carried out to prevent such breaches. In recent times when old buildings are being renovated, many of these grisly bodies have been discovered, hidden perhaps for two or three hundred years.

Thus, were our feline friends regarded and treated in days gone by. At least we can be assured that they are no longer considered to be evil in intent. When I see a black cat, I always hope that it crosses my path, although this hasn't so far led to good luck, but one never knows!

Works Consulted:

Cult of the Cat, by Patricia Dale-Green (1963)
Witchcraft in England, by Christina Hole (1977 edition)
Nine Lives: Cats in Folklore, by Katharine M. Briggs (1980)
The Magical Lore of Cats, by Marion Davies (1995)

ARTHURIANA

20 - Windsor Castle's Round Table: Edward III's Concept And Its Demise

Round Table woodcut

Viewers of the now cancelled *Time Team* will probably recall the edition at Windsor Castle. Here they were looking for remains of the Round Table building of Edward III. Before discussing the fruits of the excavation, which took place in 2006, it would be apposite first to tell in brief the story of the building's construction and demise. Most of this chapter was written before the excavation and the subsequent book (see below for publishing details).

Hastiludes at Windsor

Edward III (1312-77), crowned in 1327 and father of the Black Prince, was born at Windsor Castle, since when he became known as Edward of Windsor. Still preserved in the Royal Closet in St. George's Chapel is a painted window depicting an astrological horoscope of his nativity, although the building was not begun until a hundred years after his death. But there is a link between the Chapel and Edward, since it became the spiritual home of the Order of the Garter which he founded in 1348. Edward's original idea, however, was to form a chivalrous order in the fashion of King Arthur's Knights. He "did thereupon first design (induc'd by its ancient fame) the restoration of King Arthur's Round Table, to invite hither the gallant spirits from abroad, and endear them to himself"[10].

Thus on New Year's Day 1344 he issued letters patent of safe conduct to various knights, earls, barons and gentlemen from England and other countries to invite them to a gathering on the Monday after the Feast of St. Hilary, which fell on January 19th. His protection extended to their servants and goods and was to endure to 9th February. The intention was to provide "for the recreation and pleasure of the military men, who delight in the exercise of arms" and "the King would hold hastiludes and general jousts at his Castle of Windsor"[11]. (Hastiludes was an early name for tournaments.)

Also present were Isabel, Edward's mother, his queen Philippa and their daughter, Isabel, nine countesses and so many baronesses, ladies and girls that filled the Great Hall. The King showed them all to their places himself, settling them in order of rank, while the Prince of Wales and all the male guests had to feed outside in a tent set up in the courtyard. The jousts continued for three days, when the King won three out of six prizes. There still exists an account of these gatherings, written by Adam of Murimuth, a former canon of Hereford and St. Paul's, who appears to have been a guest.

He says: "At the costly banquet were the most alluring drinks in plenty, enough and to spare. The lords and their ladies failed not to dance, mingling kisses with embraces. Many entertainers made the most charming melody and sundry other diversions. The joy was unspeakable, the comfort inestimable, the pleasure without murmuring, the hilarity without care.[12]" On the eve of the fourth day the King announced that no lord or lady were to depart, since their presence was required the following morning. The next day Edward appeared wearing a mantle of precious velvet and the royal crown upon his head. After mass in the chapel everyone assembled and the King inaugurated the Round Table, at which he received that oaths of a number of earls, barons and knights.

The "King and all the others at the same time stood up, and having been offered the Book, the Lord King, after touching the Gospels, took a

---

10 The History of the Most Noble Order of the Garter, by Elias Ashmole (revised edition, 1715)

11 Annals of Windsor, by Robert Richard Tighe and James Edward Davis (1858)

12 The Romance of Windsor Castle, by Hector Bolitho (1946)

corporeal oath that he himself, at a certain time limited to this, whilst the means were possible to him, would begin a Round Table, in the same manner and condition as the lord Arthur, formerly King of England, appointed it, namely to the number of 300 knights, a number always increasing, and he would cherish it and maintain it according to his power"[13]. After this trumpets and kettle-drums sounded and a great feast commenced.

Erection

Edward then lost no time and early commencement of the work to build a Round Table can be seen in the account roll for 1343-4 where, in the last week of January, we find the following:

> *To two carts with two men employed in the carrying sand for the covering the bridges of the castle with the said sand lest they be broken with the heavy carriage of the Round Table, for two days*
> *...2s 8d*

> *To four men scattering the said sand upon the said bridges for two*
> *days..1*
> *6d*

More sand was brought for the same purpose in March and some repairs were carried out on the bridges within the castle from April to July, probably on account of the heavy traffic on them. Actual work on the building began on 15th February and commissions were issued to the head carpenter, William of Hurley, and the master Mason, William of Ramsay, empowering them to collect workmen and materials.

Work carried on apace between February and November and Alan of Killum, the clerk of the works, received the sum of £461 8s 8d for his services. The wages sheets reveal large fluctuations in the number of men employed, as can be confirmed from records of works showing the number of chief artisans. It appears that there were many more stone carvers than ordinary masons and therefore it is likely that the building was highly decorated. The following table reveals the number of chief artisans during the first six weeks' work:

---

13 Windsor Castle: An Architectural History, by William H St John Hope (1913)

Week	1	2	3	4	5	6
Masons	15	75	170	201	210	168
Carpenters	4	8	15	15	14	14
Labourers	17	211	401	193	180	180

By the end of the third week the total wages had risen to £45 4s 10d after which all the workers were disbanded and for eleven weeks following Easter week the works were entirely in the hands of William of Ramsay, who supervised up to 28 masons. After 23rd October all the masons except Ramsay were withdrawn, and for the last seven weeks three carpenters were engaged on "covering the walls of the Round Table". By 27th November, Alan of Killum records that the works came to an end.

During that period raw materials were obtained and transported by river to the castle. Much of the stone required was quarried at Bustlesham, but £40 worth of Caen stone was purchased from the Dean of St. Paul's. Wood was cut at Bletchingley, Reigate Park, Holshot and Ruislip. The accounts also show the purchase of tiles from Penn, Buckinghamshire, which was renowned for this product, as follows:

> *For forty thousand tiles bought for the covering of the walls of the house of the Round*
>
> *Table, and for covering the stones of the same place...£4 0s 0d*
>
> *For carriages of stones of the same from Penn to Windsor... ....£1 0s 0d*

An account roll details that on 13th December a payment of 9d was made for "carting the tiles that were left from the covering of the walls of the Round Table for half a day". These tiles were placed on the walls to protect them from frost and it was the onset of winter that probably contributed to the cessation of work, and there is no evidence to show that the building was ever finished. Adam of Murimuth recorded that the King "for certain reasons afterwards ceased from it" and his ideas metamorphosed ultimately into the Order of the Garter.

There is little further detail as to the appearance of the Round Table building except from a 14th century chronicler called Thomas of Walsingham. Under the year 1344, his *Chronicon Angliae* contains an entry concerning the building, in which he states that the structure's diameter measured 200 feet, which gives an indication of its size. (He also records that Philip of Valois, King of France, began his own Round Table to attract knights from Germany and Italy before they joined Edward.)

In addition one John Stow, who used Walsingham's version of events, mentions in his Annales that the Round Table's circumference was just over 600 feet. As to where it stood within the castle precincts was not clear until the Time Team excavation. The idea of a large structure such as this being erected merely for feasting would, in earlier days, have been considered frivolous, since castle were built as strongholds. However, by 1344 they had largely ceased to have this function and Windsor Castle was seen as not much more than the King's fortified residence. St. John Hope therefore placed it in the great courtyard of the upper bailey. Indeed, it is the only place where a building of this size could have been erected and, as we shall see, this proved to be correct.

Demolition

The Feast of the Round Table was held again at Windsor in March 1345, but there is no evidence that the building was used for this nor that any work continued on it after November 1344. The feast was held somewhere, however, since the accounts of John Marreys, the King's tailor, show an entry for making robes and sundry garments for the King and others between September 1344 and August 1345. These included robes of valet and fur and a supertunic of ermine for the King, 202 tunics and hoods for the King's shield bearers and sergeants-at-arms and 16 tunics and hoods for the King's minstrels. After this there are no records to show that a Feast of the Round Table was held in 1346 or thereafter.

During 1356-7 a number of old buildings at the Castle were demolished and it is to be assumed that the Round Table was amongst them. It is recorded in December 1356 that the Prior of Merton was paid £26 13s 4d for 52 oaks felled in his woods near Reading for the Round Table at Windsor. The oaks were then transported to Westminster for works ordered by the King there. This is therefore assumed to be the end of Windsor's Round Table. From then on whatever ideas King Edward may have had for his version of the Arthurian legend were forgotten, as sometime about the middle of 1348 he founded the Order of the Garter and the rest is history.

Excavation

So, what did the Time Team come up with? Well the amazing news was that they actually found the foundation trench of the Round Table in the upper bailey, which turned out to measure the 200 feet as stated by Thomas of Walsingham and was bigger than the Pantheon in Rome. The walls were some eight feet wide and thus could have supported a roof, but no post-holes of supporting timbers were found. However, a complete, decorated floor tile from the works at Penn was found in situ which, although dating from the 14th century, was probably not part of the Round Table structure itself. In addition, in the same trench as the tile, a medieval flagstone surface was excavated with the flagstones also in situ. Thus the exact site and the dimensions of the building were confirmed after centuries of guesswork.

The building accounts allow some guesses as to what the building would have looked like. It was built out of stone, was probably elaborately decorated and would have had a single arcade about thirty feet high, rather like a cloister, together with a stone bench against the wall for the knights to sit on. It was likely that there would have been an actual round table in front made of stone for the knights and a fountain in the open, central area. However, the building was never roofed, as Edward diverted his resources to his attempt to conquer France.

Enactments

And so comes the question – what would it exactly have been used for? The favourite idea was always that its use would have been for jousting and tournaments as well as general festivities. However, Richard Barber, historian and author of books on the Arthurian legends, was on site and gave his views. Firstly, he explained that the medieval English kings were highly inspired by the Arthurian legends and it is even possible that Chretien de Troyes, author of *Perceval, the Story of the Grail*, may have come to Henry II's court at Windsor. Indeed, Wace's *Brut* was dedicated to Henry. A century later Edward I held Round Tables and he personally arranged them at Nefyn in Wales in 1284 and at Falkirk in Scotland in 1302.

Barber then explained that medieval Round Tables were not just physical objects, but a kind of festival with jousting, feasting and dancing. They became popular in the 13th century and increasingly so until by Edward III's time they had become very elaborate. He said that it was highly likely that it was a kind on theatre within which festivals took place with not only feasting and dancing, but also where enactments of the Arthurian tales were held.

In 1290, these festivities came to a climax with the construction of a real round table and a grand tournament at Winchester. This is the table that can still be seen in Winchester Hall to this day. An account of the proceedings survives in which a squire appeared demanding that revenge be taken on the Welshmen who had rebelled and attacked him. Another squire then came on the scene, bound hand and foot to his horse, claiming that the Irish were the perpetrators and that the Irish king had issued a challenge to Lancelot to meet him in single combat. Lastly the "loathly damsel" who featured in the story of Perceval rode up to the king and told him that Leicester and Cornwall had rebelled and the Perceval and Gawain should go forth and sort things out. Traditionally such "adventures" had to take place first before the meal could begin. So the Round Table was not so much a place of jousting as a theatrical stage, perhaps England's earliest. Thus Edward III was continuing and expanding upon a tradition which had been in vogue for some time already.

On historical grounds, this must have been one of the Time Team's greatest successes, discovering as they did traces of the fabled structure of which no features were apparent above ground level.

Postscript - Edward III's Round Table at Windsor

As mentioned below, the book of Edward's Round Table appeared in 2007, and this final section tries to give some idea of what the building looked like, as specified by Julian Munby, one of the authors of the book (see note below).

It is not clear if the building was constructed with wood or stone. On the assumption that the building was circular, it would probably have enclosed an open space in the middle, and would have had a roofed vault supported by columns with two, three or four concentric arcades, depending on the size of the structure. It appears that a partially-roofed building would have been the most practicable design, not dissimilar to the Canons' Cloister built at Windsor by Edward in the 1350s. There may have been a table at the centre, similar to the one in Westminster's Great Hall. However, there was so little of the building left when Time Team completed the excavation that the scenario just described may differ somewhat from what was actually built. In fact, it seems that it was not finished before it was demolished, due to the project being too grandiose to complete, Edward then turning his attention to the Order of the Garter.

Works consulted:

The History of the Most Noble Order of the Garter, by Elias Asmole (Revised edition, 1715)
Annals of Windsor, by Robert Richard Tighe & James Edward Davis (1858)
The Romance of Windsor Castle, by Hector Bolitho (1946)
Windsor Castle: An Architectural History, by Williams H St. John Hope (1913)
Windsor Castle, by Owen Hedley (1967)

Slough & Windsor Express 1/9/2006
Daily Telegraph 29/8/2006
http://www.channel4.com/history/microsites/B/big_royal_dig/windsor/win
dsor_latest

This is an amended version of an article which first appeared in the
Arthurian magazine Pendragon XXV1/1 Winter 1996, and in an updated
version in Pendragon XXX1V/1 Autumn 2006. It was written before the
book entitled Edward III's Round Table at Windsor, by Julian Munby,
Richard Barber and Richard Brown was published in 2007, which is
recommended reading for those wishing to learn about the full, detailed
story.

21- The Nanteos Cup - The Holy Grail?

The Holy Grail

The legend of the Holy Grail has intrigued and inspired people since its first appearance in the 12th century, which shows no sign of abating. It began with the publication of the Arthurian poem *Perceval, the Story of the Grail* by the French writer Chretien de Troyes somewhere around 1185, which was left unfinished with later authors adding their own endings.

The earliest Arthurian tales originated in Wales, which were then transmitted to Brittany and adapted by Norman French writers. There have been theories, which try to connect the Grail with the Celtic life-restoring cauldron into which slain warriors were placed, but this has no literary evidence, and if indeed there were some such connection, it would have been through oral traditions that cannot be proved.

There is no mention of The Grail as such in the New Testament, apart from the brief mention of the cup used at the Last Supper, so if such hypotheses are true, it is strange that no historic or literary mention of it occurs before the 12th century, over 1,100 years after the crucifixion of Christ. In fact, the Christian churches have ignored the topic over the centuries, and it has never been accepted as a suitable subject for serious Christian study.

The legends claim that the Grail was the cup used by Christ at the Last Supper and was used by Joseph of Arimathea to collect Christ's blood whilst he was on the Cross. In *Perceval* the Grail is described as a bowl, but other authors referred to it as a dish or even a stone, and it became a mystical goal to be achieved by King Arthur's knights, the only three succeeding being Sirs Galahad, Perceval and Bors.

In recent years, much has been made of the Grail legends, reinterpreting them in unscholarly and often outlandish ways, which should be read with a critical mind. However, some approaches to the Grail can be of a broadly religious nature, and accordingly lend themselves to a meaningful spiritual perspective. The following examines the story of a real life cup which has been seen by some as the Holy Grail itself.

The Nanteos Cup

A small wooden bowl dating from Medieval times, which acquired its name from the Welsh stately home of Nanteos in Cardiganshire where it was kept, made its first public appearance in 1878 at the aforementioned house then owned by the Powell family. It was included in an exhibition of antiquities found in the locality. In Wales, it was known as "Phiol Sanctaidd Ystrad

Fflur", translating as The Holy Cup of Strata Florida, where it was kept at Strata Florida Abbey, supposedly then owned by the Stedman family.

Nanteos Cup

Folklore had it that the cup was made of olive wood and emanated from 1st century Palestine, but research has proved that it was actually made from wych-elm. It consists of a, now damaged, mazer bowl of a type used in the Middle Ages, and is now supported by metal rivets as it is in a frail condition. Its diameter is about five inches, its depth about three and its base about one and a half. A late tradition told of it having been made from the True Cross and that it had healing powers for those who drank from it. Not until 1905 was it claimed that it was in fact the Holy Grail itself, which joined other such claims from others which number over 200 in Europe alone, perhaps the most well-known being the Great Chalice of Antioch housed in Valencia, Spain.

The legendary history of the cup begins with Glastonbury, where it was held by the Abbey. At the Dissolution of the Monasteries in 1538 legend has it that a group of seven monks made their way to Wales, arriving eventually at the Cistercian Abbey at Strata Florida. It was held here until the dissolution of the abbey in 1539, when the last of the monks just before he died, handed over the cup into the safe hands of the Powells, entrusting it "until such time as the Church shall claim her own". However, there is no record of either the Stedman or Powell families owning the Strata Florida estate at the time of the Dissolution. Inventories made by the two families over the years have no record of such a cup.

Another unconfirmed story was that the cup had been at Strata Florida all along and had been there since the abbey's foundation in 1164, and in the Middle Ages pilgrims would visit the abbey to see the cup, much in the way that people would seek out many other holy relics. It must be admitted that during the Dissolution the last place to take the cup to safety was another abbey! However, legends tend to accrue too many earlier stories, and another has it that on one occasion the cup was placed on the spot where the high altar would have been positioned at Strata Florida during pouring rain. Apparently, the rain suddenly ceased and a beam of bright sunlight lit up the cup, only to turn to rain again when the cup was removed.

Its renown for healing led to the Powells allowing individuals who were suffering from various ailments to borrow the cup, each time leaving a pledge that could be redeemed upon its return. Its present damaged state has been caused by users over the years nibbling away at it in order to retain a piece as a souvenir. In fact, there are a few paper pledges still in existence which show the names of those who made use of the cup and the details of the pledges made, such as a watch or a coin. Also recorded were the dates the cup was returned and whether healing turned out to be efficacious. Apparently, the slips of paper on which the pledges were written recorded that every one of the cures turned out to be successful.

It was the convention that it was always the women of the Powell family who were "Guardians of the Cup". The earliest record of it being lent out was in 1857, to one Ebenezer Vaughan who in 1857 left £1 and borrowed it "for the use of his wife", the custom at the time being that the cup must always be borrowed on behalf of a female. When he returned the cup, he had written on the paper pledge "cured". The latest pledge surviving was that in 1962 when William Jones pledged a silver watch. There seem to have been later pledges, and the most noteworthy was a priest who was cured of rheumatism.

Another unconfirmed legend has it that the great German composer Richard Wagner once visited Nanteos and, upon viewing the cup, was inspired to write his Arthurian opera *Parsifal*. In fact, there is no historical evidence that Wagner actually travelled over to visit the house, but George Powell did go to Germany on one occasion to pay a visit to the composer. In 1895, the Western Mail reported that its healing properties were especially potent in connection with certain women's complaints, the idea being adopted by Wagner in *Parsifal* by associating the Grail with female fertility, specifically the womb. Much of the Nanteos legend is undocumented, its prestige becoming renowned merely because the romance of the vessel had been retold so many times over the years.

In 1938 a group of people, including the Rev. Lionel Smithett Lewis, Vicar of Glastonbury and author of the speculative tome on the Glastonbury legends entitled *St Joseph of Arimathea at Glastonbury*, visited Nanteos with a view to returning the cup to Glastonbury. The incumbent of the house at that time was Margaret Powell who, apparently, was not hostile to the request, but after some deliberation she did not give her permission and the cup resided at Nanteos until her demise in 1951. Her will was contested and when the will was sorted, Nanteos was inherited by a grand-niece by the name of Elizabeth Mirylees. She eventually moved away in 1967 along with the cup, leaving a replica behind which often misled those seeking the real thing. From 1968, the cup was held in a Hereford bank.

In more recent times it has been kept in water placed in a glass dish due to its fragility, and this is now how the water is drunk. Its healing powers have been able to cure multiple sclerosis, a brain tumour, epilepsy, deafness, leprosy, failing sight and arthritis. In fact the daughter of Elizabeth Mirylees herself was miraculously cured having been seriously injured with a fracture of the skull after a fall. Her mother held the cup and prayed, and the hospital soon contacted her, being amazed at her unexpected recovery. In the 1950s, a magazine published an article on the cup and the Mirylees family became inundated with letters requesting to drink from it, even including weirdos demanding the cup be returned to their care. Apparently, large sums of money have been offered to buy it. In 1979 the Mirylees family moved away to avoid the pressure of keeping the cup, the present guardian's abode being a secret. Anyone wishing to drink from the cup had to seek it out on a personal quest.

Then tragedy struck. In July 2014 the cup was stolen from a house in Weston under Penyard, again in Herefordshire. It had been lent out to an ailing lady pilgrim in the village for healing purposes, who subsequently had to enter hospital because of her condition. It was while she was away that there was a break-in and the cup removed, and the local constabulary were called in. A statement from the West Mercia Police intimated that they were not in fact searching for the Holy Grail, but were working on a simple case of burglary.

The next development was when the police were called to the 15th century Crown Inn at Lea in Herefordshire, where they had been told that the cup had been seen. The police, together with a dog handler, were said to have locked all the staff inside whilst a thorough search was made of the premises, but their investigations proved negative. It was then that a reward of £2,000 was announced for information leading to the finding of the cup and on 19th June 2015, it was eventually returned. This final step was because of Operation Icarus after the case was screened on BBC1's *Crimewatch Roadshow*. Apparently the police were approached by an anonymous informer, which led to the cup being handed over "on neutral ground in a pre-arranged meeting", with no arrests being made. The cup has now been donated by the owners to the National Library of Wales in Aberystwyth, and is safely housed in a glass case.

Bringing things up to date, at the Nanteos Mansion, now a hotel, a labyrinth has been constructed by woodcraftsman Bob Shaw, with a carving of the Cup on a plinth at its centre, sculpted by Ed Harrison, and a novel by Anglo-Welsh author Jane Blank entitled *The Shadow of Nanteos* was published in 2015. The mansion's website describes itself, not exactly truthfully, as follows:

> *Culture is all-pervasive at Nanteos Mansion with associations with leading European figures such as the composer Wagner and the poet Browning. It's an easy concept to grasp, they are famous cultural figures and they both stayed at the Mansion while touring the country.*

This thus brings us up to date on the story of the Nanteos Cup, and hopefully great care will be taken with its handling in future. There has been no response from the Church to the phrase "until the time as the Church will claim her own", but is the Nanteos Cup the Holy Grail? I leave that up to the reader to decide.

Works Consulted:

Juliette Wood:
(1)   "The Phantom Cup that Comes & Goes: The Story of the Holy Grail" a lecture given at   Gresham College in London   on   5th   March   2013.
(2)   "Nibbling Pilgrims & the Nanteos Cup: A Cardiganshire Legend", in
Nanteos: A Welsh House & its Families, by Gerald Morgan (2001).
(3)   Eternal Chalice: The Enduring Legend of the Holy Grail (2008).

"The Grail in Wales? The Nanteos Cup", by Fred Stedman-Jones, in Pendragon XXVI/2 (Spring 1997), journal of the Pendragon Society.
"A new home for the Nanteos Cup", by Ted Harrison, in Fortean Times (FT 345, October 2016).
Hereford Times 14/8/2014.

22 - The Swan Knight and the Grail Castle

King Ludwig II of Bavaria

I was lucky enough to spend a short spell in Bavaria in 1999 and there discovered a place steeped in the Arthurian legends, specifically the Holy Grail. This was the castle of Neuschwanstein (literally New Swan Castle) built by "mad" King Ludwig II of Bavaria in the 1880's, photographs of which have appeared on many a jigsaw and which has been a backdrop for a number of films. This is not surprising, since its appearance has a romantic, almost fairy-tale quality, but for those interested in the Arthurian legends is the fact that this building turned out to be a Grail Castle, as we shall see.

King Ludwig II was born at the Nymphenburg Palace, Munich in 1845 and became King at the early age of 18 after the death of his father Maximilian II. He was brought up in a castle situated in the Bavarian Alps named Hohenschwangau, which was decorated inside with scenes from *Lohengrin* and he was thus introduced to this legend from his boyhood. The story was told by Wolfram von Eschenbach in his *Parzival* of circa 1210, which featured Lohengrin the Swan Knight, son of Parzival and Condwiramurs. Although Lohengrin appears only briefly in this work, a later romance from the 1280's by an unknown author tells a rather fuller story, which merges the legend of the Swan Knight with that of the Holy Grail.

The title of Swan Knight stems from the fact that Lohengrin arrives on the scene in a boat drawn by a swan in order to deliver Princess Elsa of Brabant from the evil Tetramund and the sorceress Ortrud. Having saved her, Lohengrin marries her on the condition that she must not ask him his name or his ancestry. However, on their wedding night she asks the questions and, held by his vows to the Grail, discloses his identity and promptly disappears, taken back to the Grail Kingdom by the swan who has returned for him.

At the age of 12, Ludwig was introduced to Wagner's music after hearing a report by his governess of a performance of *Lohengrin*, which she had attended in Munich. Apparently, her vivid descriptions of the opera fired an enthusiasm to see the work himself, a wish that did not come true until he was 15, having harangued his father for three years. The performance captured his imagination almost like a religious fervour, not only for the Grail legends but also for the music of Wagner, whom he later befriended. In fact, but for Ludwig, it is doubtful whether the impecunious composer would have achieved all he did, for the King financed his projects and enabled them to come to fruition.

Ludwig's idea of art was its potential for it to raise the audience onto a higher plane and in Wagner he saw the ultimate perfection of this ideal. Thus, it was that Ludwig's interest in the Swan Knight became an obsession and he came to identify himself with the character of Lohengrin, part knight in shining armour and part swan, with its associations of majesty and piety. Later on in, life Ludwig used to dress up as Lohengrin and sail round the lake at his other residence Linderhof in a boat shaped like a cockleshell. Indeed, after his death, a costume of the Swan Knight was discovered amongst his possessions.

In the eyes of Wagner, however, Ludwig had become Parzival, the hero of his last opera *Parsifal*, by which name he referred to his friend. He was apparently struck by the similarities between the two characters - both were strong, brave and handsome, but this was accompanied by a strange innocence and naivety. Perhaps most important, though, was their destiny. Parzival was fated at birth to succeed to the Grail kingship and his story leads him to Amfortas the Fisher King and keeper of the Grail, of whom he asks the correct question about the Fisher King's wound. This act immediately cures Amfortas and frees his kingdom from the curse of being a wasteland, and thus Parzival lays claim to the Grail. And so when Wagner described Ludwig as Parzival, he saw in him the role that Parzival had acted out, someone whom he hoped would be able to regenerate the wasteland of Germany through art. Indeed, Ludwig saw himself in this role, as is evidenced by several letters he wrote to Wagner referring to himself as Parzival.

Enthusiastic as he was about the Arthurian legends it was inevitable that he would embrace the Grail romances as well and it was this theme that brought about the building of his fantasy castle, Neuschwanstein. In 1868 he wrote to Wagner : "I intend to rebuild the old castle ruins of Hohenschwangau by the Pollat Falls, in the genuine style of the old German knights' castles....There will be reminders of Tannhauser and of Lohengrin".

Lohengrin The Swan Knight

The castle became his Grail Castle, stemming as it did from the fact that he saw himself as a Grail King and these themes, along with others from Arthurian and Wagnerian narratives, were the foundation of this fantastic, romantic structure. The decoration within the castle has to be seen to be believed and the Singers' Hall and the Throne Room stand out as the most splendid rooms of all. The Singers' Hall includes Romanesque arches, a marvellous panelled roof in red and gold and the walls are covered either with pictures or intricate patterns. The majority of the paintings are from the Grail legends, taken from Eschenbach's *Parzival*, but it would be a long list to describe them all. However, examples such as *Parzival's First Encounter with Knighthood* and *Parzival Meets Amfortas* give an idea of the scenes that adorn the walls.

The Living Room is devoted to the Lohengrin legend and the paintings here describe the whole story. Examples include *The Miracle of the Grail*, *Lohengrin's Departure from the Castle of the Grail and Elsa Asking the Question*. The figure of the swan is featured prominently in this room, with one corner dedicated entirely to the elegant bird. The King's bedroom is dedicated to Tristan and Isolde and features paintings inspired by a poem by Gottfried of Strasbourg, and above the exit are wooden figures of King Mark, Tristan and Isolde. Other rooms contain murals about Tannhauser, the Gudrun saga and other German legends. With all these stories, however, Ludwig insisted on using the original sagas as a base for the paintings, not Wagner's interpretation of them.

The whole castle is lavishly decorated throughout, but the Throne Room, the centre of attraction, is of special note. Designed in Byzantine style its two storey arcades are supported by columns of plaster scagiola, or imitation stone, which are painted to resemble porphyry and lapis lazuli. The floor mosaic, featuring depictions of forest animals, is composed of more than two million coloured tiles. No expenses were spared in the King's fantasy of building a fairy-tale castle. However, he did not occupy his new abode for long. He first settled into his apartments on May 27th 1884, but by June 13th 1886, he was dead.

The King's end was unfortunate and mysterious. The last few years of his life saw him enter a period of decline, one servant commenting that he was in "a swamp of unfathomable darkness", which led him to being declared insane by the Bavarian government. His cousin Empress Elizabeth stated that "He is not mad enough to be locked up, but too abnormal to manage comfortably in the world with reasonable people". There was a history of eccentric behaviour in the family, his brother Otto succombing to mental illness, but succeeding him after Ludwig's death, although he ruled Bavaria in name only until his own death in 1916. The cause of Ludwig's demise, however, has never been satisfactorily explained.

The events leading up to his death began with Prince Luitpold announcing that, owing to the state of both Ludwig and Otto, a regency was to be inaugurated and on June 10th 1886, this became official. On June 12th, a government commission took him from Neuschwanstein to Castle Berg outside Munich, along with his physician Dr. Gudden. The following afternoon the two went for a walk around Lake Starnberg, despite protestations from Dr. Gudden. By eight o'clock that evening they had not returned and a search was immediately instigated. The bodies of the two men were found floating in the lake but despite attempts to revive them, at midnight, they were pronounced dead.

As to what happened to Ludwig and Dr. Gudden, we may never know, but murder does seem the most likely explanation. At Ludwig's lying in state, thousands of Bavarians visited Munich to pay their last respects. Thus ended the life of the Swan Knight, Lohengrin, Parzival or the Grail King. Did he live in an imaginary world of fantasy, eventually becoming mad. Who knows, but there is now evidence that his diagnosis of insanity may well have been a ploy in order to get rid of him, as he spent more and more on building his castles, against the advice of his financial advisers, until he ended up in debt. Not behaviour recommended for a king.

The guided tour around the castle is, unfortunately, rather rapid and it was difficult to take in all that there was to see. But nevertheless if anyone gets a chance to visit this remarkable building, I recommend that they do so, and they will at least be prepared to look out for all the Arthurian and Grail associations of which I was unaware before I arrived.

Works consulted:

The Swan King: Ludwig II of Bavaria, by Christopher McIntosh (1982)
The Mad King: The Life and Times of Ludwig 11 of Bavaria, by Greg King (1996)
The New Arthurian Encyclopedia, edited by Norris J. Lacy (1991)
Official guide to Neuschwanstein Castle (1998)

This is a slightly amended article which appeared in the Arthurian journal Pendragon XXV111/2 Winter 1999/2000

REMNANTS

23 - Saint Birinus, Apostle Of Wessex: Legends And Miracles Of This Little Known Saint

This chapter deals with a little known saint who was an eminently important figure in bringing Christianity to Britain, although this was the Roman Catholic variety, the Celtic Church having been introduced during the Roman period. Christianity did not disappear from the British Isles altogether after the Romans left; as the Celtic Church held sway until the pagan Saxons arrived on these shores. The Roman Catholic Church then decided that the Saxons needed to be converted to their version of the Faith, and ultimately the Celtic Church was overtaken by the Roman one at the Synod of Whitby in 664 CE.

St. Augustine was the first missionary to England, sent in 597 by Pope Gregory who was inspired to convert the English (according to the Venerable Bede) when he saw slave boys from England on sale in Rome. Upon noticing their fair hair and complexions and their noble features, he asked where they came from and whether they were pagan or Christian. When told that they were heathen Angles from Britain, he exclaimed that this was appropriate since they looked more like Angels and that they should therefore be converted to the Faith. Incidentally, an old wooden chair in St James's church in Stanford Bishop, Herefordshire, is rumoured to have been used by St. Augustine himself, but opinions differ on this.

Augustine's mission did not have the hoped-for far reaching effects and when Penda, the pagan King of Mercia, defeated and slew the recently converted King Edwin of Northumbria in 633, Pope Honorius decided that another mission was called for. Birinus, or Berin as he was sometimes referred to, was the man chosen for the task and he was sent as a free agent without reference to the mission founded by Augustine at Canterbury. In this, he was highly successful, as we shall see.

Birinus was of Lombard extraction. The Lombards were considered the most barbaric of the Germanic tribes and he, rather than another Italian monk like Augustine, may have been chosen for his racial, and therefore lingual, connection with the Anglo-Saxons. His name means "Son of the Bear", indicating that he was an offspring of a warrior. Asterius, Archbishop of Milan, consecrated Birinus for the mission at Genoa, where both British and Lombardic merchants had important trading links. Perhaps these merchants saw the mission as an opening for further trade.

In 633 Birinus was on his way across the English Channel, but before he reached our shores a remarkable event occurred. He was accustomed to carry the Holy Sacrament given to him by the Pope hanging from his neck wrapped in a linen cloth, but unfortunately, as he had to hurry to the ship he accidentally left it on the altar at the church where he preached. However, his faith was so strong that he was able to descend from the ship into the sea and, like Jesus, was able to walk upon the water back to the port, pick up the Sacrament and re-embark without a drop of water on his person, having found the ship exactly where he had left it. Unsurprisingly, after this miraculous feat, he made a number of converts on board.

Birinus' mandate was to convert the lands which lay beyond England where no Christian teacher had been before. However, on his arrival near Porchester he encountered the heathen West Saxons and decided to stay there to preach. He remained in southern England throughout his ministry and has associations with Churn Knob near Blewbury in Berkshire, Berin's Hill and Dorchester-on-Thames in Oxfordshire, and Taplow in Buckinghamshire. Churn Knob is a prominent tumulus upon which Birinus is said to have preached, and at Taplow there is also an ancient burial mound dated to the late Saxon pagan period, around 625. All these places were in the territory of the West Saxons who called themselves the Gewissas. Both Churn Hill and Taplow are sites situated near the summit of a hill, suggesting that such places were considered to be more free from evil spirits, which would have been less effective in their devilish arts due to their being blown away by the more windy hill-tops.

It may have been at Churn Knob that Birinus first encountered Cynegils, King of the West Saxons, in 635. Cynegils was baptised into the Faith by Birinus, with Oswald, nephew of King Edward of Northumbria, as godfather. Oswald had just overthrown Penda, become King of Northumbria and had come down to request the hand of Cynegils' daughter in marriage. At all events, Cynegils himself, apparently, was not an immediate convert and it may be that the defeat of Edwin by heathens was seen as a portent of the superiority of the Saxon god Woden over the new God. However, Cynegils was finally won over to the new religion and, together with Oswald, gave Dorchester to Birinus as his cathedral city. Because of his introduction of Christian baptism to the Wessex Saxons, it was about this time that Birinus was referred to as "the baptism-father".

Belief in the old gods could not last when Birinus began performing miracles, which was a sure method of winning converts. One such miracle concerned an old woman who had been blind and deaf for a long time. She was said to have had a vision, which told her to hurry to Birinus who would effect a cure. Upon receiving her, Birinus was moved to pity and made the sign of the cross over her eyes and ears, whereupon her sight and hearing were restored, one account claiming that the old woman was even rejuvenated into a young girl again.

Because of his good works, Birinus was made a bishop at Dorchester-on-Thames, and it was here that the first church was built on the same site as the Norman church, which succeeded it. He was also responsible for the first church at Winchester as well as others, the only surviving one being, perhaps, that at Wing in Buckinghamshire. Thus, he did much to spread the Word and to consolidate the influence of Christianity in the south of England.

Birinus died in 649 and was buried at Dorchester. There is a legend concerning the nature of his death. It is said the he passed away as a result of an adder's bite while he was on Berin's Hill in the Chiltern woods, where the saint had a cell, which was later visited by many pilgrims. Thereafter he was said to protect others from the same serpentine fate. The feast of St. Birinus is 3rd December (Catholic) or 4th September (Church of England), and there is a shrine dedicated to the saint in Dorchester Abbey. Apparently, it is still believed that snakes will take a detour avoiding the town as long as the tenor bell at the Abbey is still rung regularly, as told in the following locally quoted rhyme:

Within the sound of the great bell

No Snake nor Adder e'er shall dwell.

A parallel here can be seen with St. Patrick's driving out all the snakes from Ireland. This a fitting tale with which to end the life of a remarkable man, but this was not to be the end of his story.

In 692 the current bishop, Hedda, moved his bishopric to Winchester and at the same time exhumed the remains of Birinus who by now had become a saint. However, in the early 13th century the Canons of Dorchester claimed to have found his remains and suggested that Hedda had transferred the wrong body. Together with the body inside the coffin at Dorchester was found a ring, a lead cross, a chalice, a silk purse and the remnants of a garment. Nevertheless, both churches claimed to possess the real body.

After centuries of arguments, in 1224 Pope Honorius III set up an enquiry to decide the matter, but only a non-committal result was received from the Pope, and the matter remained inconclusive. This was despite an anchorite by the name of Mathew, who lived near Oxford's Holy Well, had had a vision that the saint's remains were still held at Dorchester. But a shrine was nevertheless erected at Dorchester in 1320, and this has been restored in recent times in the south aisle of the abbey church using stones from the original shrine. The church also contains some old stained glass windows depicting the life of St. Birinus. Winchester Cathedral is also well worth visiting as it possesses a large statue of the saint which was installed in the 19th century. As to St. Birinus' original abbey at Dorchester, no trace has been found of it.

In Medieval times, the Canons of Dorchester and the Monks of Winchester were permitted by the Pope to hold an open-air procession during midsummer in honour of the saint, and nowadays there is an annual pilgrimage from Churn Knob to Dorchester. In 2009 the Fellowship of St. Birinus was founded by the Bishop of Dorchester to honour people who have given exceptional service to their church and community over the years.

Pilgrims made their way to the shrines at Winchester and Dorchester, but miracles were reported to have occurred only at that latter. A man who had been blind for seven years received his sight; a young man, deaf and mute from birth, received his hearing and speech; people were raised from the dead and a leper was cleansed. Who had the real body we shall never know, but surely, this is irrelevant where belief in miraculous cures is concerned, since the faith is often the key. However, it does serve to emphasis the esteem in which St. Birinus was held following his visit to Taplow, Buckinghamshire in 642/643.

Taplow is a village that lies at the southern end of the Chilterns. It is situated atop a hill arising dramatically from the River Thames. In the grounds of the stately home of Taplow Court lie the great Saxon burial mound and a pond, which has been known as Bapsey Pond. The name Bapsey, such as Bapsey Meadow, appears on the oldest maps of the area and is a contraction of "baptism". This in itself indicates a tradition of the pond being used as a baptismal pool, and locally this is linked with the person of St. Birinus.

In the early missionary days the aim was to eradicate paganism as quickly as possible and the Church found a variety of ways and means to spread the Word, encouraged and advised by the Pope of the day. Early in St. Augustine's ministry in 601, a letter from Pope Gregory to the Bishop of London, Mellitus, exhorted him not to destroy the heathen temples and idols but to adapt them, sprinkling them with holy water and installing altars and holy relics. In the case of springs and wells, their water was adapted for baptismal purposes and often baptisteries were built at such sites, as were churches, which were sometimes constructed over the wells themselves. This matches the Taplow situation very well, as Bapsey Pond was highly likely to have been utilised for pre-Christian rituals.

No other Germanic peoples were converted to Christianity as swiftly and easily as the Anglo-Saxons, and this may be due to the influence of the local Christian Britons who followed the Celtic Church ways. The Saxons' pagan beliefs included such beings as dragons and elves and they made wide use of charms and incantations, but what may have helped Birinus at

Taplow was their reverence for trees and wells and for the site itself. Taplow Court shares characteristics with two of the other places associated with the saint, namely Churn Knob and Berin's Hill, all three being set on the ridge of a hill and regarded as sacred.

It is easy to imagine this early missionary standing on the great pagan mound of the local Saxon chieftain Taeppa, who gave his name to the village, preaching to the foregathered local inhabitants. The site will already have been sacred to them, and perhaps familiarity made it easier for Birinus to lead them down to Bapsey Pond and to baptise those willing to be converted to the Faith. This must have seem strange to some, especially the older generation, since the interment of Taeppa under the burial mound would still have been within living memory. The pagan beliefs lingered on for some time, the population being only nominally Christian for many generations. However, it is of note that about one third of our English bishoprics can trace direct descent from the mother church that Birinus founded, and churches dedicated to the saint include those at Berinsfield in Oxfordshire and Redlynch in Wiltshire.

Taplow therefore has the honour of being associated with one of history's legends, albeit a localised one, and it says something of humankind that such a story can be passed down from generation to generation. Archaeology has proved that there was once a Saxon church built adjacent to the mound, and it is highly probable that a pagan temple preceded it. This church was replaced during the Middle Ages, until it fell into ruin and was built anew elsewhere in the parish. This new building contains a stained glass window commemorating Birinus' mission to the area, and the bottom panel shows him baptising the locals in Bapsey Pond.

Open-air services and baptisms at the pond were revived in the 20th century, and it is interesting to surmise whether Christian ceremonies will be celebrated there in another 1,300 years, or whether some new age St. Birinus will introduce the locals of the 33rd century to another spiritual persuasion.

Works Consulted:

Saint Berin the Apostle of Wessex, by Rev. J. E. Field (1902)
English Shrines and Sanctuaries, by Christina Hole (1954)

This chapter is an adapted and much expanded account previously published in the author's book entitled Unknown Taplow & Environs (1988)

24 - The Exorcising Monk: A Dynamic Monk Up Against The Occult

The exorcism of evil spirits from both people and places has been carried out since time immemorial by all religions and also by the irreligious, and is a practice which continues to this day, although it is now termed "deliverance ministry". Indeed the Gospels record that Jesus himself carried out exorcisms as, for instance, in the case of the Gadarene swine. Moving on to more recent times, a noteworthy British exorcist of the 20th century was a Benedictine monk by the name of Dom Robert Petitpierre (1903-1982), who resided at Nashdom Abbey in Burnham, Buckinghamshire and became well known in the field, and who once made an appearance on prime-time television, but more of that later.

Nashdom was a grand house designed in neoclassical style by the eminent architect Sir Edwin Lutyens in 1908 for Prince Alex Dolgorouki, a Russian emigre, and his English wife Frances Wilson, its name being Russian for "our home". It was described at the time as possessing "the spirit of Versailles and being reminiscent of the great Roman palaces", and it is now a Grade II listed building. After the death of the prince and his spouse, the premises were purchased for £8,000 by a group of Benedictine monks who took up residence in 1926. Previously based at Pershore, Worcestershire, the monks there converted to Catholicism in 1913, leaving some who did not wish to convert. Therefore, these monks decided to move, arriving at their new abode in style, rolling up in a new charabanc called "The Red Devil", on whose bonnet stood a figure of the Devil holding his customary pitchfork!

Benedictine monks are a learned community, being founded by St. Benedict in the 6th century and, owing to the colour of their habits, they are sometimes referred to as the Black Monks. The Nashdom community was the only Abbey of Benedictine monks within the Church of England, but a dearth of novices willing to undergo their disciplines forced them to leave Nashdom in 1988 for a smaller site, Elmore Abbey, near Newbury.

One monk at Nashdom was Dom Robert Petitpierre, who was well known in the Burnham and Slough area, including the Canadian Red Cross Memorial Hospital located in the grounds of the nearby stately home of Cliveden at Taplow, which was the residence of the Astors (we shall be returning there later). The monks served the hospital and were popular with staff and patients as they hurried along corridors and into wards at all hours. Apparently, Dom Robert was often seen around the hospital, eccentrically clutching bundles of papers and hurrying along corridors deep in thought. He continued his hospital visits and remained based at Nashdom Abbey until his death at the age of 80 in 1984. He was buried in the monks' cemetery in the grounds of the Nashdom estate, where the graves are marked with simple crosses and encircled by a grove of trees. The house has now been turned into luxury flats with a swimming pool, gymnasium and a tennis court, a far cry from a nobleman's country seat and a Benedictine Abbey!

Dom Robert performed exorcisms for many years, most of which he regarded as "just plain ghosts", stating that he had not come across a spirit that had defeated him. His experiences led him to believe that not all spirits which he had encountered were evil, and that different entities required different methods of exorcism. He had his own theories on the nature of ghosts and spirits, which he analysed as follows:

1. Ghosts. These he defined as imprints, or place-memories, left behind in a place by people involved in often traumatic events, which could be revived under certain circumstances or if the place is disturbed in some way. This is generally known nowadays as the stone-tape theory. These hauntings he considered were harmless, but if the entity had a firm intention to achieve a certain goal, then his practice would be to either fulfil that purpose or to persuade the ghost to abandon its aims. Although he had never "seen" a place-memory himself, he had encountered some, after which the experience left him drained. He felt that place-memories behaved rather like vampires, in that they seem to feed on human energy.

2. Poltergeists. He considered that these were internal conditions within an individual that resulted in external, apparently paranormal, activity which appeared to have an external cause and which gave the appearance of being controlled by a spirit. His view on this type of occurrence was that generally spirits were not involved, but if an individual was in some kind of troubled state, normally unconsciously, it could provide an opportunity for an external agency, such as an evil spirit, to take advantage of.

3. Demons. Also referred to by Dom Robert as "little devils", these entities are of non-human origin whose only purpose is to bring harm or misfortune to people, trying to force them to turn to evil. In such cases where a person feared they were being possessed by devils, his first reaction was always to dismiss the idea of demons and suggest that the individual consult a doctor or psychiatrist. He felt that exorcism as a cure should be avoided for as long as possible, otherwise the sufferer will become even more convinced that devils are responsible.

These were the guidelines under which he worked, bound by his Christian beliefs.

In his book, *Exorcising Devils* he pointed out that some people may see a ghost, another might hear sounds and others might experience a smell, although such contacts with the paranormal are usually limited to those with psychic awareness. Perhaps a good introduction to Dom Robert is his personal account of seeing a ghost (his only "sighting") in a London church in 1938 where he had arranged to meet the local vicar.

As he entered the vestry, at about 6 pm, he saw a priest at the far end of the nave, but as he looked around the church he noticed his friend the vicar kneeling a short distance away in the chancel. He was already aware that one or two of the previous vicars had died unexpectedly, and so he suddenly realised "Oh, that's a ghost". It was then that a churchwarden appeared on the scene to whom he remarked that he had just seen one of the local ghosts. Without turning a hair, the churchwarden glanced at his watch and replied coolly, "Ah, six o'clock - that's about the right time for him!"

Dom Robert encountered various types of possessions and hauntings in his role as exorcist, and he estimated that he had banished over 1,000 ghosts and demons. His view was that real ghosts have human minds, but demons "are an army and their general is Satan". It was his belief that spiritual entities could decide whether they were on God's side or not, those on God's becoming angels and the others becoming demons who, when they became troublesome, succumbed to being exorcised. However he thought that dabbling in the occult, for instance with Ouija boards, could lead to openings for evil powers to make their presence. In his book, *Exorcising Devils* Dom Robert mentioned a case where a black magician held sway over an occult group in which a girl member tried to leave. However, his hypnotic influence drew her back and she felt compelled to secretly go to the house of one of the group members. Fortunately she was eventually rescued by friends.

He said that normally "I do not need to see, hear or smell anything; my subconscious is sufficiently receptive to pick up 'an awareness' of something going on", which he put down to his lifetime's experience of psychic phenomena. This came out in 1958 when he secretly visited Russia to exorcise the Kremlin "where I became aware of what I can only call an 'occult nastiness'". Years later in 1970, he went on a visit to Washington where he felt "exactly the same nastiness". He later learnt that both sides of the Cold War were exploring psychic phenomena with a view to using telepathy or ESP to communicate and to influence thoughts on the opposite side of the world.

His sentiments also extended to different peoples. One hundred years or so ago it was perceived that the Celts, the Irish, Scottish, Manx, Welsh and Cornish, were particularly psychic and that the English, descended from the Germanic Saxons, did not possess the same psychic sensibilities. He considered that the explanation owes more to the fact that the Celts generally inhabited more rural areas and were more in touch with nature, as opposed to the Saxons who generally favoured an urban industrialized existence. He was concerned though (writing in 1976) about the younger generation in general becoming involved with the occult, divination, magic and the paranormal

It would obviously be impossible to recount all his cases of exorcism, so I have selected a few very contrasting instances which reveal the wide variety he was asked to investigate.

To begin with are two instances of what can be described as a "presence" in someone's home. Although he did not describe the cases in detail, one case involved the house having a "strange atmosphere", the other experiencing odd noises, objects being moved about and one area of the house having what is generally called in the psychic investigation scene a "cold spot". To reassure the occupants Dom Robert recommended using a "Form of Exorcism of a Place", which was a standard procedure of saying prayers and readings from Scriptures. In such cases, he would not advise the house's occupants that their house was occupied by dark forces, but the Church would offer a ministry of blessing and filling the house with the peace of Christ. In both cases, the disturbances ceased and the family were at peace and in the second case, the whole family joined the Church.

An interesting case concerned a home for girls in the East End of London, whose premises had once been used as a brothel. The problem here was that each night one of the girls went wayward sexually, sometimes only after a few weeks of being housed there. Obviously, this caused some concern and it was decided to call in the parish priest, who concluded that the premises' previous history had left evil influences which required the expertise of an exorcist. However, after the priest and a Catholic bishop had conducted several services and two exorcisms, the strength of the evil power proved too much for them. It was then that Dom Robert was called in and, together with the bishop and twelve other clergymen, a successful exorcism of the premises was achieved and no further untoward activity by the girls occurred.

Another, altogether different, case he took on involved the legendary Wild Hunt, the spectral hunt which courses across country, through forest or across the sky, usually led by some demonic personage with an entourage of ghostly horses, hounds, devils and other unworldly beings. This ghostly hunt is common to most north European cultures and in Windsor Great Park it is led by the antlered Herne the Hunter (see also chapter 13).

The story, dating from the 1920s and located somewhere in the Thames Valley, concerns the owner of a large house who asked an architect friend to add a billiards room by way of an extension to the house. After being built for two or three months, the owner asked his friend round to visit and, during the evening, they duly retired to the new billiards room. However, just as the visitor was about to play a stroke, he looked up in amazement. What he saw charging across the room and right through the billiards table was a ghostly stag followed by a pack of hounds, a hunt and then a monk mounted on a horse.

Dom Robert was called in and the owner informed him that it had happened every night there was a full moon since the room was built. It was therefore decided to raise the floor eighteen inches so that the spectral hunt would appear out of sight, but apparently this was not sufficient and subsequently only the heads of the apparitions rushed through the table. The solution that Dom Robert came up with, ironically in this case as it did not require an exorcism, turned out to be not to play billiards on the night of the full moon!

Lastly, a more serious case took place at the afore-mentioned Cliveden in 1964. It was two years after the notorious Profumo affair, which led to the downfall of the then Conservative Government, when Lady Astor called in Dom Robert. Her husband Lord Astor, she claimed, had died of a broken heart in 1966 four years after the sex scandal, and she was advised to have the house where the goings-on had occurred exorcised. There were many rumours of what actually went on within the walls of the distinguished house, especially involving the late Christine Keeler and whispered gossip went around suggesting orgies and the occult. This was in addition to espionage, as spies and high-level establishment figures such as cabinet minister John Profumo, were party to the gatherings. Whatever the details, unsavoury activities certainly went on.

Apparently the main house itself was exorcised successfully by Dom Robert, but additionally it was felt that Spring Cottage on the Cliveden estate should also receive the same rite. The reason for this was that it had been occupied by Dr Stephen Ward, an osteopath whose clients included men in high places and who, in connection with the Profumo scandal, was subsequently charged with living off the earnings of prostitutes. He also was said to have been heavily involved in the alleged sexual and occult activities, and Lady Astor remembered him as a force for evil. During his trial he committed suicide, thus taking the full truth of his involvement in the affair to the grave.

Dom Robert duly carried out the exorcism at the main house in the presence of Lady Astor, who became ill after the ceremony. It was at this point that the Dom recommended that she did not attend the exorcism to be carried out at Spring Cottage, which was infested with the most "potent satanic entities" the Dom had ever dealt with. Lady Astor believed Ward to be the cause of the entire Profumo affair due to his meddling with occult forces. Upon entering the cottage on earlier occasions, she stated that it was nearly impossible to get through the door because of the strength of the evil atmosphere which acted like a physical force, and which nearly succeeded in preventing Dom Robert himself from gaining access. However, the exorcism was eventually completed and the Cliveden estate has now been a respectable National Trust property for many years, although cream teas are now the norm rather than orgies! After all this publicity Dom Robert quietly continued his monastic and exorcist duties, but hit the headlines again in 1970, when he encountered a rather strange gentleman.

Alex Sanders (1926-1988) was a notorious English occultist whose nickname was "King of the Witches". Apparently he was introduced to "magical practices" when as a child he would visit his grandmother in Wales who was a cunning woman. It appears that one day he came across his grandmother in her kitchen totally naked standing inside a pentacle. She imparted to the young Sanders that she was the last of a line of hereditary witches descended from the Welsh hero Owain Glyndwr, after which she initiated him into the secrets of witchcraft, as well as sexuality.

After World War Two, he dabbled in black magic, but in the early 1960s he turned to Wicca, later referring to himself as the High Priest of the movement. In the 1960s and 1970s, he caught the attention of the news media, often appearing in lurid articles in the tabloid press. He also claimed to have healing powers, even putting his newly born daughter's left foot straight, as it was twisted backwards at birth, amazing the medical profession who said that it could not be set right until she became a teenager. But he was not averse to sticking pins into dolls in order to cause harm or even death to those he considered his enemies.

Once asked about the difference between black witchcraft and black magic, he replied "Very little. The former is done in the name of a god or a devil, while the latter is non-religious and both are still practised nowadays. People are still murdered by them, and unlike voodoo, the victim need not necessarily be told of the curse." A sinister individual indeed. He died on Walpurgis Night, 30th April 1988, but after his death, an American coven claimed to have received channelled communications from his spirit addressing all Wiccans to follow the Goddess and urged them to keep up their strength to remain united. Thus he spoke from the grave.

Now back to 1970 when the popular chat show hosted by the late Simon Dee brought together three authorities on esoteric matters, namely Sanders himself, Dennis Wheatley, author of occult novels, and Dom Robert, in a discussion on the black arts. Sanders strode on to the set clothed in a billowing cape and wearing a ring decorated with a pentagram, which apparently had once belonged to the nineteenth century sorcerer Eliphas Levi, and a crux ansata pendant, as well as sporting dark glasses. It seemed that Wheatley was very wary of Sanders and avoided him as much as possible except for participating in the discussion itself, which lasted no more than seven minutes. When the talk got round to the casting of spells, Wheatley asked him whether he realised that such activity could be damaging to his karma.

Unfortunately, not much else of what was discussed has survived, but it seems that most of the dialogue was between Sanders and Simon Dee. However, Dom Robert asserted that Sanders was "the most dangerous witch in Europe" and was dabbling in dangerous practices. He considered that much of such people's power was psychological and that to use supernatural powers which were not associated with God could have dire consequences. As the conversation between the four individuals did not last that long, nobody really gained anything from it, the episode really being only a bit of sensationalism sandwiched between other features on the programme.

Dom Robert was liked by everyone (except by demons!). Ghost investigator Peter Underwood knew him very well and, in his book *Exorcism!* he describes him as one who kept his feet firmly on the ground and who had "refreshing honesty in viewing these difficult and involved matters". So here, we conclude this chapter on a very well disposed individual who, because of his level-headedness in his chosen, sometime dangerous, calling, was considered to be the leading exorcist of his day.

Works Consulted:

Exorcising Devils   *Dom Robert Petitpierre (Robert Hale*
1976)
Exorcism!   *Peter Underwood (Robert Hale 1990)*
Unknown Taplow & Environs   *Eric Fitch (Windsor*
Publications 1988)
King of the Witches   *June Johns (Pan 1971)*

This chapter has been adapted, thoroughly revised and expanded from a section of the author's book (above).

25 - M. R. James, Fairies & The Occult: Lesser Known Interests Of The Ghost Story Writer

M R James

Introduction

Montague Rhodes James (1862-1936) is generally considered to be the master of the ghost story, and his tales have been widely reprinted up until today, as well as being adapted for radio, television and film. His ghosts are not the traditional sort of wispy white phantasms, they are often more like demons or revenants. The poet John Betjeman described his tales as "the most frightening, learned and humorous ghost stories". James was also a scholar and antiquarian, with a special interest in Biblical and Apocryphal literature, Christian texts that did not find their way into the New Testament. His stories often feature a background of ancient manuscripts, libraries, rare books and ecclesiastical buildings.

As a boy James showed early academic tendencies, being able to read a 17th century Dutch Bible by the age of six, and learning to read the language spoken in ancient Ethiopia by the age of 12. As a pupil, he attended Eton College, from where he entered Cambridge University, gaining his B.A. in 1885. 1886 found him Assistant Director of the Fitzwilliam Museum in Cambridge, becoming Director in 1893. In 1905 he secured the post of Provost of King's College until 1918, when he returned to Eton College also as Provost, and remained in that position until his death in 1936. In 1925, James took up an appointment as a Trustee of the British Museum, where he had access to the Department of Manuscripts, much to his delight. He was awarded the Order of Merit by George V in 1930 "in recognition of his scholarship and of his eminent contributions to Medieval Learning". He is buried in Eton Town Cemetery.

Fairy Tales

Although famed for his ghost stories, it is less known that James also had an interest in folklore and fairy tales. James used folklore motifs in a number of his stories and was particularly interested in traditional tales from Scandinavian countries, visiting both Sweden and Denmark with his friend James McBryde (see below). His linguistic skills were outstanding, being able to read a history of Sweden in six volumes in the original Swedish. Two of his ghost stories were actually set in Scandinavia, *Count Magnus* in Rabak, Sweden, and *Number 13* in Viborg, Denmark. He went on several cycling tours to these two countries with various friends, and became "much engrossed with the folklore of Jutland, which peoples its wide and lonely heaths with many strange beings". These tours also gave him an opportunity of visiting old churches and more ancient relics such as standing stones.

It was because of these excursions that he became interested in the folk tales of Scandinavia, especially the fairy tales of Hans Andersen, a number of which he translated from the Danish, *Forty-two Stories* being published in 1930. He selected those tales that appealed to him the most, but acknowledging that not all were traditional tales gathered by Andersen, but a number were made from his own imagination. For instance with the two published in 1836, *The Travelling Companion* and *Thumbelina*, the former was a well-known folk tale, but the latter was composed by himself. (As an aside, as a child I well remember the songs *Thumbelina*, *The Emperor's New Clothes* and *The Ugly Duckling*, sung by Danny Kaye, often being played on BBC radio's Children's Favourites, and of course Kaye played the author himself in the 1952 film *Hans Christian Andersen*.) Other famous Andersen tales which James selected were *The Little Mermaid*, *The Princess & the Pea* and *The Snow Queen*, and a number of old folk-tales that James translated included *The Princess & the Pea*, *The Wild Swans* and The *Tinder Box*.

Chapter 10 deals with the folklore of the raven, but to add to this takes us to one of James's selections to translate, *The Elf Hill*, in which the night-raven is mentioned. Scandinavian folklore tradition describes this bird as a person whose grave resides at the place where three boundaries meet, the individual having done wrong during his lifetime. Apparently, beneath the ground there are tunnels, which the dead person has to work along in order to find his way up to the surface again, whereupon they are transformed into the night-raven. Once free, the night-raven, also known as the night-heron, flits about during the hours of darkness, and is heard by its eerie cry. In Norse mythology, it is portrayed as a bird without any eyes, and if anyone looks into the empty eye sockets, it is certain they would die. In addition if young children see it the bird will abduct them, take them to its nest where it will gorge itself upon their flesh. James may have had the night-raven in mind in his ghost story *The Rose Garden,* where "a bird (perhaps) rustled in the bush".

James felt that previous translations of Andersen's tales did not do them justice, so he decided to translate them himself into what he hoped was "decent English". His view on Andersen's stories was that he was a worthy successor to the Brothers Grimm, whose fairy tales were all collected from oral tradition. As stated above, not all Andersen's tales were traditional, but he made use of folkloric themes, one being that of storks, which were common in Denmark. Apart from bringing babies into the world, they were also considered to be able to talk to one another, and were considered to be very wise, and they were even seen to be almost human. Indeed James tells us that an ancient Roman belief was that when they achieved old age, they travelled to the "Fortunate Islands" and were transformed into men, which was a reward for their kindness to their brother humans. As an example, one of Andersen's stories that James translated was entitled "The Storks". In James's preface to his translation he stated: "My attempt is in the nature of a tribute to a beloved author, an admirable people and a most delightful country." But these stories were not the only translations of folk tales he made, for he made others originating from France.

In Tales from Lectoure, a small town in Gascony, south western France, James gathered some folk tales and translated them for two lectures, which were eventually published by Rosemary Pardoe as a subscriber's supplement to the journal *Ghosts & Scholars* in 2006. James also liked France and again made several cycling tours there, preferring to steer clear of the usual tourist destinations, and visiting out of the way places in the spacious French countryside. He gathered the tales from a work entitled *Contes populaires de la Gascogne*, which was first published in 1885, with James easily being able to read the original French. In fact, he had learnt the language from his mother, who began her early life in Tours.

The seven tales are *The Young Man & The Great Beast with a Man's Head*, *Golden Feet*, *The Chastisement of the Queen*, *The Green Man*, *The Sword of St Peter*, *The Prince of the Seven Gold Cows* and *The King of the Ravens*. James's view of the landscape and its associations was that they produced "the most strange and savage of all folk tales that have survived - tales which, though they have their parallels in times and countries far removed from Gascony and this century, are in their Gascon form, unique". He also considered that the tales "are marked by a copious use of the Homeric fashion of repetition. That, as you know, is characteristic of the early tales and epics....you will find it rife among the Celts".

Apparently James had visited all of the French cathedrals except Nice and Toulon, taking into account their history, architecture and atmosphere, and this obviously had influenced him when he wrote his first ghost story *Canon Alberic's Scrapbook*, which was set in the town of St Bertrand de Comminges, situated about 70 miles south-east of Lectoure. As to the folk tales themselves, rather than trying to comment on all six of them, I am restricting this to just one - *The King of the Ravens*. This fairy tale, too long to reproduce here, concerns a king who has been cursed by some diabolic individual, causing him to being a raven by day and a human by night. It also involves the king marrying the youngest of three daughters of someone called the Green Man (not the fertility figure of the 20th century invented by Lady Raglan in 1939), his imprisonment, and his release involving a magical herb recommended by a fairy washerwoman. This story has common features with the Classical tale of *Cupid & Psyche* and the French tale of *Beauty & the Beast*, demonstrating the many similarities there are in fairy tales of different countries, which have been catalogued by folklorists into "motifs", this one being Type 425 "The Search for the Lost Husband".

Finally, James's children's novel entitled *The Five Jars*, published in 1922. It is broadly a fairy tale, and I include it here because it is not widely known and deserves to be more recognised. In the form of a letter to a girl called Jane (McBryde - see below), it begins with the narrator discovering a strange box which has been hidden from view since Roman times. Upon opening it, he finds five jars, which contain magic ointments empowering him with peculiar powers that ill-intentioned fairies attempt to prevent him from using. Then using one jar per night, he commences to experience a fascinating journey into an alternative world of unearthly enchantment, enabling him to see the fairies, interact linguistically with animals, to see hidden things, and where fantastic beauty is the norm. He ultimately defeats the fairies and saves the jars. The book is still suitable for the children of today and is an enjoyable for adults as well.

Fairy tales were certainly an important element in his reading and his research, which led to him keeping copies of some of them. James's ghost stories were to be illustrated by a friend named James McBryde, who unfortunately died at a young age, leaving only four completed illustrations, which were included in James's first story collection *Ghost Stories of an Antiquary* published in 1904. McBryde's young daughter Jane subsequently became James's ward, a task he carried out seriously and dutifully. He was very encouraging to Jane in helping her to read and write, as well as draw, following in the steps of her father. In addition, James wrote letters to Jane, and occasionally she would find enclosed the text of a fairy tale he had discovered. James kept up a life-long friendship with Jane and her mother Gwendolyn, perhaps the two becoming a kind of substitute family for this confirmed bachelor. In honour of McBryde, he arranged for the latter's children's tale entitled *The Story of a Troll Hunt* to be published, with an introduction by James himself.

So fairy tales are not what one would expect from the pen of M.R. James, acknowledged for his ghost stories and scholarly antiquarian pursuits, but they reveal that he had other interests, as the following section will reveal.

The Occult

"Persons who busy themselves about the subject of Satanism and Black Magic are rarely to be depended upon for accuracy of statement."
    M.R. James

Occult reading?

Amongst his other pursuits, James also had an interest in the occult, which features in some of his ghost stories. When he was studying at Eton College, he was a member of the College Literary Society, to which he seems to have given a number of papers, including *Occult Sciences*. At the age of 18, he had obviously read copiously in areas such as archaeology, history and magic, volumes of which he found in the Eton School Library. One tome was John Dee's *Diary*, Dee being an astrologer, occultist, astronomer and the adviser to Elizabeth 1st. James later came to catalogue Dee's manuscripts in the Trinity Library in Cambridge in 1921. He also was wont to visit booksellers, scouring their catalogues looking for curious and interesting volumes, however it seems that most of the time he was not able to afford to purchase such items.

Another interest was Walter Map's compilation of Medieval tales *De Nugis Curialium* which included accounts of vampires, nymphs and most of all ghosts, and which he translated from the Latin and published in later years. He obviously kept an eye open for such tales up until his later years, as in his book *Suffolk and Norfolk* (1930) he made mention of a local legend from Orford in Suffolk, which concerned a merman who was captured by the locals sometime in the 13th century. Apparently, he could not be induced to speak nor take any interest in church services, and after a while the creature managed to escape.

James was brought up by his parents to expect induction to Holy Orders after his student days, but he decided against it. As a teenager, he took an interest in sphinxes, saints' symbols and Stonehenge, which he considered may have been used for serpent worship. He also delved into that magical book *Hermes Trismegistus*. However as James was, at least nominally, a Christian, he was not persuaded to allow the occult to enter into his personal life. Rosemary Pardoe is of the view that James was troubled by "the dichotomy between the comfortable Christian world view of his upbringing, which he wanted to accept but couldn't, and the darkly amoral version of pantheism which, try as he might to deny it to himself, he felt truly reflected the state of the world".

His paper *Occult Sciences*, delivered in 1881 whilst at Eton College, covered Hebrew and Biblical instances of magic, Egyptian and Assyrian magicians, Chaldean astrology and magic, demons, love philtres and other bewitchments from the Classical world, as wells as divination, chiromancy, geomancy and witchcraft. It revealed a wide and remarkable knowledge of these cryptic subjects gathered from reading obscure tomes he had searched out and delved into.

In his ghost stories, an important motif concerns the enduring reach of pre-Christian rites. For instance, in *Lost Hearts,* the main character possesses a library full of writings on pagan topics such as Mithraism, the Orphic Mysteries and Neo-Platonism; however the overriding themes of his ghost stories are those of supernatural malevolence and purposeful vengeance. The late Christopher Lee sums them up: "It was amazing the way he blended the somewhat ironic and at times even dry approach of a scholar with the chilling nameless fears that lurked just behind his stories".

Ron Weighell writes, "The dominant themes of MRJ's occult fiction, the continuing power and influence of ancient ritual, and the often questionable dividing line between such practices and their Christian counterparts, are evident in the earliest of the tales". Occult themes turn up in a number of his ghost stories (spoiler alert):

- ***Canon Alberic's Scrapbook*** *- a demon*
- ***Oh, Whistle and I'll Come to You, My Lad*** *-a demon summoning whistle and Templars*
- ***Mr. Humphreys and His Inheritance*** *- pagan magic, Satanic symbols and a maze*
- ***Count Magnus*** *- alchemy, Norse myths and Satanism*
- ***Casting the Runes*** *- rune magic*
- ***Lost Hearts*** *- a bloody pagan ritual involving cannibalism*
- ***A View From a Hill*** *- necromancy and alchemy*
- ***The Ash-tree*** *- witchcraft*
- ***The Residence at Whitminster*** *- scrying, witchcraft, demonic sacrifices, demonic dogs*
- ***Number 13*** *- a black magician*
- ***An Episode of Cathedral History*** *- a vampiric she-demon*
- ***The Fenstanton Witch*** *- witchcraft, necromancy and black magic*

The last story was published posthumously (see works consulted).

A trip to Dublin in 1892 to see his brother led James to visit St Michans Church where the vaults housed a number of mummified remains of various people, including one of a nun who lived some 400 years ago, and sundry Earls of Leitrim. Apparently, the environmental conditions of the vault were such that the bodies were preserved. These were, and still are, available to be viewed by the general public, and James took a distinct dislike to them, referring to them as being abhorrent and a "nightmare". They obviously had an influence on the writing of his ghost stories, however, since the mummies were in a very dry state and covered in dust, features some of his ghosts possessed, such as that in *The Tractate Middoth*.

There is another building that James may well have seen, and that is what was once described as the most haunted house in England, Borley Rectory in Essex. In 1922 he was commissioned to catalogue the medieval stained glass to be found in the churches of that county, and it is quite possible that he came across the Rectory, as he would have paid a visit to the church in the nearby village of Belchamp St Paul, the place where the outcome of the story Count Magnus unfolds. The first ghost to be seen at the Rectory was that of a nun observed in 1900, but ever since then all sorts of supernatural goings on were reported, including spectral coaches, objects flying across rooms and ghostly writings appearing on walls, until the building was burnt down in 1939.

The famous ghost hunter Harry Price took out a lease on the property in 1937, and he then arranged for observers to stay for periods to record what they experienced. However the various types of a supernatural events recorded by Price and his assistants were challenged after Price's death in 1948. In fact, it was suggested that Price had faked some of his findings. At any rate, it is highly unlikely that James would not have heard of the renowned ghostly events at Borley Rectory, especially taking into account his interest in ghosts.

It has been suggested that James may well have met the notorious Aleister Crowley, the Great Beast, in 1895 when both were at Cambridge, and it has been suggested that James based the figure of the demonologist Karswell on Crowley in *Casting the Runes*. Not only that, but James once had his portrait painted by Sir Gerald Kelly, who at one time was Crowley's brother-in-law, but it seems that there was no particular association between the two men. However, a new candidate has now been put forward, very convincingly, and that was a dubious character who called himself Fr. Rolfe, who was well known in the Cambridge circles within which James moved. (see *The Ghosts & Scholars M.R. James Newsletter* 33, April 2018)

A highly rated film adaptation of *Casting the Runes* appeared in 1957 entitled *Night of the Demon*, which has been issued on DVD and Blu-ray. Incidentally, one of the experts who were contacted for advice in making the film was Dr Margaret Murray, who was an Egyptologist, folklorist and archaeologist, but is most well known for her researches into witchcraft, with her two books entitled *The Witch-Cult in Western Europe* (1921) and *The God of the Witches* (1933). In these volumes, she put forward the idea that witchcraft was the continuation of a pagan religion, which remained underground with the arrival of Christianity, only to come to the fore at the time of the witch trials. This has subsequently been proved to be unfounded, and I trust that she did not put forward her offbeat views to the film makers, and stuck to substantiated folklore.

Nevertheless, James himself in his lecture of about 1922 entitled *Forgotten Books*, surprisingly seems to have been taken in by Murray's theories. He states: "But Witchcraft you know has taken a step up of late and it does not do to treat the ancient tales with the levity to which we were accustomed. I am not thinking of the prevalence of occultism in the present day, but of the recent investigation of the real old paraphernalia of Sabbaths and the rest of it. I have not much doubt that Sabbaths were held, and that those who attended them were adherents of an older religion than Christianity, and that much of the confessions have a substratum of truth." However, these were early days of the popularisation of Murray's theories, which were eventually discredited.

As mentioned above James's ghosts are not spectres, but rather demons, and James stated that "the good and kindly ghost" does not feature in his stories. His ghosts are often malignant and they put the fear of God into their victims, who are on occasion actually killed. In addition they are never got rid of by way of exorcism for example, and the stories often possess a scenario whereby an ancient site is being disrupted, leading to terrifying consequences. Turning again to two favourite topics of James, i.e. demons and Biblical literature, both of which he acquired an interest in from an early age, he penned an article in 1899 on the 3rd century CE text The Testament of Solomon, which dealt with the King coercing 72 demons to build his temple at Jerusalem. James describes how the Wisdom of Solomon was legendary and, as such, would include esoteric knowledge including that of command over the world of the spirits. The demons he took power over included:

- Ornias, who appears only in The Testament of Solomon and who could transform himself into various creatures.
- Beelzebub, known as Lord of the Flies or Prince of the Devils.
- Onoskelis, "she with asses legs", a beautiful female demon in satyr form. Appears only in The Testament of Solomon.
- Asmodeus, "worst of the demons" found in the apocryphal Book of Tobit. He has three heads, a bull, a man, and a ram.

In 1913 James published a volume for children entitled *Old Testament Legends*, which included a chapter called "Solomon and the Demons", however some parents may have been wary of giving a tome containing such demonic narratives to their youngsters!

James obviously developed an enthusiasm for demons, which became a feature of a number of his ghost stories, as mentioned above. His delving into early Christian and apocryphal texts obviously led him to the subject. The term "demon" derives from the ancient Greek *daemon*, which denoted a benevolent entity, but over the centuries, especially in the Christian world, they became evil beings, sometimes referred to as fallen angels. In the Old Testament, deities of other religions were considered demons, and by the time of the compilation of the New Testament discussion of demons was limited largely to the apocryphal Christian writings, the main exceptions being Jesus's expelling of demons from affected persons, and those in the *Book of Revelation*. These texts were nourishment to James's intellect, but of course other influences were at work on his mind.

The Demon Asmodeus

Folklore themes were an important feature of his ghost stories and James stated that he followed the "rules of folklore". However, in one ghost story he seems to have been responsible for actually creating a non-existent piece of folklore. In *A Warning to the Curious* he tells of three Saxon crowns, which had been buried on the East Anglian coast in order to protect England from invasion. This has developed into a local legend, even being accepted by a noted folklorist, but no record of the story has been discovered that is earlier than that of James.

In *Oh, Whistle and I'll Come to You, My Lad* the blowing of an ancient whistle causes a ghost to be summoned. In folklore, such whistling could call up any manner of ghostly spectres including the Wild Hunt or the Devil himself. "Whistling for the wind" was considered a superstition that should not be followed, the folklore surrounding this being found in both Scandinavia and Yorkshire. In the case of the latter location, whistling after dark was thought to be very dangerous, the perpetrator being driven out of the house and ordered to walk three times round the building in order to break the spell. James not only obeyed the "rules of folklore", but also the literary conventions of the short story, a combination that resulted in ghost stories, which are masterfully superb. Black magic makes an appearance in more than one story, in which the figure who is practising the black arts has his comeuppance, as in *Lost Hearts* and *Casting the Runes*. However, generally when obscure relics are disturbed and the terrors released, the person who is the perpetrator of the disturbance is Christian, at least nominally.

James also delved into Biblical matters and published *The Apocryphal New Testament* (1924), *The Biblical Antiquities of Philo* (translated from the Latin, 1917), *The Apocalypse in Art* (1931), *The Testament of Solomon* (an article 1899) and *Old Testament Legends* (1913). Forgotten and abstruse knowledge and apocrypha were areas James particularly studied, the latter being prominent in *Canon Alberic's Scrapbook*. He seemed to have taken an interest in the lesser-known Biblical works, which do not actually appear in the Bible itself, especially concerning folklore and the cryptic. *In The Testament of Solomon*, for instance, James refers to a Biblical passage to be found in Isaiah, which I leave up to the reader to discover, but please read *Canon Alberic's Scrapbook* first! His apocryphal delving also led to such strange tales telling of fish that walk on land, a talking dog, a man with a wasps' nest up his nose and the figure of the magician Simon Magus.

James's main interest was basically antiquarian, compiling catalogues of old manuscripts held in such places as Cambridge University, and writing a volume entitled *The Wanderings and Homes of Manuscripts* (1919). He was also vocal about other authors, including Aldous Huxley (whom he called "unspeakable") and James Joyce (whom he called a "charlatan" and "that prostitutor of life and language"). When he was a student at King's he expressed his opposition to the awarding the post of Provost at Eton College to none other than T.H. Huxley, "Darwin's Bulldog", because he was agnostic, a term that Huxley had coined himself. He was also critical of Bram Stoker, whose Dracula he considered "suffered by excess".

James also had an interest in archaeology and antiquities in general, and in his young days, he would often go around the countryside exploring ancient churches and poring over antique manuscripts, activities that he continued to indulge in to the end of his life. At Cambridge University, it crossed his mind that he could follow a career in archaeology, but in the end, the call of medieval studies overcame such an occupation. However, he worked on two excavations, the first taking place in Cyprus in 1887/8. This involved excavating several sites on the island, after which the focus homed in on the Temple of Aphrodite near Old Paphos, where his talents steered him into deciphering inscriptions that had been discovered.

The second dig with which he was involved has a strange story. The site was the chapter house of Bury St Edmunds Abbey, which was carried out in 1902/3, but James made a discovery that almost smacked of the occult. He had been examining an old manuscript relating to the abbey, when he chanced to discover a reference to the burials of six abbots dating from medieval times, which had been referred to in a work by Jocelyn de Brakelond, a 12th century monk at the abbey, entitled *Chronicle of the Abbey of Bury St. Edmunds*. James then claimed that he could identify their graves from the lie of the land at the abbey, pointing out that they would be discovered in the chapter house. Excavations were then carried out, supervised by James, and on New Year's Day 1903, the archaeologists unearthed the remains of five coffins and one body in the chapter house ruins, exactly where James had predicted. The abbots' remains were subsequently reinterred.

Graves of abbots in Bury St Edmund's Abbey

To some this would be considered as supernatural, and the figure of Bligh Bond comes to mind. Bond directed excavations at Glastonbury Abbey commencing in 1908, and he had remarkable success in discovering various abbey buildings. However, it later came out that he had employed a medium who was in touch with the spirit world and had used automatic writing channelled by dead monks to point out where to dig. Bond was very successful in discovering the exact places to explore, but was subsequently sacked from the excavations in 1921 by an outraged Church of England. James, of course, was not using occult means in his case, he was too conventional, but his seemingly unlikely locating of the sites of the abbots' graves could be interpreted that way by some. In fact, James commented on Bond's psychic works in his book *Abbeys* (1925) in which he stated "The thesis of [Bond's books] is that communications can be and are received by means of automatic writing, from men who in ancient times were connected with Glastonbury.... Here is obviously a highly controversial field, into which I do not feel myself called upon to enter".

James's' ghost stories were often set in ancient buildings such as churches, cathedrals and old libraries. These settings presented the protagonists of his ghost stories to delve into their history and, by disturbing them, they unleashed an avenging terror as a retribution, even though the perpetrator may only be satisfying his curiosity. Perhaps his most popular story, *Oh Whistle, and I'll Come to You, My Lad*, the whistle is found in the ruins of a Templar preceptory, and summons up one of the most unforgettable ghosts in the history of the genre. And in many of James's ghost stories, the antiquarian, archaeological and occult themes are ever present. But in his own life he did not seem to have experienced anything supernatural, except once when he was a boy, which James seemed to describe in his last ghost story *A Vignette*, published in the London Mercury 35 (1936), following his death a few weeks previously. This event occurred when he was growing up in Great Livermere in Suffolk.

A further occult connection concerns James's first story, *Canon Alberic's Scrapbook* (1894), which Nick Warren, editor of the Jack the Ripper journal *Ripperana*, suggests that James was influenced in writing after a trip to France. He visited the small town of St Bertrand de Comminges, specifically the cathedral, which appears in the story. The chief character is that of Dennistoun, an English archaeologist who is seeking to purchase Alberic's treasure, his Scrapbook, from the cathedral sacristan, which has a demonic guardian. It may be that James had picked up stories about Rennes-le-Chateau, about 80 odd miles from St Bertrand de Comminges, and its priest Berenger Sauniere who, in 1891, suddenly became very wealthy after renovations had been carried out at his church, perhaps discovering treasure in the fabric of the building. This topic is so well known now, that I shall not elaborate on it, except to question the "researches" of the authors of *The Holy Blood & The Holy Grail* and their spurious conclusions, which then ended up in Dan Brown's *The Da Vinci Code*. On the lookout for Biblical subject matters on his travels, James could well have come across word of Sauniere's activities and incorporated themes therefrom into his first ghost story. Who knows?

To conclude this section of James and the occult, an article by an art critic interpreted a painting by an unknown painter as having Satanic overtones. In January 1932, a French Art Exhibition was staged at the Royal Academy, which included a triptych painting entitled *Annunciation*, a once common theme for artists. However, the unnamed critic wrote a review for The Times and picked out this painting in particular, which he considered was painted by a Satanist artist. He pointed out that the artwork "mingled the bestial and the spiritual and the infernal and divine". His examples included the following:

- The Angel Gabriel has the wings of an owl.

- The groining of the building shows vampires and bats, rather than larks and doves.
- Horned devils peep from arches' trefoils.
- A vase contains evil herbs such as belladonna, basil and foxglove.
- A ray of light falls not on Mary, but a monkey.
- Both God and the Angel Gabriel are raising their fingers with the sign of the Devil.
- In the shutters are two nameless diabolical figures standing near book shelves, (probably containing tomes with titles such as Malleus Maleficarum or Daemonomania)

The critic added that there was a local "long-standing and deeply rooted tradition" that the painting was Satanic and it was painted when "practices of witchcraft were rife in the region" where the painting was normally hung (at Aix).

James was incensed. He replied to The Times that he saw nothing of what the critic alleged. For instance he could see no signs of vampires and bats, the herb plants cannot be specified, God's and the Angel's so-called devilish finger pointing cannot be made out to that degree, and the rays of light only pass over a lectern, which features a tiny monkey at its finial, and thence to Mary. As to the two figures, James points out that one has below him the name Jeremiah, and the other whose name has disappeared would be that of Isaiah. His final comment was such people "should not be allowed without protest, to blacken gratuitously the name and work of a fine painter". And, as we know, James knew his Bible and its symbology. At any event, would any church really hang a painting that portrays overt devilish images so prominently?

It seems that James's attitude to the magical arts was a blend of almost seductive attraction and abhorrent repugnance, and it must be said that personally it would be erroneous to see James as some kind of diabolical mage. He was one who recognised the dark side of some infernal beliefs and practices, much to the frightfulness of his stories and our delight in being frightened!

Burnham Abbey and Eton

To end this chapter I now add a short, adapted article about James that I contributed to the newsletter of the area in South Buckinghamshire where I used to live, which was close to his burial place. It is about one of those typical sites favoured by James - an abbey.

James was Provost of Eton College in his later years until his death in 1936. He was also an antiquarian, and as mentioned above, in 1925 he published a book in conjunction with the Great Western Railway entitled *Abbeys*, its object being "to provide the traveller with an adequate explanation of the buildings he is to visit". He visited most of the abbeys he wrote about, including that at Burnham. His description follows in his own words:

Burnham, Buckinghamshire, founded in 1266 for Augustine canonesses, is in the occupation of a sisterhood. The church is practically gone; it was a plain rectangular building a little over 100 feet long. The east range of the cloister buildings survives, with sacristy, chapter house, parlour and warming house. The wall of the frater next to the cloister is also there, and, east of the main block are the remains of the infirmary. These buildings are of the thirteenth century. They are very plain, and were long used as farm premises.

This is a clear and concise description of the buildings. The original abbey suffered the same fate as other abbeys under Henry VIII's Dissolution in 1538. However the order of nuns, The Society of the Precious Blood, took up residence there in 1916, just nine years before publication of James's book and they are still there to this day, celebrating their 100th anniversary in 2016, as well as the 750th anniversary of the Abbey's founding charter. I do not know whether James was aware of the ghosts reputed to haunt the abbey, which I have described in my book *Unknown Taplow & Environs*, but having written so many excellent ghost stories himself, I should be surprised if he did not make enquiries about such matters.

I may have given the impression that James was a dull and pedestrian academic; in fact, he had a keen sense of humour and was a very capable mimic. Amusingly, whilst he was an Eton College schoolboy he occasionally contributed to the journal *Eton College Chronicle* discussions of antique manuscripts which turned out to be totally bogus! James is buried not far from Burnham in Eton Town Cemetery, and his gravestone was renovated and reconsecrated in 2000. This author, along with others, attended the ceremony, after which we were invited to the College Library where Jamesian books and manuscripts were arranged for us to view, which was followed by a guided walk round the College, a very pleasant afternoon. However, I gather that the gravestone is again rather timeworn with ivy beginning to creep over it and the grave itself.

Nevertheless, I can recommend a walk around the graveyard, which is a peaceful spot. The graveyard is in Eton Wick Road about three or four hundred yards from Eton High Street. Having entered via the arch, pass to the right of the chapel, keep on straight ahead almost to the end of the cemetery and the grave is to be found two or three rows from the end brick wall. Incidentally, the chapel is now used by the College as a library and archive, with James possibly having had some input to the Victorian stained glass windows on the east wall, which depict scenes from the *Book of Revelation*. Thus I would ask you to pay your respects to Montague Rhodes James, a great storyteller, antiquarian and scholar.

Finally three quotes:

M.R. James's own view on ghosts?

> *"Do I believe in ghosts? To which I answer that I am prepared to consider evidence and accept it if it satisfies me."*

And M.R. James's view on fictional ghosts?

> *"The ghost should be malevolent or odious: amiable and helpful apparitions are all very well in fairy tales or in local legends, but I have no use for them in a fictitious ghost story."*

And a final comment from Ron Weighell:

> *"As lovers of macabre fiction, I feel we should be eternally grateful that there was a place in this good and gifted man's heart of hearts that was not entirely on the side of the angels."*

Works Consulted:

Forty-two Stories, Hans Andersen (translated by M. R. James, 1971 edition)
Occult Sciences, M.R. James, (edited by Rosemary Pardoe, 2004)
Tales from Lectoure, M. R. James (edited by Rosemary Pardoe, 2006)
The Five Jars, M. R. James (1922)
The Fenstanton Witch and Others (edited by Rosemary Pardoe, 1991
Abbeys, M.R. James (1925)
M.R. James: Book of the Supernatural, edited by Peter Haining (1979)

Warnings to the Curious: A Sheaf of Criticism on M. R. James (edited by Rosemary Pardoe & S.T. Joshi, 2007)
Ghosts & Scholars Magazine/Newsletter (various), a journal devoted to M. R. James
(edited by Rosemary Pardoe) [also a website]
M.R. James and the Archaeological Uncanny, Gabriel Moshenska in Antiquity no. 86 (2012)
Dark Devotions: M.R. James and the Magical Tradition, by Ron Weighell (Ghosts & Scholars no. 6, 1984)
A Pleasing Terror, by Robert Lloyd Parry in Fortean Times no. 292 (September 2012)
An Accursed Treasure, by Nick Warren in Fortean Times no. 206 (February 2006)
Round & About: Burnham, Hitcham, Taplow & Dorney Community Newspaper no 162 (Oct/Nov 2006)
13 Things You Didn't Know About M R James, by Eddie Brazil at spookyisles.com

I should also like to thank Rosemary Pardoe, editor of Ghosts & Scholars journal, for casting her eye over this chapter and making a few comments and corrections.

As to M.R. James's ghost stories, they have been anthologised many times, but I can recommend:

The Complete Ghost Stories of M.R. James (edited and annotated by S.T. Joshi, Penguin Classics, 2006):
Volume 1 - Count Magnus & Other Ghost Stories
Volume 2 - The Haunted Dolls' House & Other Ghost Stories

26 - How Green Was My Utopia: Comparing The Environmental Qualities, Or Not, Of Three Literary Utopias, By William Morris(1890), H G Wells (1923) And Ernst Callenbach (1975)

William Morris

At the outset, I feel I should clarify what I mean by "green". In the context of this chapter I limit the term purely to the concept of a sustainable world achieved via the use of renewable resources and the elimination of waste and pollution as far as practicable. Such a society would affect the balance of nature as little as possible without, however, being merely conservationist. Discussion is thus on these specific green issues, leaving aside others such as the social and political.

Men Like Gods was published in 1923 and was the second of the Wells' *Utopias*, the first being *A Modern Utopia* (1905). However, the latter was not a fully perfect world since Wells states that: "...the Modern Utopia must not be static but kinetic, must shape not as a permanent state but as a hopeful stage, leading to a long ascent of stages". It is therefore to the first mentioned book that I have turned in order to attempt to answer the question in the title of this chapter. In addition, it is a later work and should therefore reflect Wells' mature thoughts on the subject of humankind's ecological predicament. (I apologise for the emphasis on Wells, but this chapter was originally written for the H. G. Wells Society.)

Given that Callenbach's book Ecotopia, published in 1975, is the archetypal green Utopia, I wish to examine how far on the way Wells had gone towards this vision and compare it to Morris's *News from Nowhere* from 1890, which is considered by some environmentalists as being ahead of its time in its depiction of a green society. So at the end, perhaps, we shall be able to ascertain how much Wells was influenced by Morris's thinking and how much he rejected, and whether *Men Like Gods* can be regarded in any way as a green Utopia.

Beginning with Morris; in the late 1890s Wells used to visit Kelmscott House, Morris's riverside home at Hammersmith "where socialists, communists, Fabians and anarchists argued the present and the future into the night in a haze of tobacco smoke". Here he heard Morris speak, and his own personal brand of socialism was formed and he of course read Morris's works including *News from Nowhere*. Indeed, he refers to this tome in *Men Like Gods*, where he described it as a "graceful impossible book". He felt that the work reflected the outlook of an artist rather than a scientist, which he considered too biased. Nevertheless, the book does incorporate what would now be called green concepts, which Wells himself would espouse in later life, as we shall see towards the end of the chapter.

So, how green was Morris? Like Wells, Morris was critical of the market system, which he considered extremely wasteful, and *News from Nowhere* describes a world, which produces only wares that are actually needed by the populace. These are manufactured by individuals in what can be described as cottage industries where craft handiwork is the norm, although factories exist where the larger scale or energy savings are required. Morris's view was holistic, in that he was concerned with everything that happened to a commodity from the time of its extraction from nature to the end of its useful life. It appears that minerals are mined with minimum pollution and there is widespread use of wind and water power, although these are not described in detail except in as far as to mention that electricity is thereby generated. In addition there are enigmatic "force vehicles" which replaced steam-powered water transport such as barges, but the nature of this force is not detailed. Presumably it is non-polluting.

The early part of the book describes a trip along the Thames and the visitor to this transformed vision of London, William Guest, comments on the clarity of the river water; it turns out that it is now so unpolluted that salmon have returned. He also remarks on the fact that unlike in the London of old, the stone bridge they pass under shows no sign of grime, apparently a result of the demolition of the "smoke vomiting chimneys" of the old soap works. This industry, together with those of glass production and textile manufacture, were responsible in the unregulated 19th century for the venting forth of highly corrosive hydrogen chloride and Morris would have been only too familiar with this scenario. It is against this background that he describes an alternative vision of a world comprising "a healthy, unpolluted and pleasant environment of small communities, pleasant workshops, clean air and water, decent housing, garden fields and woods".

Morris's idea of decentralised socialism produces a vision of a society with a sense of community, which had evolved into a steady state condition in which production is for needs, which are met by goods that are of high quality and durability. In instances such as the felling of timber to make products, pollarding and coppicing are practised under a scheme of careful rotation. This emphasis on the minimisation of the destruction of the natural environment is achieved by the elimination of surplus goods, which, under capitalism, use up so many resources.

There is a strong sense of a new relationship with the natural world, which is attractive to modern day Greens, and some areas of the countryside are maintained in a natural state in order to emphasise this to the population. Children often spend their holidays in woodlands, where they experience the wilderness and get acquainted with wild creatures as well as gaining much enjoyment from such pleasant surroundings during their periods of recreation. As an old man says:

> *"The spirit of the new days, of our days, was to be delighted in the life of the world; intense and overwhelming love of the very skin and surface of the earth on which man dwells, such as a lover has in the fair flesh of the woman he loves ... more akin to our way of looking at life was the spirit of the Middle Ages, to whom heaven and the life of the next world was such a reality that it became a part of the life upon the earth".*

Thus this was the philosophy, which led, through stages according to Morris, to his Utopian world of green fields, small communities, beautiful houses and a pollution-free environment. As such it is a very green society and, given the time it was written, prophetic of the kind of ecological ideas around a hundred years later. But what now of a book written in our modern polluted age - *Ecotopia*, first published in 1975?

"Reconstruction of social and personal relations from the roots up is what *Ecotopia* is all about. In a blending of socialist and anarchist ideas he (Callenbach) creates the most dramatic vision of a possible future since William Morris's *News from Nowhere*"[14]. In a sense, there is not much to say about the novel, since it portrays the ultimate green vision. Recycling is the norm, people make and repair things themselves wherever possible, there are no cars, although certain motor vehicles are permitted, and pollution of the environment is virtually eliminated. An important point not addressed by Morris, although events had not reached a critical stage in 1890, is that of population. Since Ecotopia was formed from the former West Coast of America which broke away from the rest of the USA, the population steadily dropped by about 65,000 a year. There are arguments amongst the citizens of Ecotopia as to how far this should go, but there is general agreement that lower population has a beneficial effect on the environment.

As in *News from Nowhere* there is a proliferation of windmills and there are also many rooftop wind-driven generators providing energy for the home. On the larger scale, energy that can be tapped without affecting the biosphere has been adopted and includes wind, tide and solar power as well as geothermal. What waste products are produced in Ecotopia are where possible biodegradable, even their plastics. Chemical fertilisers have been dispensed with, aided by sewage recycling, composting, and the use of animal manure. Trees are in evidence almost everywhere, including their appearance in streets, which are otherwise full of pedestrians, cyclists, fountains, gardens and sculptures.

Description of Ecotopia could go on, but suffice to say that this is the green Utopia par excellence and I recommend anyone to read the book for themselves. One detail in particular would have been very appealing to Wells - the sexual freedom. Examples are scattered throughout the book. But what about Wells' thoughts of the environment? How does *Men Like Gods* measure up to the two green worlds just described? The first thing to note is that Wells says very little about green issues. Secondly his viewpoint is still that of man's domination over Mother Nature. Uthred, a Utopian, states: "We have taken over the Old Lady's Estate. Every day we learn a little better how to master this little planet". This reflects Wells' perhaps unconscious acceptance of the Judaeo-Christian concept via Genesis that humankind is placed on earth to lord it over the natural world. This is at odds with Morris's perception that we are here as stewards to live with the minimum destruction of the environment and to have an almost

---

14 From the publisher's notes to the 1978 English Paperback, Pluto Press.

spiritual partnership with nature, which is also the outlook endemic in Ecotopia.

H G Wells

Wells' Utopia has also eradicated all noxious diseases and every living species is assessed according to its usefulness or the harm it causes. If it is found that more harm comes from its existence than good, then it is exterminated. However, due regard is given to those species dependent upon it, which would also disappear at the same time. For instance, there are now no more swallows since there were no more gnats or midges. Nevertheless, reserves were maintained which kept condemned species in secure isolation presumably for scientific purposes and possible reintroduction should things change in some way. It seems that, at this time (1923), Wells seemed to have paid little attention to ecosystems and their fragility, and thought solely about humanity. This is strange, since in *Food of the Gods* (1904) Wells tackled the topic of the possibly calamitous results of tampering with nature, perhaps being the first novelist to do so.

Recycling seems to take place to some extent, for we hear that unread books are returned to the pulping mills, but the energy used to work these mills is not described. Whether there are numerous windmills, as in Morris's world, is not stated. However, there is obviously much use of water power since there are two instances where this is mentioned. Firstly, as the Earthlings are transported by aeroplane to their new Utopian abode in the mountains, a leading character in the book notes: "There were Cyclopean turbines athwart the mountain torrents", and secondly, when they are being flown to their place of quarantine, the Earthlings can see that: "Every torrent, every cataract was a working turbine." Of course, these were the days before nuclear power, but it is interesting to note that Wells does not predict any kind of such power, as he did with nuclear bombs in *The World Set Free* of 1914. It is likely though that had solar power been mooted in his days, Wells would have incorporated its use in his Utopia, just as it was to be, fifty years later, in Ecotopia.

It is clear also that in *Men Like Gods*, Wells was concerned with the population problem. The Earthlings' aeroplane flights revealed to them the relative paucity of people in Utopia. Mr Barnstaple muses, "There were more people, he thought, in the highland country than in the levels below, though still far fewer than he would have seen upon any comparable countryside on earth." Towns had virtually disappeared, but gatherings did take place for certain activities such as studying in "great series of communicating buildings." He, therefore, foresaw the possible disaster that over-population could cause and adjusted his Utopia accordingly. Wells' advocacy of birth control is well known and he became vice president of the National Birth Control Council. His views, therefore, accord well with the declining population scenario of Ecotopia.

This sums up the evidence for Wells's green ideas in *Men Like Gods*. Even though influenced early on by Morris, Wells' scientific outlook would not allow him to encompass Morris's holistic attitude to nature and by 1923, *Men Like Gods* appears as a world much less concerned with humankind's relationship with the natural world. This is not to say that Wells was ignorant of ecology. As Professor W. M. S. Russell points out, *Food of the Gods* (1904) describes a chemical escape into the environment, which spread through the food-chain and, in such details, was the first work to highlight the problems which would concern later ecologists studying the effects of pesticides (*H. G. Wells Under Revision*).

However, it is very likely that Wells, had he lived longer, would have seen the importance of green issues and, indeed, have recognised that the ecological crisis which we have heard so much about in recent years is, in its broadest sense, now the world's most important issue. Evidence that this was increasingly of concern to Wells appears in an article he wrote for the Picture Post of 4th May, 1940:

> *We are not only burning up our coal and oil, and sweating and degrading the workers who are employed for that service, but we are rapidly stripping our planet of its forests and so turning a*

> *wholesome mitigated rainfall into an alternation of*
> *droughts and soul-destroying torrents. We are*
> *exterminating hundreds of precious and interesting*
> *species that can never be replaced - whales,*
> *elephants, penguins, seals and the like - and we are*
> *turning millions of acres of grasslands into dusty*
> *deserts. All this is ascertainable fact.*[15]

So, would Wells have eventually have written an *Ecotopia*? Even though
there is not such an emphasis on the environment in *Men Like Gods* as in
News from Nowhere, we have seen that it does contain some green
concepts. These ideas were obviously coming more to the forefront of his
thinking as he grew older and it is not impossible that he could have written
a third *Utopia* had he lived longer. Even if it would have not been quite
Ecotopia, I feel that it would have progressed a fair way towards embracing
its ethos. At all events, were he alive today, I am sure he would be at the
forefront of modern green thinking, but no doubt putting his own personal
"Wellsian" stamp upon it.

Works Consulted:

Ecotopia, Ernest Callenbach (1975)
Men Like Gods, H. G. Wells (1923)
A Modern Utopia, H. G. Wells (1905)
News from Nowhere, William Morris (1890)
The Time Traveller: The Life of H. G. Wells, Norman & Jean Mackenzie
(1977)
An Index of Possibilities: Energy and Power (1974)
'H.G. Wells and Ecology', W. M. S. Russell in H.G. Wells Under Revision,
eds. P. Parrinder & C. Rolfe (1990)

This chapter first appeared in The Wellsian (Winter 1996 no. 19), the
journal of the H.G. Wells Society, who have kindly granted permission to
reproduce it here. I have made a few minor amendments for this volume.

---

15 Quoted in Index of Possibilities

Printed in Great Britain
by Amazon